DEVELOPING GLOBAL BUSINESS LEADERS

DEVELOPING GLOBAL BUSINESS LEADERS

Policies, Processes, and Innovations

Edited by
Mark E. Mendenhall,
Torsten M. Kühlmann, and
Günter K. Stahl

QUORUM BOOKS
Westport, Connecticut • London

Library of Congress Cataloging-in-Publication Data

Developing global business leaders : policies, processes, and innovations / edited by
Mark E. Mendenhall, Torsten M. Kühlmann, and Günter K. Stahl.
    p.   cm.
    Includes bibliographical references and index.
    ISBN 1–56720–314–0 (alk. paper)
    1. Leadership. 2. Executives—Training of. 3. International business
enterprises—Personnel management. I. Mendenhall, Mark E., 1956– II. Kühlmann,
Torsten M. III. Stahl, Günter K., 1966–
    HD57.7.D496   2001
    658.4′07124—dc21   00–027654

British Library Cataloguing in Publication Data is available.

Library of Congress Catalog Card Number: 00–027654
ISBN: 1–56720–314–0

First published in 2001

Quorum Books, 88 Post Road West, Westport, CT 06881
An imprint of Greenwood Publishing Group, Inc.
www.quorumbooks.com

Printed in the United States of America

The paper used in this book complies with the
Permanent Paper Standard issued by the National
Information Standards Organization (Z39.48–1984).

10 9 8 7 6 5 4 3 2 1

Contents

Figures and Tables

FIGURES

TABLES

Preface

The overwhelming globalization in business in the past decade was marked by great increases in cross-border trade and investment, the emergence of global products and consumers, an increase in the privatization of formerly government-owned companies in many countries, higher global standards in production and quality, and a massive increase in the effective usage of information technology (Cullen, 1999). These powerful developments have changed the rules of how business is done internationally, and how businesses should be led and managed.

Compared to the domestic business context, global business is more unpredictable, chaotic, and complex. Doing business in the global marketplace multiplies the variables and interdependencies that executives must take into consideration in their decision making. Due to these complex interdependencies, every single action an executive takes results in intended as well as unintended consequences that can have long-term positive or negative effects on an organization's performance. In global organizations the strategic planning of today may be outdated next month, and the inherent dynamics of the global business environment cause ferocious time pressures that exacerbate the need for executives to act without sufficient information and analysis.

Because the awareness of many of the variables that have a bearing on global business decisions (and the nature of their interdependencies) are often inaccessible to executives, they find themselves having to act somewhat like a wheelman who must steer a boat through fog. Some objects can be seen clearly, some appear blurred, and the rest remain undetected. But unlike the wheelman, the executive does not get quick and continuous feedback about the results of his or her decisions. The requirements for managing in a global context can be likened to a chess player who is required to play against an ever-changing number of participants, while having to observe partially unknown rules that are subject to change without announcement.

For these reasons, the challenge of leading and managing in an environment of globalization has caused many companies to rethink their management-development systems; however, most companies still have not developed the knowledge and skills necessary for their managers to succeed in a global business world. A recent survey of U.S. *Fortune* 500 firms conducted by Gregersen, Morrison, and Black (1998) found that most companies lack the quantity and quality of global leaders they need: 85 percent reported that they do not think they have an adequate number of globally competent executives, and 67 percent believed that their current executives needed additional knowledge and skills before they met needed global capabilities. In spite of this, 92 percent of the firms reported that they do not have comprehensive systems for developing global executives.

Most companies are aware of the fact that the development of global leadership competencies will be of critical importance to their success in the new millennium. However, companies have often found themselves "in the dark" when trying to decide what specific skills are needed to be a global business leader, and how to develop these skills in managers within their organizations. A common goal for many leadership-development programs is to develop executives with "global mind-sets," but exactly what a global mind-set is, what global leadership is, and how to develop these competencies in people remain unclear.

Companies are trying to develop leaders with global mind-sets as best as they can, either on their own or with the help of consultants. Too often they are not aware of the research that exists in this area, or of related research that would assist them in their leadership-development efforts. The purpose of this book is to assist both scholars and practitioners who are interested in gaining a foundational knowledge about, and further insight into, global leadership development.

The genesis of this book was in 1998. A small group of scholars with expertise in international management issues gathered at a castle in Thurnau, Germany, to wrestle with the same issues that many companies face: What is global leadership? What is a global mind-set? What do we currently know from the research literature about it? What can other academic fields tell us about these issues? How can global leadership skills best be conceptualized and developed? The result of the Thurnau Conference was a set of writings that all address the critical issue of global leadership development from rich, novel perspectives.

Practitioners will find in this book both conceptual and empirical foundations upon which to base their thinking about global leadership. What are the unique features of global versus domestic leadership? What competency dimensions transcend internal corporate leadership dimensions? And how should we go about developing people to obtain these competencies? The chapters in this book offer insight, definition, and guidance to any executive who is concerned about developing global leaders in his or her company.

Scholars in the field of international management will find that the chapters in this book offer two value-added contributions to the field: (1) The research on global leadership is reviewed in a way that offers a clearer picture of what the field knows, doesn't know, and might know concerning this phenomenon; and (2) many of the chapters link existing knowledge in the field of international human resource management to the concept of global leadership, thus offering new theoretical and empirical insights into this new and emerging field.

The heuristic value of this book for new scholars might be its most significant contribution; the chapters in this book provide the foundation for numerous future potential research projects that as yet have not been conducted. For doctoral students, scholars who are interested in getting involved in some area of international organizational behavior or human resource management, and long-time international scholars, this book will be a valuable resource in designing and conducting research in the area of global leadership issues.

Before presenting an outline of this book, a word of caution about its limitations seems warranted. The study of global leadership is a relatively new area of research in the field of international management, and few scholars have carefully examined the nature of global leadership competencies and their development. The findings reported in this book provide important insights into the antecedents, processes, and outcomes of effective global leadership, but at this stage in the field's progression it would be unwise to state that these research efforts are more than a first step toward a thorough understanding of the phenomenon. The chapters in this book open up a number of questions and avenues for future studies, and future research will have to refine many of the reported concepts and research designs.

The introductory chapter delineates the competencies of global leadership and discusses the relationship of global leadership competencies to existing research in the field of international human resource management. Salient issues from the discussion are applied to the practical areas of selection, training, and development of global leaders.

The chapters that constitute Part I all address the current state of the art, so to speak, in global leadership development in companies across various industries. Current approaches to the challenge of developing global leaders being utilized by German, Japanese, U.S., and other European companies are discussed, along with recommendations for how companies can improve their efforts.

In Part II organizational processes important to the development of global leadership competencies are reviewed. Expatriate systems, multinational work-group processes, intercultural communication, and personal transformation dynamics are all discussed in the light of global leadership development. These chapters offer rich insights into processes that influence global leadership development, and provide a plethora of ideas regarding what types of issues, content, and concepts need to be included within a global leadership-development program.

In addition to exploring how related processes influence global leadership development, it is also important to consider how extending human resource management functional practices might aid in developing global leaders. New perspectives and twists on selection instrumentation, training, team building, and repatriation policies as they might—and do—impact global leadership development is the contribution of Part III.

The book concludes with the thoughts, analyses, and perspectives of seasoned human resource management experts regarding the challenge of developing global leaders. Nancy Adler, Ed Miller, and Mary Ann Von Glinow share their wisdom and observations on this topic as a conclusion for the book.

The Thurnau Conference, and the ongoing interaction of scholars after the meeting, could not have produced the writings published in this book without the generous assistance of many donors. The editors gratefully acknowledge the contributions of the following organizations (in alphabetical order) who supported the efforts that have led to the publication of this book:

• Deutsche Forschungsgemeinschaft
• The Foundation of International Management Bayreuth
• The Frierson Leadership Institute
• The German Marshall Fund of the United States
• J. Burton Frierson Chair of Excellence in Business Leadership
• The University of Bayreuth
• The University of Tennessee at Chattanooga

As the world grows smaller due to technological advances, it will require human beings who possess global mindsets and leadership skills to merge their efforts to create not just profits for their companies, but a world worth living in for our children and us. It is our hope that this book will spur innovation in both research and practice in the area of global leadership development, and thus be a contribution to the world's economic and social progress.

1

Introduction:
New Perspectives on Expatriate
Adjustment and Its Relationship to
Global Leadership Development

Mark E. Mendenhall

It has been argued by many scholars and business observers that people—not plans, systems, or strategies—are the key to obtaining a global competitive advantage for a company in any given industry (see, for example, Bennis, 1989a; Pfeffer, 1994) Black, Gregersen, Mendenhall, and Stroh (1999) summarized this view when they wrote, "People formulate and implement strategy. . . . The strategy of a company is a function of its strategy makers. For example, whether they recognize or miss global threats or opportunities is a function of their experience and perspective. How they structure an organization for global reach and results depends on how they see the world of organizations, markets, competitors" (pp. 1–2).

It has also been argued by organizational scholars that leadership is critical to organizational productivity (Bennis, 1989a; McFarland, Senn, & Childress, 1993; Yukl, 1998), and recent findings suggest there is a positive relationship between a multinational corporation's (MNC) ability to develop global leadership and the MNC's return on assets (Stroh & Caligiuri, 1997). Thus, one of the key concerns of many current North American CEOs is the development of future leaders who have global leadership abilities (Black et al., 1999; Stroh & Caligiuri, 1996, 1997).

Adler (1998, 140) notes that the word "lead" is derived from the Latin verb "agere," which means "set into motion," and was combined with the Anglo-Saxon word "laedere," which meant "people on a journey." Thus, leadership involves setting ideas, people, organizations, and societies in motion, on a journey. The concept of global leadership, then, requires that this definition be extended into the international, rather than be limited to the local or domestic context. Which naturally leads to the following question: What "skill sets" or competencies make up the repertoire of a global leader?

WHAT IS GLOBAL LEADERSHIP?

The delineation of global leadership competencies is a new area of research in the field of international management, and therefore relatively few scholars have been actively at work attempting to isolate these competencies and their attendant characteristics; however, the work that has been done has yielded a worthwhile "snapshot" of what those competencies might be. A more comprehensive and specific list of the competencies that scholars have generated from exploratory research is given in the following list:[1]

Global Business Savvy	Global Organizational Savvy
Integrity/Managing Cross-Cultural Ethics	Thinking Agility
Managing Uncertainty	Maturity
Balancing Global versus Localization Tensions	Expertise in Negotiation Processes
Inquisitiveness/Curiosity/Self-Learning	Conflict Management
Change Agentry	Community Building/Networking
Creating Learning Systems	Stakeholder Orientation
Motivating Employees	Improvisation
Entrepreneurial Spirit	Establishing Close Personal Relationships
Commitment	Courage

These competencies are not listed in any particular order, and at this stage in the field's progression it would be unwise to state that some are valid while others are not, or that some are more important than others. Future research will no doubt further refine them (and their relative valences), but for now this is the best delineation of global leadership competencies that scholars can offer.

The list of competencies raises an intriguing question: How does one acquire or develop these competencies associated with global leadership? Many senior executives believe that "an international assignment is the single most powerful experience in shaping the perspective and capabilities of effective global leaders" (Black et al., 1999, 1). Companies such as Ford, Philip Morris, GE, Gillette, and Colgate-Palmolive are beginning to pay more careful attention to the overseas experiences of their future leaders. Perhaps the most telling statement on this focus of MNCs is that of Jack Welch, CEO of General Electric: "The next CEO of GE will not be like me. I spent my entire career in the U.S." (Black et al., 1999, 1).

RELATIONSHIP OF EXPATRIATE ADJUSTMENT TO GLOBAL LEADERSHIP

One way to ascertain the validity of the intuition of CEOs and senior executives regarding the efficacy of international assignments for the development of global leaders is to review the competencies that are necessary to achieve success in an international assignment, and to then see if these skills overlap with global leadership competencies. If one must develop certain skills to be successful on an international assignment, and if those skills are the same as—or at least closely linked to—global leadership competencies, then there is preliminary evidence that an effective way to develop global leaders is to send them abroad.

The list of global leadership competencies has already been reviewed and reported. The following list is of the determinants of expatriate adjustment from the research literature:

Self-Efficacy	Spouse Adjustment
Resilience	Family Adjustment
Behavioral Flexibility	Social/Logistical Support
Curiosity	Culture Novelty
Extroversion	Organization Culture Novelty
Broad Category Width	Role Conflict
Flexible Attributions	Role Novelty
Open-Mindedness	Role Discretion
High Tolerance for Ambiguity	Goal Orientation
Empathy/Respect for Others	Technical Competence
Nonverbal Communication	Reinforcement Substitution
Relationship Skills	Stress Reduction Program
Willingness to Communicate	

The field of expatriate adjustment is much more developed than the field of global leadership, and the majority of scholars in this field would agree that each of the variables listed has been empirically or theoretically demonstrated to positively influence expatriate adjustment (for an overview of this literature, see Black et al., 1999; Stahl, 1998b).

In Figure 1.1 the list of global leadership competencies and the list of determinants of expatriate adjustment are compared. In order to gain a clearer perspective of the overlap (or lack of overlap) between global leadership competencies and determinants of expatriate adjustment, I have placed each global leadership competency and each determinant of expatriate adjustment into one of eight dimensional categories: "interpersonal skills," "business skills," "personal traits," "organizational structuring skills," "cognitive processes," "nature of the job," "organizational context," and "external factors."

Figure 1.1 obviously reflects a high degree of overlap between the determinants of expatriate adjustment and the global leadership competencies for the categories of "interpersonal skills," "business skills," and "personal traits." The overlaps in these three categories are not perfect, and as yet no research exists that delineates the exact nature of these interrelationships. The strongest overlaps are indicated by underlining.

It can, of course, be argued that competencies/skills influence other competencies/skills outside of their assigned dimensional category; for example, "courage" (which resides in the "personal traits" category) quite likely has an influence upon "willingness to communicate" (which resides in the "interpersonal skills" category). Also, a competency/skill that resides in a category with no overlap (such as "managing cross-cultural ethics") may have a significant positive relationship with a competency/skill in one of the categories with internal overlap between competencies/skills (such as "respect for others").

The purpose of this chapter is not to delineate with high levels of specificity each relationship that can potentially be derived between global leadership competencies and the determinants of expatriate adjustment; rather, it is to bring into view the overall conceptual overlaps that exist in order to show that some of the skills necessary for expatriate adjustment are likely linked to particular global leadership competencies. It is likely that some of the determinants of expatriate adjustment influence the ability of an individual to effectively deploy particular global leadership competencies that may be prerequisite skills or conditions for the development of given global leadership competencies as well. Much research, both theoretical and empirical, needs to be done in the

Figure 1.1
Global Leadership Competencies and Determinants of Expatriate Adjustment Compared

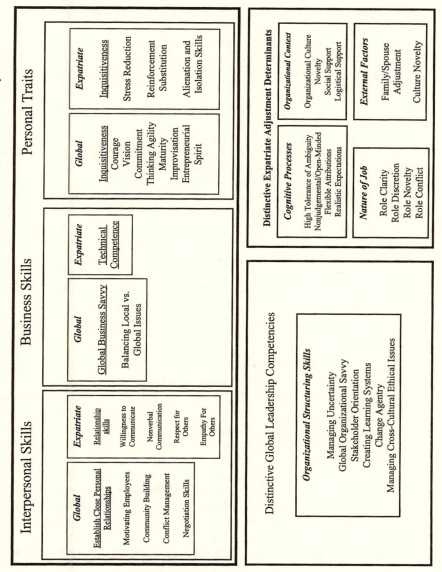

future to delineate all the relationships in their specificity, but the cursory review reported in Figure 1.1 seems to indicate that such relationships likely exist and should be investigated.

Thus, it seems clear that the intuition of the senior executives was correct: International assignments are efficacious venues for the development of global leaders. That is the good news. The bad news? Research over the past two decades indicates that though their intuition is correct, executives' ability to leverage the validity of their insight has usually been flawed (Black et al., 1999).

COUNTERINTUITIVE ASSUMPTIONS

Implementing a structure that will leverage an insight is often more difficult than obtaining the insight itself. From many executives' view, if an international assignment can assist in the development of global leaders, the resultant approach should be to simply send "fast-trackers" to Tokyo, Paris, or Frankfurt for awhile so that they can "become internationalized." And this is generally what companies do. The research literature clearly shows that such fast-trackers are usually sent overseas with little or no training for their new assignments. They are expected to "sink or swim" cross-culturally (Black et al., 1999; Mendenhall & Oddou, 1985).

The sink-or-swim approach makes sense to most executives because to them it does not seem to be a sink-or-swim approach. In the minds of executives, it makes perfect sense to take someone who has performed well in one place (New York) and send them to a foreign location (Tokyo) in order to gain international skills and at the same time perform well at the subsidiary. The assumption is that since the best and the brightest people are being sent overseas, they should only need a little training, and once overseas, they should be able to figure out for themselves what they need to do to in order to be successful.

This approach would be akin to the Joint Chiefs of Staff agreeing, "In order to develop our younger officers, let's just send them into battle without training and see how they do. Those that survive will be our future generals, and those that don't, won't." In this strategy, some fast-trackers will survive their battle experience due to luck, random fortuity on the field of battle, and the amount of wisdom possessed by their junior officers and troops. Conversely, other fast-trackers will suffer from unlucky decisions, random vagaries on the field of battle, and inexperienced junior officers' and troops' behavior. These and other factors will cause some high-potential officers to fail in their assignments. In the latter scenario an officer with the potential to be an excellent general would forever be overlooked for advancement to the top echelons of the military.

International assignments are often touted by HR executives as being strategically used by their companies for global leadership development purposes (Wirth, 1992); however, most expatriates wind up providing control, coordination, technology transfer, or "fire fighting" services (all of which are important functions) without any formal development of their global leadership competencies. Executives pride themselves on their logic and acumen, but in the case of developing global leaders, the research literature resoundingly reveals a serious "blind spot" in their management of human resources. This blind spot is well summarized by Black et al. (1999), when they state, "Most U.S. firms make global assignments primarily on the basis of the needs of a given position and their inability to fill it with a host-country employee. In the day-to-day reality of the decision-makers responsible for global assignments, succession planning and managerial development are often irrelevant. Succession planning becomes replacement planning, and what is urgent drives out what is important" (pp. 9–10).

It is beyond the scope of this chapter to comprehensively review the dynamics that tend to cause poor decision making regarding international assignments. Suffice it to say that it is not simply a North American phenomenon, for research indicates that Japanese and European companies make the same types of strategic mistakes in their attempts to develop global leaders through international assignments (Black et al., 1999; Stahl, 1998b). The next important question in the discussion of global leadership development thus becomes this: How should one structure an expatriate experience to induce the development of global leadership competencies?

UNDERSTANDING THE PROCESS OF EXPATRIATE ADJUSTMENT/GLOBAL LEADERSHIP DEVELOPMENT

The mistake that most companies make in structuring international assignments is that they do not take into account the reality of the process of expatriate adjustment. Ignorance of international issues—especially of expatriate adjustment and global leadership competencies—abounds throughout most organizations. And this is to be expected. After all, most executives have never been trained in this area of expertise, either at work or in graduate or undergraduate business schools.

Developing global competencies does not involve acquiring knowledge and adding it into one's existing worldview. Expatriate adjustment is not a linear accumulation of knowledge. To adjust to a new culture requires learning and internalizing new worldviews—new cognitive "software systems"—that must run simultaneously with one's own, traditional, cultural software system. Then, these separate software systems must be integrated into a new, more complex software system, one that sees more deeply into the complexities of the reality of the context in which the expatriate finds himself or herself.

In short, the expatriate adjustment process is one of human transformation. Expatriates do not return from overseas—whether successful or unsuccessful in their work assignments—the same people as they were before they left. Though they are still recognizable as being essentially the same individuals to those who knew them before their sojourn, knowingly or unknowingly, for better or for worse, they have undergone a transformation, and they return to their home country with new ways of seeing and thinking about the world around them.

This is the first understanding that executives must hold strongly in their minds: Global leadership development involves fundamentally changing people, not simply adding new nuggets of information to their current levels of thinking or into their current portfolios of managerial expertise. It involves throwing away old managerial skill portfolios and replacing them with new ones. This is not an easy process to engage in; in fact, it is in many ways one of the most challenging, exciting, painful, and frustrating experiences one can have in life. Being an expatriate requires walking into an entirely new world, which, in turn, requires one to become a new person in order to excel.

The research findings in the field of expatriation reflect the obvious: Not all people are suited for this type of journey, and not all people can handle the experience (Mendenhall & Oddou, 1985). Individuals who often seem the most talented due to their professional skills often struggle overseas, and return home not as global leaders but to one degree or another as frustrated managers who are glad to be back on their home turf. Riding out one's stay overseas and returning home may not constitute outright failure, but neither is it indicative of having developed global leadership competencies.

How many expatriates do not excel in developing a global mindset and global leadership competencies while overseas, but who could have done so with the proper support and training? We do not know. The fact remains that simply sending someone overseas does not ensure that they will automatically develop global leadership competencies. The following broad guidelines are offered in order to facilitate global leadership development during an international assignment.

SELECTING FUTURE GLOBAL LEADERS

The entire process of global leadership development begins with the selection of "high-potentials" or fast-trackers who senior management feel have the potential to become the future leaders of the company. Increasingly, these people are being required by their organizations to spend some time overseas in order to develop an affinity for international business operations. However, the expatriate literature reveals that past performance in a domestic setting is not a good predictor of excellent performance overseas (Black et al., 1999; Miller, 1973). The following lesson from the Bible is instructive in this regard.

When the prophet Samuel was instructed by God to select a new King of Israel, he was told to go to the house of Jesse the Bethlehemite, and was informed that from one of Jesse's sons God had prepared a new King of Israel. Samuel went, and upon interviewing Eliab, the oldest, Samuel said to himself that surely this was the man whom he should select. But before he could do so, the voice of God said to Samuel, "Look not on his countenance, or on the height of his stature; because I have refused him: for the Lord seeth not as man seeth; for man looketh on the outward appearance, but the Lord looketh on the heart." After interviewing all of Jesse's sons, Samuel could not find one that seemed right to him. He asked Jesse if these were all of his sons. Jesse then fetched his youngest son, David, from his shepherd's job, and it was then that God told Samuel, "Arise, anoint him: for this is he."

North American high-potentials are usually noticed because they have achieved something significant compared to their peers. They generally manifest a "propensity for risk-taking, a passion or commitment to seeing the organization succeed, courage to go against the grain, and a keen mind" (Spreitzer et al., 1997). They are usually hard drivers, self-motivated, assertive, and outwardly passionate and self-confident. And this is where the trouble often begins.

Research clearly shows that for the past three decades the primary criterion for sending someone overseas was based on their "track record," their actual or perceived performance (Baker & Ivancevich, 1971; Gertsen, 1990; Marx, 1996; Miller, 1973; Tung, 1982; Windham International & National Foreign Trade Council, 1994; Wirth, 1992). It is counterintuitive, but the types of traits, attributes, and management styles that produce an excellent track record in North America will be "out of synch" with many other business cultures around the world. The exact traits that produce outstanding results in the United States do not produce productivity in the Far East, the Middle East, Scandinavia, and many other parts of the world. In many global contexts, the very strengths of many North American high-potentials actually become liabilities (Ruben, 1989).

Thus, in order to enhance global leadership development, executives have essentially two options: send high-potentials overseas with the understanding that they will have to learn to adjust, modify, or change the very traits and styles that have brought them success in the United States, or expand their view of who is a high-potential. Perhaps other committed and bright managers who do not stand out quite as much as the high-potentials may actually have an existing skill set that might be more amenable to being successful in global business contexts. While it is likely that either selection approach is acceptable, both approaches require senior executives to be in touch with the following truth: Technical expertise and culture-specific leadership styles are not the entire universe of criteria upon which to evaluate global leadership potential.

While it is still too early to weight the global leadership competencies in terms of their comparative importance, some scholars have suggested that the competency of inquisitiveness/curiosity is a critical one, and thus one to look for when selecting or developing global leaders. In the Black et al. (1999) model of global leadership the role of inquisitiveness is central to all of the other global leadership competencies, and is held to be the core trait that acts as a type of psychological glue to hold all the other competencies together. Morrison (in press), in summarizing the role of this competency, states that inquisitiveness

- Produces action that is associated with learning, and learning is essential for keeping global competencies fresh.
- Prompts the individual to ask the types of questions required to understand global market opportunities and organizational resources.
- Motivates one to be eager to learn about employee conditions, new cultures, and values, and to connect with people and make difficult ethical decisions.
- Accelerates learning and promotes rapid decision making in environments where data are of questionable value.
- Forces an individual to ask questions about industry conditions, competitors, customer values, and microeconomics. Familiarity with these drivers is essential in differentiating between the activities, products, and services that should be globally standardized and those activities that should be turned over to local managers to run.

Spreitzer et al. (1997) note that individuals who are likely to succeed as international executives manifest this inquisitiveness competency and that it motivates them to learn and to enjoy the very process of learning. Such people "proactively seek formal and informal experiences to learn about themselves, the work environment, the organization, the external environment, and how these elements interact" (p. 25). Interestingly, Dalton & Wilson (1998) and Stahl (1998b) also found that inquisitiveness was one of the most important determinants of expatriate success. It is just such criteria as that of inquisitiveness that executives overlook when making selection decisions for overseas assignments. Like Samuel in the Bible, senior executives must be wise in how they evaluate their managerial cadre in order to tease out their best future global leaders before sending them on overseas assignments.

TRAINING AND DEVELOPING FUTURE GLOBAL LEADERS

Once high-potentials have been selected and sent overseas, they will need help—no matter how impressive their intellect or illustrious their past domestic performance. And even if they already rate highly on all of the dimensions of adjustment and global leadership already discussed, they will still be walking in cold to a culture they know nothing about. They will need education and guidance in order to develop new accurate and efficient cultural "software." How is this best accomplished?

Traditionally, when companies have offered cross-cultural training to their expatriates it occurs right before they leave, and is not very rigorous (Black et al., 1999; Black & Mendenhall, 1989; Mendenhall, Dunbar, & Oddou, 1987). Indeed, it cannot be rigorous because as yet the expatriate has no real-world experience in the new culture with which to reference what he or she has learned in the training program. At best, predeparture programs can have an innoculative effect; that is, they can give the expatriate enough knowledge to not make a complete fool of himself or herself upon arrival. However, in order to be successful overseas one must develop a working knowledge of the subtleties of the host culture's business and social norms, and the underlying values that sustain those norms. To accomplish this requires an entirely different philosophy of training.

Before describing what kind of training is necessary to develop global leaders, it will first be necessary to describe why traditional training by itself is ineffective in helping expatriates to learn about, and be effective in, their new, host culture.[2]

TRADITIONAL VERSUS REAL-TIME TRAINING

Once overseas, expatriates will inevitably experience unique cross-cultural encounters for which they were not prepared by their predeparture training. Black et al. (1999) observe that most companies prepare their expatriates with predeparture training programs that are relatively low in rigor, programmatic in format, and with content that assumes that "one size fits all." Such training cannot foresee all of the future cross-cultural encounters of expatriates, and even if trainers could see into the future they would not be able to adequately prepare the expatriates anyway. This is due to the fact that the skills necessary to deal with global situations can often only be learned while dealing with those global situations. Thus, training needs to take place in real time, while the expatriate is in the actual situation that he or she needs training for. Expatriates need immediate guidance in response to the questions and frustrations that arise from confusing cross-cultural experiences, so that they can effectively manage and learn from those experiences.

I have suggested elsewhere (Mendenhall, 1999; Mendenhall & Macomber, 1997; Mendenhall, Macomber, Gregersen, & Cutright, 1998) that in order to provide expatriates with this kind of real-time training, new approaches to training will have to be developed. One potentially useful approach is that of personal coaching. Personal coaching "essentially involves the personal counseling of managers by external consultants or advisors; in other words, the counseling in real-time of managers by experts" (Mendenhall & Stahl, in press). How would this training process work for expatriates?

Upon arrival in the host country an expatriate cohort would be assigned a coach—someone who has "expert knowledge" of the host culture's social and business norms, and who has had experience living and working in that culture. Ideally, the coach would still be living in the host culture, though long-distance coaching via telephone and e-mail could still be done. Whenever the expatriate runs into a cross-culturally "messy" situation, he or she would have immediate access to an expert who could help the expatriate understand what happened and craft a strategy to ameliorate the situation. Thus, appropriate behavior can be deployed immediately by the expatriate in order to correct a problem or deal with a potential problem. As it currently stands, most expatriates must wait for a training program or seek help from other expatriates in order to deal with problems, with the latter case often resulting in a "blind leading the blind" scenario.

Obviously, personal coaching can be fruitfully combined with traditional training programs, but without personal coaching—or something akin to it—traditional training is not able to meet all of the training and development needs of potential global leaders while they are overseas. Personal coaching is a potentially powerful method by which global leaders can become continual learners overseas rather than frustrated expatriates. It makes no sense to force expatriates to learn on their own when the knowledge they need is available from experts.

LEVERAGING GLOBAL LEADERS

After an extended overseas assignment, if successful, managers come home with many of the skills of global leadership (Oddou & Mendenhall, 1988). However, most do not find themselves in situations upon return to use these global competencies that they have worked so hard to acquire (Black et al., 1999). It is common for expatriates to return home to positions that have nothing to do with international business, and that are less challenging than the jobs they held overseas. No wonder many of these expatriates leave the firms that sent them overseas within a year or two of returning home for companies who have need of their hard-won international expertise (Black et al., 1999).

While it seems ridiculous not to leverage their global skills, repatriating expatriates is not an easy task. Only one person can be a CEO at a time, and the number of vice presidencies and other strategic positions are limited as well. A company cannot play musical chairs with its high-level positions every time an expatriate comes home. However, over time their global competencies will be needed, so the question arises: How can a firm keep a global leader satisfied in the present until he or she is ready in the future to move into a position that will require the skills learned overseas?

The first step in solving this problem is a simple one: This state of affairs must be admitted by senior management up front—both before departure and upon return. Companies alienate repatriates when they try and cover up the reality of the often haphazard nature of their succession planning. Executives should be up front with expatriates before they leave and upon return by stating that the position they have returned to is all that is available now, but that the individual will be slotted in the future into positions that will increasingly make use of their global competencies. Firms can go a long way toward retaining managers in whom they have invested a lot of money during their overseas assignments by being honest and nonmanipulative with their expatriates and repatriates.

The next step is to insert these repatriates into a company's "global cadre." Firms need to organize those of their people who have been overseas into semiformal or formal cadres of global managers who meet from time to time in order to update their knowledge about global business issues. The cadre members can give presentations to each other on what is currently happening in their areas of expertise around the world. Experts can be brought in from outside the organization to update the skills of the cadre as well. The purpose of such an organization within the organization is to keep the global leaders involved with international issues, and to sustain the company's view of them as global assets to the company.

This cadre can also be used like a National Guard reserve unit within the company. Whenever a trouble spot erupts in the firm somewhere overseas, some of the members of this cadre can be used to either help put out the fire on a short-term project basis, or analyze the aftermath of the problem and then present reports to top management regarding how the company can better handle similar incidents in the future. Also, cadre members can be brought in as needed to assist top management with a variety of issues, such as global strategic planning, analysis of country markets, political risk analysis, and so forth.

Members of this cadre can also be integrated into the cross-cultural training process of new expatriates. They can act as trainers and mentors to those who are preparing to leave on overseas assignments. They can be assigned to help monitor current expatriates in terms of performance appraisal and support needs, and can assist in the personal coaching process discussed earlier. In addition, when short-term international business travel opportunities crop up (e.g., business negotiations, auditing, look-see visits, or appraising foreign subsidiaries), members of the global cadre should be called upon to lead the team that travels overseas. In order to maintain foreign language skills and cross-cultural business acumen, members of the global cadre can have bonuses built into their contracts if they attend seminars or other programs designed to keep their international skills honed. This would symbolize the company's perception of their value to the firm and act as a reward for possessing skills that others in the company do not possess.

There are probably a hundred different ways that companies can integrate repatriates into domestic subsidiaries upon their return to their home countries, but the key principle is to create an institutional cadre where global leaders can take pride in being a member. Repatriates who see themselves as part of an elite global cadre will be more likely to stay put in the organization that sent them overseas than to become frustrated and ultimately seek employment elsewhere.

CONCLUSION

More research needs to be conducted in order for us to under-stand exactly how expatriate adjustment also simultaneously aids in the development of global leadership competencies. No doubt some of the expatriate adjustment determinants influence global leadership development more powerfully than others. Despite the current lack of rigor in understanding regarding these relation-ships, there seems to be enough preliminary evidence to suggest that international assignments are prime avenues for the develop-ment of global leaders.

The skill set of global leaders is quite large, and when reading this list many readers may feel that a person must be a superman or superwoman in order to be a global leader. We currently do not know how many people possess these skills in totality, or if anyone does. It also may be that some of these skills are more important than others, or are subsumed within other skills. As the field delin-eates the terrain of this phenomenon, more clarity will develop re-garding how global leadership competencies integrate with each other to produce effective leadership behaviors in a global setting.

It is also possible that certain determinants of expatriate adjust-ment may actually interfere with the development of some global leadership competencies. For example, high tolerance of ambiguity may sometimes influence expatriates to be too ethically situational in their decision making at times, when a better approach might be to adhere to fixed company standards. Thus, some variables of ad-justment may vary in their efficacy depending on the specific cross-cultural context the expatriate encounters in the moment.

It is also possible that certain global leadership competencies may not always interact with each other in fruitful ways; for ex-ample, the ability to establish close interpersonal relationships may at times influence the manager to be biased toward a localization approach in his or her decision making instead of a balancing strat-egy between global headquarters and local issues. In some cases and situations the competencies may be paradoxical, and require the leader to be able to lead in a context of mutually opposite di-mensions that are also simultaneously valid. We need to know more about how these competencies influence each other, and how glo-bal leaders can leverage them in the day-to-day dynamics of their work lives.

In summary, it behooves senior executives to carefully consider how international assignments are structured in order to ensure that potential global leaders are developed while overseas. To date, the track record of companies has been poor in this regard. It is hoped that this chapter—and the others in this book—might serve to prod companies to more carefully consider how they treat their most valued human resources: potential global leaders.

NOTES

1. These competencies were derived from Adler and Bartholomew (1992); Black, Morrison, and Gregersen (1999); Brake (1997); Dalton (1998); Moran and Riesenberger (1994); Spreitzer, McCall, and Mahoney (1997); and Rhinesmith (1996). Most of the competencies listed by each of these authors overlap with each other, though they are given different labels by each author. Labels from all of the authors' writings are reflected in this list.

2. I have explained elsewhere in detail the theoretical rationale that supports the recommendations that I give in this chapter; the interested reader should consult Mendenhall (1999) and Mendenhall and Stahl (in press) for this information.

Part I

CURRENT MNC GLOBAL LEADERSHIP DEVELOPMENT POLICIES AND PRACTICES

2

International Assignments and Careers as Repositories of Knowledge

Allan Bird

> After investing over a million dollars in my overseas assign-
> ment, I thought someone, somewhere in the organization would
> want to know what I learned. I was wrong.
> Anonymous international manager

Managers on international assignments (IAs) often find themselves
in a paradoxical position. They have been sent on assignment, in
part, to gain valuable experience that cannot be obtained elsewhere.
But when they return from such assignments, often the organization either appears uninterested in what they have learned or seems
incapable of drawing upon that experience. Anecdotal and empirical evidence suggests that the anonymous international manager
quoted at the beginning of this chapter is not a lone voice in the
wilderness, but one of many voices in the chorus.

At a minimum, the development of global business leaders requires that organizations and individual managers pay greater attention to what and how people learn on international assignments.
This, in turn, requires that organizations understand the nature of

organizational knowledge creation and the role played by individual managers in the knowledge-creation process. In this chapter I present an emerging perspective from the field of career studies, which can help organizations and individuals to understand the role that IA experiences play in developing global business leaders.

The following section introduces the concept of a career as a repository of knowledge. Career experiences are linked to the process of organizational knowledge creation, with a special emphasis on four types of knowing. The next section considers IAs in light of this perspective, laying out aspects of the experiences that distinguish them from their noninternational counterparts. The concluding section addresses the implications of the careers as repositories of knowledge perspective for international human resource development, particularly global business leaders.

WHAT IS A CAREER?

Defining "career" is not easy. Indeed, the definition of career varies as the term crosses disciplinary boundaries. Within the disciplines of psychology, sociology, political science, economics, history, and geography, Arthur, Hall, and Lawrence (1989) identify eleven separate descriptions of what constitutes a career. For example, social psychologists would define a career as an "individually mediated response to outside role messages," whereas economists might define it as a "response to market forces," and political scientists portray careers as "the enactment of self interest" (p. 10). Common to all these perspectives, however, are characteristics of work experiences occurring over some span of time. In its broadest sense, then, a career is "the evolving sequence of a person's work experiences over time" (p. 8).

One element is missing in traditional definitions of a career: There is no recognition of the information and knowledge acquired as a result of one's evolving sequence of work experiences. A more comprehensive perspective would define a career as an accumulation of information and knowledge embodied in skills, expertise, and relationship networks acquired through an evolving sequence of work experiences over time. In this context, work experiences constitute the primary mechanism by which a career occurs, though they are not in themselves a career. Rather, the nature or quality of a career is defined by the information and knowledge that is accumulated. Furthermore, viewing a career as a repository suggests the possibility that, in addition to being accumulated, knowledge may also be removed, rearranged, or replaced.

Syntactic and Semantic Aspects of Careers

One way of understanding the relationship between knowledge and work experiences is to borrow two concepts from grammar: syntax and semantic. Syntax refers to "the way in which words are put together to form phrases, clauses, or sentences" (Merriam-Webster, 1977, 1.183), whereas semantics has to do with meaning or content. The syntactic aspect of a career is its structure, which is exhibited in the sequence of work experiences. A representative example of this approach can be found in Rosenbaum's (1984) study of careers among a cohort of workers in a single large organization. He analyzes nearly 4,000 careers, measuring them in terms of such things as number of hierarchical levels advanced and length of stay at each level.

In contrast, the semantic aspect of careers considers their significance. It is concerned with the content and meaning of work experiences. Semantic aspects of careers are not easily universalized. They are inextricably embedded in context. The contents of a career are located in what is learned from experiences, in the information, knowledge, and perspectives that are acquired or changed over time as a result of a series of work experiences. For example, two employees might both work for three years as tellers at the same bank. The syntactic aspects of their careers are similar: the same position, the same bank, the same length of time. In semantic terms, however, there may be substantial differences as a result of the specific relationship networks developed, skills acquired, and expertise accumulated.

CAREERS AND ORGANIZATIONS
AS KNOWLEDGE CREATORS

The notion of careers as repositories of knowledge connects easily to the view that organizations are knowledge creators, and that the substance from which knowledge is created is the experiences of individuals (Nonaka, 1991b). Regardless of whether firms compete primarily on the basis of cost, quality, or product differentiation, a firm's chosen strategy is essentially aimed at making its product or service different in some way from that of its competitors. The source of a firm's ability to differentiate itself from others is embodied in an invisible asset: information. Ultimately, all advantages are information in one form or another. One implication of this perspective is that in order to remain competitive and to ensure an ongoing ability to differentiate, firms must develop their human resources in ways that enhance the supply of information and knowledge available to the firm. Through knowledge creation, firms are able to revitalize themselves and to set themselves apart from their competitors.

Organizations create knowledge by shaping the firsthand work experiences of employees and then drawing out this experiential learning in ways that allow it to be shared throughout the organization and that lead to the accomplishment of organizational objectives. The key activity of managers is to give direction to the knowledge-creating activities of employees by creating meaning.

Tacit Knowledge and Explicit Knowledge

Organizations and individuals have two types of knowledge to work with in creating new knowledge. Explicit, or articulable, knowledge can be transmitted to others through formal, systematic language (Polanyi, 1966). It is impersonal and independent of context. A mathematical equation, for example, is explicit knowledge because it conveys knowledge by means of an impersonal (it is not rooted in any person or situation), formal (there are rules governing the structure of equations), and systematic language (mathematical symbols).

In contrast to explicit knowledge, tacit knowledge refers to knowledge embedded in people's experiences, which is difficult to communicate to others. Tacit knowledge is necessarily personal because it is attained through firsthand experiences and is deeply rooted in action and commitment (Nonaka, 1991b). It is accessible to its possessor primarily in the form of intuition, speculation, and feeling. Tacit knowledge is the sum of an individual's understanding as described by Polanyi (1966) when he states, "We know more than we can tell" (p. 4).

Two aspects of tacit knowledge are relevant to its application to careers. First, tacit knowledge has a cognitive dimension that is reflected in traditional beliefs, paradigms, schemata, or mental models (Nonaka, 1990). The cognitive dimension helps us to make sense of the world around us, influencing how we perceive and define the world. The second aspect is the technical dimension, which consists of skills, crafts, and know-how that are situation specific. Much tacit knowledge, particularly the cognitive dimension, remains beyond our ability to make it explicit (Winogard & Flores, 1986).

Types of Knowledge Creation

The interplay between the two different types of knowledge—tacit and explicit—gives rise to knowledge creation (Nonaka, 1991b). There are four types of knowledge creation (see Figure 2.1).

Figure 2.1
Typology of the Knowledge-Creation Process

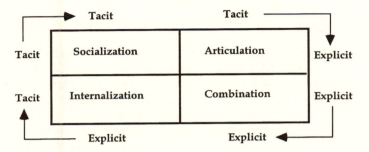

Source: Adapted from I. Nonaka, Managing innovation as a knowledge creation process: A new model for a knowledge-creating organization (paper presented at New York University, Stern School of Business, International Business Colloquium, 1990).

Tacit to Tacit

One form of knowledge creation involves the transmittal of tacit knowledge between individuals. When an apprentice studies under a master craftsman, learning occurs not only through spoken words or instructions, but through observation and imitation as well. *Socialization* of the apprentice leads to knowledge creation through the expansion of the knowledge base to someone new who imbues or modifies what is learned with their own understanding. However, socialization leads to little new knowledge being created because it remains, to paraphrase Polanyi (1966), as more than can be told. Moreover, the transmittal process itself is time consuming and not something easily provided to large numbers of people.

Explicit to Explicit

By contrast, knowledge that is explicit can be easily transmitted. Its very explicitness makes it easy to combine. Consequently, bringing explicit knowledges together is referred to as *combination*. For example, collecting information about the financial performance of various business units (explicit knowledge) brings about the creation of new knowledge: how the firm as a whole is performing (explicit knowledge). Though combination creates new knowledge through synthesis, like tacit-to-tacit knowledge creation the volume of new knowledge created tends to be small.

The most profound knowledge creation occurs when knowledge extends from tacit to explicit or explicit to tacit. It is also at this nexus that individual careers as reflected in work experiences hold the potential to make their largest contribution to the organization.

Tacit to Explicit

The conversion of tacit knowledge to explicit knowledge—*articulation*—is significant for the organization because it makes possible the sharing of knowledge that was previously inaccessible. In a furniture company, when a master cabinetmaker is able to articulate the thinking and techniques behind his particular style of woodworking, that information can be widely disseminated within the organization. Designers can incorporate the newly created knowledge into future products. Also, the information can be shared with other cabinetmakers so that they can produce pieces of comparable workmanship.

Explicit to Tacit

When employees acquire explicit knowledge and then apply it to their own unique situations the result is an expansion of their tacit knowledge base. *Internalization* leads to a reframing of knowledge that constitutes knowledge creation in its own right. Perhaps more important, the transference from explicit to tacit leads to self-renewal of the employee, which in turn deepens commitment. In addition, self-renewal of individual employees taken as a whole constitutes a self-renewal of the organization itself.

Tacit-to-tacit and explicit-to-tacit knowledge-creation types may appear similar in some ways. The difference between socialization and internalization as employed in this typology lies in the primary informational source contributing to knowledge creation. In the tacit-to-tacit quadrant (socialization), the primary information source contributing to new knowledge creation is the master. New knowledge is being created through replication, with the receiver's knowledge base contributing little to the newly created knowledge. By contrast, in the explicit-to-tacit quadrant it is the receiver's knowledge base that contributes the bulk of information, while the explicit serves as a leavening agent, obliging the receiver to see things in a different light or think in a different way (both being forms of new knowledge).

CAREER PATHS AS SPIRALS OF KNOWLEDGE CREATION

The sequencing of knowledge-creation modes defines a career path. Different experiences lead to shifts from one mode to another.

Nonaka (1991a) outlines the nature of experience in each mode as well as the modal shifts in his description of how a product-development team at Matsushita Electric Company created a new home bread-making machine. Though a prototype had been developed, the bread it produced was considered unacceptable. The crust was hard and the inside was doughy. One member of the development team, Ikuko Tanaka, suggested they study the technique of Osaka International Hotel's baker, who had a reputation for making the best bread in Osaka. While working as an apprentice with the baker, Tanaka noticed that the baker used a distinctive technique of stretching the dough when kneading it. Upon returning to the product-development team Tanaka shared her insights with them. After making several modifications in the design of the bread maker, Matsushita developed the "twist dough" method and came out with a new machine that set a sales record for kitchen appliances. Nonaka (1991a, 99) continues:

1. First, [Ikuko Tanaka] learns the tacit secrets of the Osaka International Hotel baker [socialization].
2. Next, she translates these secrets into explicit knowledge that she can communicate to her team members and others at Matsushita [articulation].
3. The team then standardizes this knowledge, putting it together into a manual or workbook and embodying it in a product [combination].
4. Finally, through the experience of creating a new product, Tanaka and her team members enrich their own tacit knowledge base [internalization]. In particular, they come to understand in an extremely intuitive way that products like home bread-making machines can provide genuine quality. That is, the machine must make bread that is as good as that of a professional baker.

The use of project-team experiences as the basis for this illustration is noteworthy for several reasons. First, the sequencing of experiences is laid bare (Nonaka, 1994). Though individuals usually begin a socialization mode when they enter a firm or when they move from one position to another, it occurs most frequently when they join a project or work team. The shift to an articulation mode is triggered by rounds of dialogue and discussion among team members. As concepts generated by the team are pieced together or joined with existing data there is a modal shift to the combination mode. Experimentation with various new combinations results in a phase change to the internalization mode as members of the team engage in "learning by doing," which results in the translation of explicit knowledge into various types of tacit knowledge.

As individuals reiterate this sequence of work experiences their store of knowledge grows. For example, individuals usually begin a socialization process as they enter a new position or take on a new assignment. The shift to an articulation mode is triggered by discussion and dialogue with coworkers. As new insights are made explicit, they are pieced together or joined with existing data and there is a modal shift to the combination mode. Over the course of experimenting with various new combinations there is a phase change to the internalization mode as the individual learns by doing. A career, then, can thus be understood as the path of an individual's work experiences through the various knowledge-creation modes. The modulation of those experiences between the tacit and explicit epistemological dimensions can be visualized as an outwardly expanding spiral.

Four Types of Knowing

This repository of knowledge known as a career is comprised of four types of knowing. *Know Why* relates to the nature and extent of a person's identification with the firm's culture and strategy: Knowing, for example, why the firm chose to set up an overseas operation in Brazil, rather than Argentina. Knowing why gives meaning and purpose to organizational and individual action.

Know What relates to the nature and extent of a person's understanding about specific projects, products, services, or organizational arrangements. A knowledge of the firm's product offerings in Brazil, or an understanding of structure of the Brazilian subsidiary constitute types of know what.

Know How relates to a person's set of skills and knowledge about how to do things or how to get things done. For example, methods for structuring invoicing schedules to offset the effects of hyperinflation in Russia represent one type of know how. Another would be techniques for giving *face* in Chinese negotiations.

Finally, *Know Who* refers to a person's social capital; that is, the actual and potential resources embedded within, available through, and derived from the network of relationships an individual possesses. Examples of know who would include such things as having a contact in a Japanese bank willing to make introductions on one's behalf to local firms, or being acquainted with key individuals in the Hong Kong Trade Development Agency. Knowing who involves not only an acquaintanceship with others, but also an ability to draw upon various resources through that relationship.

Through time the volume and value of each type of knowing may increase or decrease. In addition, specific types of knowledge may be acquired, lost, and recovered. Figure 2.2 presents a graphic depiction of an idealized career developing over time.

IMPLICATIONS FOR THE INTERNATIONAL ASSIGNMENT

When understood within the context of knowledge-creating careers, IAs possess unique properties that human resource managers often fail to take into consideration when making such assignments or to exploit when managers return from them. This section considers those distinctive properties and explores their implications for the development of global business leaders.

Syntactic and Semantic Issues

If IAs are to lead to significant knowledge creation beneficial to the firm, then human resource managers must address the syntactic semantic dimensions of careers. Syntactic dimensions include duration, sequence, and structure. There are several obvious issues. The duration of IAs tends to be arbitrarily established. Short-term assignments of nine months or less are usually based on the completion of a particular task or project. Long-term assignments

Figure 2.2
Four Types of Knowing over Time

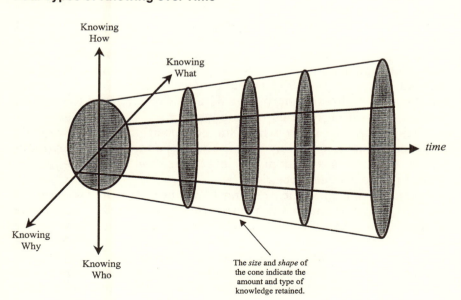

Knowing
How

Knowing
What

time

Knowing
Why

Knowing
Who

The *size* and *shape* of
the cone indicate the
amount and type of
knowledge retained.

often follow a standard length, three years being the typical tenure. These durations are set with little regard for the impact on knowledge acquisition or dissemination. Similar cultures and legal regulations and a common language make it possible for a U.S. manager to quickly learn how to get a new plant up and running in Australia. By contrast, it may take that same manager considerable time to learn how to set up a similar plant in China. The difference is not simply one of cultural distance, but involves the challenges of acquiring the right sorts of experiences through which useful new knowledge can be created. Chinese culture is high-context; that is, much of the communication essential to understanding what is going on is embedded in the situation rather than in explicit written documents or verbal exchanges. Consequently, U.S. managers working in China may need to acquire a substantial range of local experiences before they can make sense of what is going on around them. In other words, the most effective knowledge creation in the early stages of the assignment may take place via a tacit-to-tacit exchange—socialization—whereby a newly arriving manager might work closely with a local Chinese manager or an experienced expatriate. By contrast, U.S. managers in Australia may be able to create knowledge through a process of combination (explicit-to-explicit) in which U.S. managers and their local counterparts share their understanding of plant set-up and management.

Sequence is also an issue when considering the use of IAs in developing global business leaders. Though many large organizations carry out career planning to identify logical sequencing of positions and promotions for managerial personnel, it is not clear that such planning factors into the knowledge-creation process. An IA may be appropriate as the next step on a career path headed to the top of the organization, but not appropriate for moving a manager through the next phase of the knowledge-creation cycle. For example, after eighteen months in a domestic department focused on mortgaged-based securities, one manager at a U.S. investment bank was transferred to Tokyo where his new position was to oversee a Japanese securities trading operation. There was little if any room within the new assignment for internalization of knowledge acquired in the previous position.

A similar disruption in the knowledge-creation process is even more likely when managers return from IAs. It is rare that firms have a deep understanding of what the manager has learned or how to position the manager so that IA experiences can be effectively used in new knowledge-creation activities. In one typical instance, a manager returning from five years in Germany was placed in a holding pattern and put on six-month temporary assignment assisting in the training of new employees in the United States. His superiors had no idea how to capitalize on his German experiences within the context of existing training programs, nor could he identify ways to apply his hard-won insights in this assignment. By the time he received a longer-term assignment working with African subsidiaries, his German know-how, which over time he discovered was relevant to the assignment, had already begun to dissipate. Key contacts had moved or were no longer in position to help him.

Finally, firms are only just beginning to recognize that the structure of IAs must be tied to knowledge growth for both the individual and the organization. There has been longstanding appreciation that such assignments lead to personal growth and that this personal growth can have a positive payoff for the firm. However, few firms consciously consider the knowledge-creation process in making such assignments. For example, mentoring is widely recommended as a means of helping to train and counsel managers on IAs. Focused mentoring can also be used effectively to help managers make sense of their IA experiences in terms of what they can contribute to the firm or accomplish within the firm (use of tacit-to-explicit to create know why and know what).

Unquestionably, the most significant impact of IAs is the effect they have on the semantic aspects of an individual's career. Often the experience is so powerful that it has a transformative effect on the manager. Indeed, Osland (1995) couches the experience for many IA managers in terms of Joseph Campbell's "hero's adventure" and points out that managers return home fundamentally changed.

Ironically, though firms send managers on IAs to get experience and develop new insights, few firms seem to appreciate how successful they have been, often underestimating the growth in knowledge that managers experience in IAs. Returning managers report that work takes on broader significance. Moreover, they have a changed perspective of their role within the firm and within the world, as well as a changed understanding of where the firm fits in the world.

Three aspects of the IA experience help to explain why managers undergo significant transformations. First, both short- and long-term assignments often result in a commingling of work and nonwork experiences. Where the IA involves moving a manager's family to a new location, the manager often becomes caught up in a host of nonwork experiences in the host country that lead to learning and insight affecting a broader view of self, family, and the world in general. These insights cannot help but extend to a changed view of the work setting. Even in the case of shorter assignments not requiring the relocation of family, extended absences or the need to develop social support systems in the host country often lead to a new perspective on work, the company, and larger "purpose of life" issues.

Second, the compression of myriad novel, intense, and significantly different experiences into a short time span, as is often the case with IAs, leads to a proliferation of mental maps and the expansion of a managers' repertoire of schema and scripts for dealing with a multitude of commonplace and not-so-commonplace events. One obvious example relates to the proper way to greet people in a business setting. Prior to an IA in Japan, a typical U.S. manager would employ a handshake as the common form of greeting and introduction. After working in Japan for several months or years, that same manager would return home with an expanded set of greetings and introductions that would now include bows of various depths and rigidity as well as handshakes of varying strength and duration.

Finally, IAs also lead to significant loss of knowledge. Some friendships, acquaintances, and relationship networks wane; knowledge of some products and services or specific aspects of some organizational arrangements are forgotten; one's identification with the firm or its culture may ebb; and knowledge of certain techniques or the ability to use some skills may wither. IAs are not only a time of knowledge growth and development, they are also a time of loss.

Highly Enhanced Knowledge Creation

The essential element in knowledge creation, for both individuals and organizations, is personal experience, the basis for all tacit knowledge. Knowledge creation in each phase (e.g., tacit to explicit or explicit to tacit), draws on the current and past experience of individuals. But not all experiences are the same. Those which are repeated frequently (e.g., brushing one's teeth), provide little grist for new knowledge creation. Experiences likely to lead to significant knowledge creation share three things in common: variety, quality, and self-knowledge (Nonaka, 1994). All three are present in most IA experiences.

Variety of experience refers to the range of experiences acquired over a period of time. IAs are striking in this regard because they are like few other work experiences. Traveling to and working and living in a host country presents a wide range of new experiences. There are often one or more new cultures with a mélange of customs, norms, beliefs, and attitudes to be encountered across a vast array of situations and circumstances. There is likely a new environment with differing climate, terrain, and weather. There are new foods and beverages to sample and adjust to. There may be a new language to learn. There is also a new job with new colleagues in a part of the company not previously experienced.

A consequence of these varied, novel experiences is that the quality of experiences is richer and deeper. Expectations, which we carry into all experiences, are more likely to be undermet or overmet, forcing us to pay greater attention to the experience itself. Failures are likely to be more frequent, causing us to reevaluate assumptions. We are more likely to experience unexpected successes, filling us with surprise.

The heightened quality of experience increases the probability that we will have greater knowledge of experience (i.e., be more aware of the experience itself). This is because our reactions to such events have a strong affective component. They are more strongly felt. Moreover, the challenge of adapting and adjusting to the IA is often intensely stressful, heightening the impact of emotions, positive or negative.

In short, IAs can be characterized as rare occasions during which managers are likely to acquire extraordinary volumes of tacit-knowledge-fertile experience. This explains why the IA is a transformative experience for many managers. It has no comparison within a work context and few comparisons outside. The profundity of such experiences—the extent of variety, the depth of quality, and the intense emotionality—also help to explain why organizations have such difficulty in consciously deriving benefit from them. At the same time, few other occasions afford organizations with such rich potential for knowledge creation.

Sharing Tacit Knowledge Is Problematic

The potential for organization knowledge creation is substantial. Unfortunately, finding ways to elicit individual managers' tacit knowledge is problematic. The conditions on which effective knowledge creation are predicated usually are missing in the case of managers on or returning from IAs. Nor do managers themselves possess self-awareness or knowledge of process sufficient to initiate organizational learning on their own.

Given the volume of tacit knowledge acquired on IAs, efforts at organizational knowledge creation can focus on two modes: socialization (tacit to tacit) and articulation (tacit to explicit). Socialization, requiring as it does the one-on-one participation of an apprentice, is costly, time consuming, and, in the case of IAs, difficult to foster. Most socialization involves an understudy who observes and mimics a "master." This may be straightforward in the case of a cabinetmaker or a mechanic. However, it is hard to envision how one observes and mimics a master of IA. Effective socialization as a form of knowledge creation requires that the knowledge be observable, either through action or outcome, something that is nigh impossible to do with highly idiosyncratic IAs.

Articulation may not be much easier to facilitate. Nonaka (1994) suggests that the most effective vehicle for articulation involves dialogue within a field of sharing in which participants enjoy a common frame of experience. Interaction within such a field affords participants with occasions for explicit sensemaking in which one's understanding (knowledge) is made explicit through the stimulation that others provide. The type of knowledge created by this process is embodied in Weick's (1996) famous question, "How can I know what I mean until I see what I say?" Dynamics of dialogue give rise to new understandings as participants react to one another's statements. Recall the bread maker example in which Tanaka's insight was elicited through interaction with fellow team members.

The difficulty for organizations is in fixing a location for the sharing field and in assembling participants with the right set of shared experiences. To be useful, the knowledge must be created in ways that make it consistent with an organization's vision, mission, and strategy. Nonaka (1991b) suggests that this is accomplished by shaping a field through top management's resource allocation decisions and by the actions of middle management in organizing teams and providing general direction over tasks. But in the case of IAs, the field for sharing cannot be easily controlled by the organization. Most IA managers engage in sensemaking and dialogue in local, host-country social groups. Or, where there are sufficient numbers, IA managers may gather within the local subsidiary, but usually outside the office, once again in more social settings. The conceptualization of new knowledge, then, is likely to be on a more personal level, connecting tacit knowledge to family and self, and relating to work primarily in terms of career. Without the influence of the organization, and outside a peer group of fellow managers within the firm, there is little chance that tacit knowledge will be developed in ways that meaningfully contribute to organizational goals. Even when the articulation process elicits knowledge valuable to the firm, because it was created externally there is scant probability it will be accessed, tested, applied, or retained by the firm.

One option is for organizations to bring IA managers together on a regular basis, through knowledge retreats or under the guise of training seminars. For example, one Japanese MNC holds a regional semiannual gathering for its human resources managers in Europe. As part of this gathering, Japanese expatriates frequently congregate to talk among themselves. The result is new explicit knowledge. The challenge, however, is for the company to now find ways to codify and transfer this newly created and fleeting explicit knowledge to others.

Other Problems in Organizational Control of Knowledge Creation

Beyond the more basic structural challenges of shaping the tacit-to-explicit knowledge-creation activities of IA managers, there are several additional challenges for organizations. Extended involvement with overseas subsidiaries and with host-country personnel may lead to a shifting of employee commitment to the local operation or the emergence of a dual commitment to both parent and subsidiary. A greater commitment to the host-country subsidiary may lead to the development of knowledge that is overly localized. The old epithet, "He's gone native," may be an appropriate sobriquet describing the direction of individual knowledge growth for the IA manager who has developed a stronger allegiance to the host-country operation. Or upon return from an IA managers may be less committed to the organization and more committed to their individual careers or personal lives and families. They may be unwilling to invest themselves in the organization's knowledge-creation process.

Even when the returning manager is committed and the organization can structure the post-assignment position to facilitate knowledge creation to work in its favor, repository shifts in types of knowing may be so significant that they impede the process. For example, a broadened and more philosophical view of the firm's place in the world may create difficulties in a manager's ability to see connections between tacit knowledge and organizational mission. Or an expanded network of host-country contacts may be difficult to apply to new initiatives when the result of the IA experience has also been a drastic shrinking of headquarters relationships and acquaintances.

In a related vein, some of the most personally compelling learning and knowledge acquisition on IAs may not be specific to the firm at all. Managers often acquire nonwork living and coping skills when adjusting to a new country and culture. Such skills may lead to improved interpersonal repertoires and enhanced self-confidence through heightened self-awareness. Nevertheless, it may be difficult for the manager to fit these into the prevailing view of the firm that is held by colleagues back at headquarters. Indeed, many repatriated managers, having undergone a transformational IA, confront difficulties in fitting back into the home-country organization (Osland, 1995). If managers don't share a sense of community, they cannot effectively share the tacit knowledge they have acquired.

EXPLOITING THE KNOWLEDGE-CREATION POTENTIAL IN INTERNATIONAL ASSIGNMENTS

Viewing organizations as knowledge creators and careers as repositories of knowledge alters our perceptions of IAs and their value in developing global business leaders. The conventional wisdom has long been that IAs are invaluable in developing skills and knowledge essential to becoming an effective global manager. What has been missing is a framework for understanding why and how IAs contribute to leader development. Career planning takes on a different character when it is directed at providing opportunities for acquiring the right sorts of experience and creating organizationally useful types of knowledge.

If firms are to capitalize on the experiences that managers acquire from IAs, they must take action in two areas. First, firms must structure assignments to enhance the individual learning and growth that lead to tacit knowledge creation. Second, firms must construct fields of interaction for IA managers in ways that will encourage conceptualization and crystallization of new knowledge of practical value to the firm. These areas relate directly to issues of how IAs should be structured and how the tacit knowledge managers gain from such assignments can be exploited. For actions in these two areas to be effective, at a more fundamental level firms must adopt a knowledge-organization mind-set in which learning and the acquisition of new knowledge is valued as one of the firm's central goals.

Enhancing Tacit Knowledge

Firms can capitalize on the enhanced levels of tacit-knowledge acquisition that managers on IAs experience through thoughtful career planning and assignment management. Predeparture briefings provide occasions during which clear learning expectations can be established. For example, a typical briefing might encourage a manager to consider what aspects of past experience and current knowledge might be applicable in the new assignment. Experiences are greatly influenced by the expectations that people bring to them. In encouraging managers to reflect on past experiences, briefings shape the expectations that managers will hold as they embark on the new assignment. Such briefings have an added value of drawing the manager's attention to the experience itself, thereby amplifying the body–mind awareness essential to making experiences tacit-knowledge rich. Managers will be more likely to focus on the experience qua experience, rather than focus on the details of the assignment itself.

In planning and managing IAs, firms should also address the level and nature of variety in experiences that managers receive. For example, a Japanese MNC used the occasion of short-term assignments of three to six months in the United Kingdom to provide its managers with additional learning opportunities by incorporating visits to affiliated subsidiaries on the Continent. Though such visits were not necessary for completing the assignment, Japanese managers were able to acquire additional insights into the company's worldwide operations that were useful in their positions back in Tokyo.

Firms may also want to incorporate into an IA additional tasks or projects specifically designed to foster the development of tacit knowledge. For example, an IA manager in a marketing position might be asked to write a sales prospectus to be used in the host country or to design a seminar for host-country nationals.

Sharing Tacit Knowledge

Having provided managers with fertile IA experiences, the greater challenge for firms is in finding ways to help managers share their tacit knowledge, in the process creating new knowledge and simultaneously developing global business leaders. Firms can facilitate sharing in three ways. First, they can construct heterogeneous but balanced project teams and managerial groups. Returning managers often complain of being isolated or being placed in work units where they have little in common with others. Sharing requires a frame of reference that is at least partially held in common among group members. When IA managers are placed in units where they alone have international experience (or where those with international experience are in an extreme minority) sharing is constrained and the knowledge gained from IAs is either suppressed or dismissed.

Second, sharing of tacit knowledge gained through IA experience can be accomplished by establishing formal and informal reporting and briefing opportunities that focus explicitly on what has been learned. Most IA managers prepare reports on a regular basis about their progress on a particular project or assignment or on the performance of their units. However, it is unusual for them to report on what experiences they had, what they learned from those experiences, or how what was learned might be applied elsewhere in the organization. "Learning" reports are far more likely to lead to knowledge creation useful to the development of effective global leadership, both for the individual and the organization. In a related practice, some firms have returning managers give "learning" briefings for groups of colleagues and superiors. The briefings themselves and the accompanying question-and-answer sessions often lead to new insights for presenter and audience alike.

A third step firms can take is to enlist returning IA managers in the preparation and subsequent mentoring of new IA managers. Aside from the benefits new managers can gain from this type of wisdom sharing, former managers themselves are often transformed as they internalize the very wisdom that they share. An additional benefit of assigning returning IAs to work with new IAs is that it encourages the creation of informal networks for sharing IA tacit knowledge. Although not always formally supported, informal networks of IA managers develop naturally within most global firms. By bringing together new and returning IA managers, firms can influence the informal group formation, thereby shaping the field in which knowledge is shared and created.

A FINAL NOTE

Much of this chapter has focused on the knowledge growth and acquisition potential inherent in IAs. Unquestionably, such assignments hold tremendous promise when considered from a knowledge-based view of careers and organizations. However, if the metaphor of careers as repositories of knowledge is to be fully applied, then firms must also address the issue of knowledge loss among IA managers. While continuing education and professional development are an important part of developing global business leaders, it may also be necessary to provide refresher training or pursue other mechanisms through which managers on or returning from IAs can increase their overall knowledge base, not simply replace new knowledge for old.

3

The Effects of International Human Resource Management Strategies on Global Leadership Development

Marion Festing

The increasing globalization of markets poses challenges to companies all over the world. Gaining competitive advantage becomes a more and more demanding and at the same time critical task. The human resources of a company can support the creation of competitive advantage (Dowling, in press; Festing, 1999c). Kamoche (1996) suggests "that the human resource refers to the accumulated stock of knowledge, skills, and abilities that the individuals possess, which the firm has to build up over time into an identifiable expertise" (p. 216). From this definition it becomes clear that human resource management (HRM) has a support function in developing the knowledge, skills, and abilities of a company's managers.

A special set of knowledge, skills, and abilities is required for developing global leadership. The importance of global leadership is steadily growing because of the globalization of many markets and companies (e.g., see Brake, 1997). From a literature review, Yeung and Ready (1995, 531) derive that global leadership "affects the organizational interpretation of the environment (Daft & Weick, 1984; Dutton & Jackson, 1987), the articulation of business vision and strategy (Bennis & Nanus, 1985; Hamel & Prahalad, 1989, 1994), and the alignment and mobilization of people toward common ends (Kotter, 1991)."

However, due to changes in global competition, traditional leadership models do not work anymore (Adler & Bartholomew, 1992; Gregersen, Morrison, & Black, 1998). Whereas in the past the role of a leader mainly included resource allocation and rule setting for subordinates to control international activities, this has changed. In the context of global competition leadership becomes much more complex (Weber, Festing, Dowling, & Schuler, 1998). Managers not only have to deal with people from different nationalities and work in different countries (Morgan, 1986); they also face an increasing complexity of organization structures of large and diversified companies, permanent innovations in information and communication technology, and accelerated product lifecycles. These are important factors that force organizations to engage in intense global time, quality, and price competition simultaneously (Festing, 1999b; Yeung & Ready, 1995). Whereas traditional corporate visions have reflected the values and goals of the country of origin of the MNC, they now become global themselves (Adler, 1997c). To meet the new and complex challenges of global leadership, managers now have to fulfill a support and guidance function in the globalization process of companies, which requires a different set of skills and capabilities than in the past (Brake, 1997).

Concepts describing this new set of skills and capabilities are briefly discussed within this chapter. However, the primary objective is to analyze how global leadership development can be supported by international human resource management (IHRM) strategies in order to gain competitive advantage. Thus, the first question to be answered is how global leadership can lead to the development of competitive advantage. The chapter will then discuss one way of developing a strategic approach to the development of global leadership capabilities via the utilization of the strategic international human resource management (SIHRM) model (Festing, 1996, 1997). Case-study research from a study of IHRM strategies of ten German MNCs will be used to illustrate the implications of the SIHRM model for global leadership development, and the chapter will then conclude with a brief discussion of the implications of this paper's findings for scholars and practitioners.

GLOBAL LEADERSHIP DEVELOPMENT AS COMPETITIVE ADVANTAGE

Gaining Competitive Advantage

Primary sources of competitive advantage have been found in the external environment of the firm and by historically grown resources and capabilities within the firm (Hitt, Ireland, & Hoskisson, 1995). While the first-mentioned perspective, the I/O model (Porter 1985, 1986), underlies the SIHRM model discussed later in this chapter, the second-mentioned perspective, the resource-based view of the firm (Barney, 1991; Penrose, 1959; Wernerfeldt, 1984, 1995), is used here to explain how competitive advantage can be gained through global leadership.[1]

From the perspective of the resource-based view of the firm the organization is a collection of unique resources and capabilities. Competitive advantage is gained from the fact that other firms are not able to attain or easily duplicate the resources and their usage (Barney, 1991; Grant, 1991). This is especially true for knowledge. According to Grant (1996), knowledge has emerged as the most strategically significant resource of the firm. "Knowledge is a fluid mix of framed experience, values, contextual information, and expert insight that provides a framework for evaluating and incorporating new experiences and information. It originates and is applied in the minds of knowers. In organizations, it often becomes embedded not only in documents or repositories but also in organizational routines, processes, practices, and norms" (Davenport & Prusak, 1998, 5).

However, not every type of knowledge leads to sustainable competitive advantage. A critical determinant within this theoretical perspective is transferability (Barney, 1991). Only if it is difficult to transfer knowledge between companies would it represent a source of sustainable competitive advantage. Consequently, different types of knowledge have to be differentiated. A very common distinction is the one between explicit and implicit or tacit knowledge (Polanyi, 1966; Grant, 1996). While explicit knowledge can be communicated quite easily, this is not the case for implicit, or tacit, knowledge:

Tacit forms of knowledge are neither easily imitated nor clearly understood outside the firm. Unlike universal knowledge (which has an off-the-shelf quality), tacit knowledge is firm-specific and often cannot be written or encoded. . . . Tacit knowledge has an immutable, hard-to-decipher quality that cannot be easily transmitted to others, and often represents a shared experience among organization members. Thus tacit knowledge is richer than universal knowledge. (Lei, Hitt, & Bettis, 1996, S. 556)

In summary, the transfer of tacit knowledge between companies is difficult and costly because it can only be observed and acquired through practice (Kogut & Zander, 1992). It is more valuable for gaining competitive advantage—on the national or international level—than explicit knowledge. As for knowledge in general, this is also true for global leadership capabilities. The next section gives an overview on the global leadership discussion which is structured by these arguments.

Characteristics of Global Leadership

Regardless of the international context, global leadership also involves basic leadership capabilities. Following the definition by Yeung and Ready (1995), leadership capabilities "refer to the knowledge, skills, abilities, and attributes that leaders need to possess and demonstrate in order to perform their roles and jobs competently" (p. 330). Leadership roles include the following: setting a direction, aligning people, and motivating and inspiring. However, the relative importance given to the key roles may vary according to the culture of the leader and his or her subordinates (Yeung & Ready, 1995, 529). This is the reason why there is no general concept of global leadership that can be applied in every country. While some leadership capabilities may be considered important in many countries, others may be culture specific (Adler, 1997c; Hofstede, 1999). This is confirmed by an empirical study of 1,200 managers from ten major global corporations by Yeung and Ready (1995).

As global leadership is critical to success in international business, quite a few contributions have emerged that define the concept in different ways and from different perspectives (e.g., Gregersen et al., 1998). Some authors have empirically tested their conceptualizations (Spreitzer, McCall, & Mahoney, 1997; Yeung & Ready, 1995). For an extensive discussion on the state of research about global leadership, see Mendenhall (2000). Here, some major features of global leadership are discussed, based on the example of two concepts.

In their study of employees from eight nations, Yeung and Ready (1995) found a high degree of convergence for several key leadership capabilities. According to their results, the most important capability is the ability to articulate a tangible vision, values, and strategy. Others include "being a catalyst for strategic change," "being results-oriented," "empowering others to do their best," "being a catalyst for cultural change," and "exhibiting a strong customer orientation." The reason for the high degree of consensus of managers from different firms and nationalities is seen in the fact that managers are facing similar challenges in global competition. However, this result does not mean that unique competitive advantage through global leadership capabilities cannot be gained. As leadership capabilities need to be contextualized within each company's unique organizational cultures, histories, technologies, and socially complex interactions, they are hardly replicable, and differentiate a company from its competitors (Harvey & Buckley, 1997; Yeung & Ready, 1995). Consequently, if they are well managed they may lead to sustainable competitive advantage for global companies.

In their contribution, Gregersen and colleagues (1998) identify the following characteristics of global leaders: inquisitiveness; personal character, including emotional connection and integrity; duality, understood as the capacity for managing uncertainty as well as the unique ability to balance tensions; and business and organizational "savvy." While the first three characteristics are more general aspects in global leadership, savvy explicitly refers to the company's context. Organizational savvy means that "global leaders have intimate knowledge of their firm's capabilities and their ability to mobilize resources to capture market opportunities. They know the strengths and weaknesses of the organization, are familiar with the company's subsidiaries and competitive positions, and know key overseas managers" (p. 27).

As the exemplary analysis of these two contributions has shown, global leadership capabilities are always composed of general and company-specific knowlege, and—in the language of knowledge management—of explicit and implicit knowledge. According to the resource-based view of the firm only the last-mentioned aspect will lead to unique and sustainable competitive advantage. Consequently, it must be asked which requirements need to be fulfilled to develop these company-specific leadership capabilities.

Strategies for Global Leadership Development

Strategies for global leadership development can be discussed according to their didactic orientation as well as concerning the content. From a didactic perspective four broad categories of development methods have been identified. They include experience-based learning, which mainly consists of on-the-job-training, performance management with the measures of performance feedback and mentoring, and classroom education as well as benchmarking (see for an overview Yeung & Ready, 1995). Experience-based learning is of great strategic importance because this approach leads to the development of valuable knowledge about the organization and thus to the creation of tacit knowledge. However, this does not mean that other didactic approaches can be neglected. Classroom training may contribute to the development of other, more general leadership capabilities that are also important to the company. In summary, an IHRM strategy should not only concentrate on experience-based learning. It should add a variety of didactic approaches to contribute to the development of a set of global leadership capabilities that includes general as well as company-specific dimensions.

Concerning the content of global leadership development strategies, the term "global leadership development" may indicate a concentration on the HR function of management development. However, within this chapter the term is understood as a strategic goal of an IHRM strategy including all major HR functions. Thus, it corresponds to the requirements of a transnational HRM system defined by Adler and Bartholomew (1992): "A transnational human resource system is one that recruits, develops, retains and utilizes managers and executives who are competent transnationally" (p. 56). Important features of the HR functions of recruiting, developing, retaining, and utilizing are *transnational scope*, which addresses the geographical context and global management as a frame of mind; *transnational representation*, operationalized as the multinational composition of the firm's managers and executives; and *transnational process*, which "reflects the firm's ability to effectively include representatives and ideas from many cultures in its planning and decision-making process" (p. 56). The SIHRM model presented in the next section has addressed all these aspects. Thus, it goes beyond expatriate management. Nevertheless, the organization of international assignments also plays an important role within the IHRM strategies because it is considered as a very powerful strategy for developing global leaders (Gregersen et al., 1998; Stroh & Caligiuri, 1998).

To sum up, gaining competitive advantage through global leadership development requires appropriate IHRM strategies. These should address a variety of didactic approaches, but also pay attention to the fact that a high percentage of management development occurs through experience-based learning. This didactic approach is also useful for developing the tacit dimension of global leadership and in the long run may lead to sustainable competitive advantage. The model outlined in the next section shows one strategic approach to develop global leadership capabilities.

A MODEL OF STRATEGIC INTERNATIONAL HUMAN RESOURCE MANAGEMENT

The SIHRM model (Festing, 1996, 1997) consists of two parts. The first part links corporate strategy to the nature of work. The second part discusses appropriate IHRM strategies for different types of labor-market transactions. It can be derived from the model which corporate strategies global leadership is most important for, and how global leadership can be managed. Arguments are mainly based on transaction cost theory (Williamson, 1975, 1985). Figure 3.1 gives a graphical overview of the model. Theoretical arguments derived from the resource-based view of the firm are not included.

Figure 3.1
Model of SIHRM

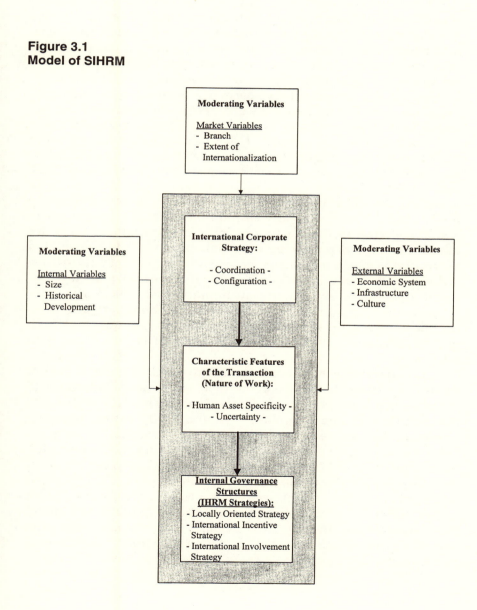

Corporate Strategy and the Nature of Work

Wright and McMahan (1992) have outlined that transaction cost theory can link corporate strategy to strategic HRM: "It seems intuitive that a firm's strategy can have an effect on the nature of work. To the extent that the nature of work changes . . . the types of HRM systems necessary to monitor inputs, behaviors and outputs also change" (p. 310). Following this idea in the first part of the model, corporate strategy is identified as the main factor influencing employment relations in multinational enterprises. It is demonstrated that it is mainly the corporate strategy that affects the nature of work in terms of human-asset specificity and uncertainty. In this context, human-asset specificity means company-specific qualifications of managers that are needed to meet the requirements of international positions, such as the knowledge of informal communication channels. Uncertainty is derived from the extent to which the outcome of a manager is easy or difficult to measure. These two variables will be outlined in more detail in the next section.

Within the SIHRM model, systematic variations between the dimensions of Porter's (1986) coordination and configuration model and the environmental factors of labor-market transactions are identified. With increasing coordination demands, person-oriented coordination mechanisms are of growing importance (Martinez & Jarillo, 1989). As these require company-specific qualifications of the managers, investments in human-asset specificity of international managers become necessary.[2] Thus, a strong need for coordination in multinational enterprises requires a high degree of company-specific qualifications of the international managers.

In the literature there is also evidence for the assumption that there is a systematic variation between the geographic dispersion of the enterprise's activities and the extent to which it is difficult to measure the outcome of employees. Hedlund (1986) states that geographical distance leads to higher control costs. As the environment of a foreign subsidiary may differ substantially from the environment of the headquarters, the company has to rely on information given by the managers of the subsidiaries. This information is always subject to interpretation (Doz, 1979; Weick & Van Orden, 1990). Thus, a highly dispersed multinational enterprise may have more difficulties directly observing and measuring the outcome of international managers than a company that is geographically concentrated.

The combination of the dichotomous characteristics of coordination and geographical dispersion lead to differences in the nature of work.

The Nature of Work and IHRM Strategies

In the second part of the model the efficiency of IHRM practices is analyzed. It is assumed that labor-market transactions characterized by a varying nature of work will be organized more or less efficiently in governance structures described by varying IHRM strategies. Thus, the main assumption of the second part of the model is that the efficient organization of work in multinational enterprises is realized by designing IHRM strategies corresponding to the nature of work. The nature of work is conceptualized by the degree of human-asset specificity and the extent to which the outcome of the employee is measurable.

The human capital of employees can be either of a general or a company-specific nature. Only the latter leads to a mutual dependence of both the transaction partners, viz. employee and company (Williamson, 1985). Williamson, Wachter, and Harris (1975) have described the idiosyncrasy of the employment relationship with four types of tasks. They distinguish between equipment, process, informal team, and communication idiosyncrasies that lead to mutual dependence in the employment relationship.[3] Examples of a high degree of human-asset specificity of international managers include the following: personal relationships that have developed during a long duration of an employment relation in a company, the knowledge of operating processes and equipment contributing to the understanding of the global and local requirements of the MNC, or the knowledge of communication channels and codes as well as the culture of the international organization (Evans, 1992, 94; Rall, 1989, 1085–1087; Hedlund, 1986, 27; Hedlund & Rolander, 1990, 33; Adler & Bartholomew, 1992, 56; Kumar, 1992, 327). An example for noncompany-specific human assets would be the knowledge of languages or cross-cultural skills that can be applied in other companies without any loss in productivity (Festing, 1997). All these characteristics of idiosyncratic tasks can only be obtained through long experience within the company (i.e., the IHRM strategy would include experience-based learning). The knowledge of foreign languages, however, can also be acquired through classroom training.

The definition and the examples of human-asset specificity show strong similarities to the concept of tacit knowledge (for further detail, see Festing, 1999b, 1999c). As has been outlined, for specific corporate strategies developing tacit knowledge of international managers—or, in the words of transaction cost theory, developing asset specificity—may lead to competitive advantage. These investments in human-asset specificity will be amortized by international managers by looking for a permanent employment relationship (Hedlund, 1986; see also Williamson, 1984). The same is true for the company, since it takes a long time to find and train a replacement. As Hedlund (1986) states, "Idiosyncratic assets should lead to internalization, according to Williamson (1975), so one can expect more encompassing and long-term contracts with employees" (p. 28) (for a more detailed theory-based explanation, see also Sadowski & Frick, 1989, 224). An early termination of employment is disadvantageous for both sides of the labor market (Gerlach & Lorenz, 1992). It is a critical function of an IHRM system to not only build company-specific qualifications but also to allow for retaining and utilizing them within the company.

Management tasks also vary according to uncertainty, the second important feature of labor-market transactions. According to transaction cost theory, the consideration of this variable is only important in connection with an important extent of human-asset specificity. Even then, uncertainty, conceptualized as the measurability of outcome, "only" has an effect on the kind of control realized through HRM practices. The consideration of the two key variables of labor-market transactions, human-asset specificity and uncertainty, leads to the development of IHRM strategies as part of governance structures:

- If human-asset specificity is high and if the outcome of work of international managers is easy to measure, monetary incentives can be offered for good performance. The IHRM strategy that is considered to be efficient in this situation is the international incentive strategy.

- If human-asset specificity is high and if it is difficult to measure outcomes, the multinational enterprise will aim more at increasing the involvement or commitment of employees. The IHRM strategy that is considered to be efficient in this situation is the international involvement strategy (IIS). The aim of this strategy is the adjustment of individual and corporate goals.

- In contrast, if company-specific qualifications are not vital for coordinating the multinational enterprise, there is no (efficiency) reason to design internationally oriented HR strategies. Neither the building of such qualifications nor programs for retaining and utilizing these qualifications would be conducted on the corporate level. Instead, HR strategies would be designed on a local or national level. This would be a locally oriented strategy.

Basic features of the three IHRM strategies are described in Table 3.1.

Key Insights of the SIHRM Model

The SIHRM model shows that efficient IHRM solutions in MNCs require a systematic variation of corporate strategy with the IHRM activities. This is explained by the nature of work. If coordination needs of the international activities are low, the locally oriented strategy is recommended. If coordination needs are high and geo-

Table 3.1
Description of the IHRM Strategies

	Locally Oriented Strategy	International Incentive Strategy	International Involvement Strategy
Superior Goal of the Strategy	Efficiency of HRM in subunit (Reason: low need for coordination)	Securing of company-specific qualifications by compensation for good performance	Securing of company-specific qualifications by creating involvement of the international managers with the company
Management of Expatriates (Main features)	Individual solutions	Above average compensation of international managers; International management development programs to build company-specific qualifications	International management development program including international job rotation, international career paths, international training, international groups, etc. in all business units
HRM Function	No guidelines and only a few contacts on the corporate level	International guidelines primarily concerning compensation policies for expatriates	International guidelines for a lot of HRM measures (e.g. international compensation, management development)
Corporate Culture	No international orientation in corporate culture.	International corporate culture may exist, but is not very important.	International corporate culture is very important.

graphical dispersion of international activities is low, the international incentive strategy would represent an efficient solution. The international involvement strategy is recommended when both coordination and geographical dispersion of international activities are high.

GLOBAL LEADERSHIP DEVELOPMENT THROUGH IHRM STRATEGIES

The Concept of Global Leadership within the SIHRM Model

The first part of this chapter outlined that global leadership capabilities are required due to changes in the competitive environment of MNCs. Considering the corporate-level strategic choices in the SIHRM model, the most complex requirements of a competitive environment can be expected when geographical dispersion of international activities and coordination needs of the international activities are extensive.[4] The SIHRM model has shown that in this situation investments in human-asset specificity need to be made and retained in order to gain competitive advantage. The appropriate IHRM strategy in this case would be the international involvement strategy, which aims at developing and retaining such qualifications while explicitly addressing the company-specific and tacit aspects.

Investments in human-asset specificity include global leadership development. As was outlined at the beginning of this chapter, global leadership capabilities need to be contextualized in order to be effective (Gregersen et al., 1998; Kumar, 1992; Rall, 1989). This contextualization means that company-specific investments are made. Very often they include tacit knowledge, as when organizational capabilities relevant to MNCs are at the center of consideration: "Transnational managers must learn how to collaborate with partners worldwide, gaining as much knowledge as possible from each interaction, and transmitting the knowledge quickly and effectively throughout the worldwide network of operations" (Adler & Bartholomew, 1992, 56).

The International Involvement Strategy for Developing Global Leadership

The IHRM strategies identified within the SIHRM model address all important HRM functions. As has been called for by Adler and Bartholomew (1992), they fulfill the requirements of recruitment, development, retention, and utilization of managers within the transnational human resource system. However, other activities have been added. Furthermore, expatriate management practices have been considered explicitly. It is supposed that all of the activities are designed to support the overall goal of the strategy.

Within this chapter, only the international involvement strategy is described in detail because this is the IHRM strategy that would be recommended when global leadership capabilities are needed. The measures carried out by this strategy allow for experience-based learning, which is indispensable to develop company-specific qualifications and thus human-asset specificity or tacit knowledge. The optimal combination of HR measures for this strategy is described in the following section (for more details, see Festing, 1996).

The objective of the international involvement strategy is to strengthen the involvement of the international manager with the company in order to build an efficient long-term relationship. Recruitment from the external labor market is usually early in the career. Criteria for recruitment mainly focus on behavioral aspects. Specific technical and management skills are developed within the company. Later in the career of managers, internal recruitment for top-level management positions as well as for foreign assignments is preferred. When selecting managers for international assignments, the personnel department is involved. This is important, because international assignments should be integrated into long-term career planning. Furthermore, professional selection procedures are applied.

Management development includes changes in function and of business units (if applicable). Top management positions are open to all managers regardless of their nationality. Training is not only function oriented, but aims at the behavioral dimension as well. Consequently, training objectives are improving technical skills on the one hand and developing involvement on the other. Performance appraisal is of great importance to provide feedback to international managers, and it is the basis for individual components of the compensation package. It includes a technical dimension as well as a behavioral dimension. International assignments are integrated into the management development program and individual career planning. This involves (relatively) long-term planning, careful preparation, and support of assignees. The number of expatriates compared to the total number of employees is relatively high, because high coordination needs require person-oriented control mechanisms (Martinez & Jarillo, 1989). International experience is important in the company and a prerequisite for top-management positions. Consequently, career paths are international and involve functional as well as business-unit changes. Usually, the duration of international assignments is limited because the international experience is needed in other parts of the company. Thus, the MNC does not strive for long-term assignments but for changing employments between headquarters and subsidiaries. Due to this policy, international experience in the company is quite common.

Compensation packages usually include financial participation schemes as well as pension plans for managers. Compared to other companies, compensation packages are competitive but the MNC does not pay top salaries for all management levels. Instead, they offer an interesting long-term career perspective. Salary is based on individual as well as company performance. Compensation of expatriates follows a systematic approach. Often the balance sheet approach is used for PCNs, HCNs, and TCNs.[5]

Additional measures within the international involvement strategy include HR guidelines for many activities. For key functions such as top-management compensation they are applicable on a worldwide basis. The HR department is involved in the strategic decision-making process of the company. The informal organization structure and the organization's culture are of high importance and their development is supported by IHRM measures (for a detailed presentation of the other IHRM strategies, see Festing, 1996, 181–187).

As can be seen from the description of the IHRM measures, many of them aim at experience-based learning: international assignments, individual career plans, and succession plans. However, classroom training and performance management are also parts of this approach. The strategy is designed to further long-term employment relationships of the international managers with the employer. In the next section the results of an empirical investigation illustrate the basic ideas of the SIHRM model.

THE EXAMPLE OF GERMAN MNCs

IHRM Strategies in German MNCs

Case-study research in the headquarters and subsidiaries of ten German MNCs has supported the assumptions of the SIHRM model to a great extent. Two out of the ten companies have pursued an international involvement strategy. This means that most of the HR measures described have been realized by those companies. However, in four cases, elements of the international incentive and of the international involvement strategy can be found. According to the model, this means that they have not found an efficient solution for their IHRM function yet. A reason for this result can be seen in the evolution of the companies. They are all engaged in a process of tremendous change. This is true for the corporate strategy as well as for the IHRM strategy. While they have already nearly finished the change process on the corporate level, the IHRM practices are still in a process of change. When considering the future goals of the IHRM policies it can be said that they aim at an efficient solution but because of the ongoing process of change they have not reached it yet. Of the other cases, one was characterized by an international incentive strategy and two by locally oriented strategies. One case was ambiguous. This company had just experienced a merger, and elements of several strategies have consequently been identified but no efficient IHRM strategy could be found.

Of course, other variables that have not been analyzed within this study may also have had an influence on the results. This may have been the case in the four companies where a mixture between the international incentive strategy and the international involvement strategy was found. If other variables had been considered other explanations would apply. However, developing a model or a theory always means that the real world is conceptually simplified in order to understand the problem. In the SIHRM model presented within this chapter the variables of interest were selected according to the transaction cost theory and thus the problem is mainly explained from this perspective.

Importance of Global Leadership

For the two companies pursuing an international involvement strategy, global leadership is of critical importance. The same seems to be true for the four cases characterized by a change process. All aimed at a stronger coordination of their worldwide activities. No company tried to reduce the extent of coordination. This may be interpreted as a reaction to the globalization of the world economy. International competition becomes more intense and consequently more and more multinational enterprises need to increase the coordination of their worldwide activities in order to operate more efficiently.[6] If control of international activities is essential, global leadership becomes critical to success.

Expatriate Management Measures to Develop Global Leadership

MNCs need international managers who have had the opportunity to learn through international experience. Their development occurs through sophisticated IHRM strategies. As has been pointed out by Gregerson and colleagues (1998), helpful measures in developing global leadership are extensive travel activities, working in global teams (for an overview, see Snow, Snell, Davison, & Hambrick, 1996), international training, and transfers. According to these authors, international assignments represent the most powerful strategy within this context. Some selected expatriate management activities of an MNC pursuing the international involvement strategy will be presented to illustrate this case.

The company focused on is a major supplier in the automobile sector, with subsidiaries in many countries of the world. Within this chapter the company is called "AUTO." In 1997, more than 60 percent of the total sales of nearly 50 million DM were gained in the automobile sector. Other important businesses are consumer goods and communication technology. Around 50 percent of the nearly 200,000 employees work in Germany; the other half are employed in foreign subsidiaries. The following are the IHRM guidelines of AUTO:

- International managers must have international experience.
- Career prospects are independent of nationality.
- International assignments are a most important management development tool.
- Contracts for international assignments differ from local contracts.
- Employees should speak at least one foreign language (English in the German headquarters, German in foreign subsidiaries).

International experience is an excellent opportunity to develop global leadership capabilities. In its best case it leads to the development of general leadership capabilities as well as to contextualized capabilities concerning the international activities of the company. The high importance of international experience within the MNC can be seen from the large number of German and foreign expatriates. Both are increasing more with the increase of assignments of HCNs and TCNs than the assignment of German expatriates. In 1997 nearly 700 Germans were assigned to foreign subsidiaries and 250 managers from foreign subsidiaries pursued an international assignment in the German headquarters or in a third country. Considering these trends in connection with the IHRM guidelines, it is clear that international assignments are of great importance to the AUTO corporation. International management development is one of the most important tools in IHRM, if not the most important tool. Career advancement is not possible without international experience. In contrast to other companies that have reduced the number of expatriates for cost reasons, the AUTO corporation has decided to further the internationalization of human resources and to develop managers suited for international challenges through foreign assignments. The MNC invests in the employees to build a qualified workforce for the future and has not reduced the IHRM program to international management training.

As Figure 3.2 shows, the increase in international assignments is supported by a systematic and professional IHRM approach. The management of assignments includes international selection processes, predeparture training, practical assistance, as well as long-term repatriation planning. Furthermore, international assignments are integrated in individual career plans. Measures are designed in cooperation between the IHRM department and the respective business unit. The objective of the management development program is to develop qualifications needed in international management, and to increase motivation and identification of international managers. The AUTO corporation is aware of the strategic importance of its international managers. Developing global leadership is one of the major goals of IHRM activities. They support long-term employment relationships of company-specific qualified managers in order to gain sustainable competitive advantage.

Figure 3.2
IHRM Measures for International Assignments of a German MNC

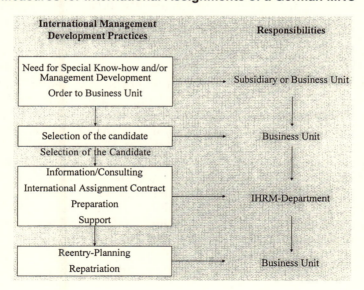

CONCLUSION

The implications of this chapter for practitioners mainly focus on the company-specific aspect of global leadership. This is not a qualification that can be developed from one day to the other or found on the external labor market. Thus, HR managers need to take a strategic approach to developing and retaining managers with company-specific qualifications. The company must offer opportunities to international managers to get to know the global organization and its people. Only experience-based development may lead to company-specific international know-how. A nonsystematic approach or a hire-and-fire policy with regard to these valuable human resources would be dangerous for the company's competitiveness on the global market. Instead, a long-term perspective is essential when considering employment relationships with international managers. The international involvement strategy includes a suggestion for a strategic approach to international human resource management. The strategic perspective also shows that it is most important not to consider the HR measures independently from each other but to design them according to a common objective. Following this approach, MNCs may be able to develop global leadership capabilities.

The arguments within this chapter have shown that global leadership is of crucial importance to gaining sustainable competitive advantage. This is especially true for industries characterized by a high degree of globalization. For MNCs competing in these markets, global leadership capabilities are a valuable resource. These insights have been derived from the combination of the two strategic approaches, the I/O model and the resource-based view. Thus, it seems to be important to use both perspectives.

Furthermore, a concept has been presented that contributes to the analysis of the strategic orientation of the HR function in order to gain competitive advantage. It has shown that the international involvement strategy is able to support the development of global leadership capabilities. Other important insights derived from transaction cost theory include the aspect of retaining and utilizing company-specific qualified employees. As global leadership capabilities are contextualized, it is important to offer a challenging perspective to international managers in order to allow for amortization of investments for both employer and employee. Thus, the IHRM strategy outlined in the SIHRM model goes beyond the development aspect of global leadership. However, using this strategy is not an efficient solution for every company. Without considering the corporate strategy it would be risky to imitate the

IHRM strategy of another MNC. Best practice in one company may not be best practice in another.

The limits of the SIHRM concept include that it may be culture bound. Empirical evidence of the SIHRM model has only been analyzed in German MNCs. Central concepts of the SIHRM model are the long-term relationship and the economic focus on the employment relationship. In other cultures these aspects may be perceived in different ways (Hofstede, 1996). Thus, the extent to which coordination mechanisms and IHRM measures are used may vary according to the country of origin of the MNC (Harzing, 1999). Consequently, further research is needed in this area.

Furthermore, characteristic features of global leadership have been defined in this chapter according to the chosen theoretical framework. This is a very specific perspective highlighting the company-specific or tacit dimension of this global leadership concept. More research is needed on the general and culture-bound nature of global leadership.

This chapter has taken an organizational perspective on global leadership. This means that the strategic importance of global leadership for gaining competitive advantage has been discussed. An analysis of global leadership at the individual level, as in other chapters within this book, however, complements the arguments. Only both perspectives can lead to a full understanding of the problem of global leadership development.

NOTES

1. To fully understand the problem of competitive advantage, both perspectives need to be considered (Festing, 1999b). This would not be necessary if all industries were characterized by a high extent of globalization (Macharzina & Wolf, 1996).

2. Bartlett and Ghoshal (1987a, 1987b, 1989) evaluate qualifications needed for a high degree of coordination in a similar way with regard to transnational companies, and Hedlund (1986, 24) with regard to the concept of heterarchy. See also Edström and Galbraith (1977, 260), Evans (1992, 95), Macharzina (1992, 11), Rall (1989, 1,085), and Welch and Welch (1991, 15).

3. These are tasks requiring a special know-how concerning the use of idiosyncratic equipment (equipment idiosyncrasies), the knowledge of specific operating contexts (process idiosyncrasies), informal networks between employees engaged in recurrent contact (informal team idiosyncrasies), and firm-specific information channels and codes (communication idiosyncrasies).

4. Within this chapter it is not possible to further discuss the diverse organizational structures of globalized corporations that change the bor-

ders of organizations (for an overview, see, for example, Buckley & Casson, 1998, or Picot, Reichwald, & Wiegand, 1996).

5. "The balance sheet approach to international compensation is a system designed to equalize the purchasing power of employees at comparable position levels living abroad and in the home-country, and to provide incentives to offset qualitative differences between assignment locations" (Dowling, Welch, & Schuler, 1999, 190).

6. However, according to the model it would be wrong to conclude that every company should have the same IHRM strategy. There might be a similar development in many companies, but without considering the corporate strategy of the company it is very risky to imitate the IHRM strategy of another company.

4

The German Approach to Developing Global Leaders via Expatriation

Torsten M. Kühlmann

An increasing number of German corporations are realizing that their long-term performance depends upon a successful international presence. "Going international" is not a new phenomenon in German business. What is new, however, is the pace and scope of internationalization. Foreign sales amounted to 950 billion DM in 1998, which is an increase of 40 percent compared to 1990 (Deutsche Bundesbank, 1999). German corporations are generating an average of 60 percent of their sales outside of Germany (Unctad, 1998). Embedded in this trend is the fact that a growing number of small- and medium-size German enterprises rely heavily on the international market for revenues.

Besides trade, international investment has increased substantially as well. Foreign-direct-investment (FDI) outflows from Germany set a new record in 1998. The outflows reached about 121 billion DM, rising from 25.6 billion DM in 1993 (Deutsche Bundesbank, 1999). After the United States and Great Britain, Germany is the world's third-largest investor abroad. Automakers like BMW and DaimlerChrysler have built new assembly plants throughout the world. Not surprisingly, German suppliers of automotive components have followed their customers abroad. Internationalization has been a necessity for the survival of the textile and clothing industry in a high-wage country such as Germany. Many companies from this industrial sector have moved their production chains overseas. The preferred destination for FDI from Germany is the United States; however, the amount of investment directed to developing countries in Asia, Latin America, and Eastern Europe is growing as well.

Agreements between German firms and firms from different countries (e.g., joint ventures, licensing, R&D partnerships) have gained importance in the 1990s as complements to trade and investment. Well-known examples are the international joint ventures Volkswagen runs with the Shanghai Tractor and Automotive Corporation in the People's Republic of China, with Skoda in the Czech Republic, and with Ford in Portugal. Together with United Airlines, SAS, Thai Airways, Air Canada, Varig, and Air New Zealand, the German airline Lufthansa has built a global partnership called "Star Alliance." An R&D cooperation has been established by Siemens, IBM, Motorola, and Toshiba to develop 256MB microchips. A growing number of small- and medium-size enterprises utilize cross-border interfirm agreements when entering new foreign markets (Bamberger, Eßling, Evers, & Wrona, 1995; Lubritz, 1998; OECD, 1993; for examples, see Köhler, 1997).

International mergers and acquisitions are increasingly being used as a means of entering foreign markets. Over the last two years German multinationals have made spectacular mergers and acquisitions abroad, with such well-known companies as Bankers Trust, Chrysler, Random House, Rhone-Poulenc, and Westinghouse Power Generation. Non-German employees already represent about 50 percent of the workforce in multinational corporations like Volkswagen, Bayer, or Siemens (Unctad, 1998). At the same time, more than 80,000 German managers and technical personnel have been appointed to positions in European subsidiaries alone. Unfortunately, there are no data about the number of German expatriates outside the European Union.

The implications of internationalization for the workforce are manifold: change of job designs, restructuring of chains of command, loss of job security, attention to international rules, and, above all, cross-cultural interactions. Employees have contact with foreign coworkers, executives, suppliers, customers, civil servants, and competitors, not only abroad but also at their domestic workplaces. Increasingly, direct face-to-face contact is being replaced by communication via e-mail and/or videoconferencing (Brewster & Scullion, 1997; Martinez & Jarillo, 1991; Price Waterhouse, 1997).

In response to these changes, many German firms that operate internationally are busily creating pools of employees who are capable, as well as willing, to work in an international environment. There is a growing recognition that employees with international expertise do make a difference in gaining competitive advantage in the global marketplace (Festing, 1996; Macharzina & Wolf, 1996; Mayrhofer, 1996; Schuler, 1995; Stroh & Caligiuri, 1998; Taylor, Beechler, & Napier, 1996; Tung, 1988b; Wolf, 1994).

Most German human resource managers claim a lack of internationally competent personnel. Of particular importance is the shortage of leaders who have the skills, knowledge, and attitudes necessary to interact with foreigners. Therefore, global leadership development has become one of the most prominent goals of international assignments in many German firms (Horsch, 1995; Mayrhofer, 1996; Wirth, 1992).

In the past three decades, the main reasons for sending German executives abroad were (1) the transfer of know-how that the local labor market could not supply, and (2) the coordination and control of geographically dispersed operations. Although these motives for international assignments are still valid, the goal of global leadership development has gained significance as a reason for sending executives overseas. Surveys among senior executives of German MNCs show that between 80 and 90 percent use international assignments as a means of global leadership development (Bittner & Reisch, 1991; Wirth, 1992). For example, the German electrical equipment manufacturer Bosch started a trainee program for university graduates that provides opportunities for future executives to work in a variety of countries and receive firsthand international experience at the beginning of their careers. The Bosch example also reflects the tendency for German companies to give managers international experience much earlier in their careers than they did in previous decades (Hirschbrunn & Schlossberger, 1996; Mayrhofer, 1996; Scullion, 1993).

This chapter's intention is to give an overview of expatriation policies and practices in German firms, and to evaluate these practices against the goal of developing global leaders. Up to now relatively little empirical research has been conducted on international human resource management practices of MNCs that have their headquarters outside the United States. Thus, there is a shortage of data to substantiate trends of cross-national divergence or convergence in international HRM (Kopp, 1994). By documenting expatriation-related HRM practices of German companies, this chapter attempts to broaden the database from which international comparisons can be made.

SELECTION CRITERIA
FOR INTERNATIONAL ASSIGNMENTS

Employees who are successful at home are not necessarily successful when working abroad and/or together with foreigners. The confrontation with unfamiliar business practices, the failure of once-effective strategies, and the ambiguity of situational demands and constraints require a set of competencies that go beyond technical skills or general managerial qualifications. Psychologically, working in foreign countries and/or with foreigners means stress on the individual and puts him or her at risk of physical and psychic illness (Barna, 1983; Berry & Sam, 1997; Coyle, 1988; Furnham & Bochner, 1986; Kühlmann, 1995a).

Not every person is capable of acquiring the knowledge, skills, and attitudes necessary for adjusting to a new environment and for interacting effectively with foreigners. Some may retreat to the comfort of the expatriate community and avoid confrontation with the hosts and their culture, some may try to convince the locals of the expatriate's home culture's superiority, and some may cope with the daily hassles of an overseas assignment by using psychological defense mechanisms (Berry & Sam, 1997; Stahl, 1998b). Thus, it becomes clear that simply assigning someone to an overseas position does not ensure that he or she will develop global leadership competencies. MNCs that intend to use international assignments as instruments to develop global leaders first need to carefully clarify the requirements expatriates have to fit in order to learn and develop leadership competencies for the global context.

A survey of ninety-two German MNCs found that 85 percent lacked a specific set of requirements against which they assessed the potential of their prospective expatriates for international assignments in general and for leadership development in particular (Marx, 1996). These findings are similar to the results of a previous survey among German multinationals (Wirth, 1992). Obviously, the spread of requirement profiles that consider the qualifications necessary for learning from the international experience in terms of global leadership development has not increased significantly in German multinationals during the last ten years. The majority of German companies base international selection decisions mainly on the assessement of technical skills, past performance, and availability (Horsch, 1995; Marx, 1996; Stahl, 1998b; Wirth, 1992). The logic underlying the selection process seems to be, "Employees who have done a good job at home, automatically have competencies that guarantee their successful performance in another country." The German experience parallels the practices found in MNCs throughout the world (Black, Gregersen, Mendenhall, & Stroh, 1999; Gertsen, 1990; Kealey, 1996; Marx, 1996).

The neglect of the candidate's potential to learn from his or her international posting corresponds to the state of research on global leadership development. Up to the present, the competencies of successful global leaders have not been empirically validated, and the personal prerequisites and instruments for systematic global leadership development have not been evaluated (see Chapter 1).

Research on expatriation has generated a general set of characteristics that influence performance and adjustment abroad. This set includes capabilities like empathy, open-mindedness, behavioral flexibility, tolerance of ambiguity, and language proficiency (Gudykunst, 1998; Marx, 1996; Mendenhall & Oddou, 1985; Stahl, 1998b). These and similar characteristics have been discussed extensively in the literature and are based on surveys of expatriates with diverse functions, company affiliations, and host countries. One has to speculate whether the predictors of expatriate adjustment and performance that can be derived from the research literature also support the development of global leadership competencies during an international assignment. On the other hand, it also seems plausible that developing competencies for leadership in the global context requires additional capabilities not frequently mentioned in the literature about expatriation. The expatriate in his or her role as a learner has to deal with a wide range of specific activities. Learning from the overseas experience requires actively confronting the foreign environment/foreign partners, experimenting with different modes of conduct, reflecting on observations, drawing conclusions, identifying general principles, and designing plans for more effective behaviors in the future. Thus, characteristics like curiosity, cognitive complexity, or reflectiveness could be proposed as significant predictors of global leadership development success. More research remains to be conducted before a comprehensive and empirically based list of learning capabilities necessary for the development of global leadership competencies via expatriation can be offered.

Another shortcoming in the identification of selection criteria in German MNCs concerns the disregard for the candidates' family situations. Although research suggests that spouses' well-being and adaptability are crucial for expatriation success (Arthur & Bennett, 1995; Black & Gregersen, 1991a; Black & Stephens, 1989; Torbiörn, 1982; Tung, 1981), the current selection practices neglect family issues. Only 15 percent of the companies in Wirth's 1992 survey consider the attitude of the spouse toward expatriation, the spouse's career aspirations, or the family in general prior to an expatriate assignment. A study of 116 German expatriates in the United States and Japan conducted by Stahl (1998b) found a complete lack of spouse participation in the selection process for a foreign assignment.

SELECTION INSTRUMENTS
FOR INTERNATIONAL ASSIGNMENTS

The German approach to selection is typically based on performance appraisals and unstructured interviews (Horsch, 1995; Stahl, 1995a; Wirth, 1992). According to a recent, yet unpublished survey of German multinationals which investigated best practices in international HRM, these selection techniques are being used by some 80 percent of German companies. However, they have been frequently criticized for their relatively low validity in predicting professional success, even within the home environment (Schuler & Funke, 1993). In addition, both instruments show significant weaknesses in their power to predict professional success, adjustment, and personal development of an employee when being confronted with new work and nonwork environments. Performance appraisals evaluate past performance in familiar surroundings; therefore, their predictive validity for future behaviors in foreign contexts is rather limited. The low validity of unstructured interviews is caused by lack of standardization in the usage of this type of interview, along with the fact that such interviews are not linked to any actual behavioral measures of the candidate's past or current performance, but to subjective self-reports. Finally, the tendency of interviewers to not examine the candidate's potential, but rather to promote the international assignment itself, negatively influences the validity of unstructured interviews. At the same time, evidence indicates that the systematic use of more valid selection instruments like psychological tests or assessment centers is virtually nonexistent in German internationally operating companies (Marx, 1996; Stahl, 1998b; Wirth, 1992).

One can summarize the current state of affairs in the following manner: German companies do not use state-of-the-art methodology when selecting candidates for foreign assignments. German human resource managers rely on candidates' technical skills as the sole criterion for selection for international assignments, which in turn are based on rigorous domestic performance appraisals.

PREDEPATURE PREPARATION
FOR CROSS-NATIONAL INTERACTIONS

Preparation and training can help to improve the ability to interact effectively and adequately with foreigners in work and nonwork environments (Black & Mendenhall, 1990; Deshpande & Viswesvaran, 1992; Kealey & Protheroe, 1996). Ideal preparation should enhance knowledge about cultural, political, legal, economic, and social conditions of the host culture. It also should further understanding of why foreign partners think and behave in different ways. Finally, it should improve interaction skills, especially the command of the foreign language. The survey by Stahl (1998b) shows significant differences between this ideal model of cultural preparation and the reality in German companies. Less than 40 percent of the expatriates interviewed in the Stahl study were provided with a look-and-see trip, foreign language training, or orientation lectures (see Table 4.1). Table 4.1 also reveals that preparation activities are not always offered to the spouses of the participating employees. Family-oriented preparation appears not to be a priority for many German companies.

When asking human resource managers about the preparation and training of expatriates managers for foreign assignments, the answers are more favorable. For example, the results of a British–German comparison study (Marx 1996) indicate that 91 percent of German companies are offering language training, 60 percent look-and-see trips, and 45 percent cross-cultural training. This contradiction to the study of Stahl (1998b) can be explained by taking into consideration that the listed preparation methods are not offered to all groups of expatriates and not before every international assignment.

Table 4.1
Predeparture Preparation and Training for Foreign Assignments in German Internationally Operating Companies (percentages reporting practices offered)

Practices	% reporting	
	Expatriate	Spouse
Look-and-see-trip	39 %	30 %
Foreign language instruction	24 %	10 %
Orientation lecture/briefing	24 %	0 %
Cross-cultural training	16 %	7 %
Briefing by returnees	2 %	2 %

Source: G. K. Stahl, Internationaler Einsatz von Führungskräften (München: Oldenbourg, 1998b); based on a survey of 116 German expatriates.

Most of the training that is carried out is based on cognitive approaches (e.g., lectures, books, videos). Experiential learning (e.g., role plays, simulations), which tends to have a higher impact on the acquisition of knowledge, skills, and attitudes, is an exception to the rule in German companies. The reasons for these shortcomings regarding the preparation for cross-national interactions can be put into three categories (Horsch, 1995; Thomas, 1995; Wirth, 1992):

1. Time pressure: Employees are often sent to foreign countries on very short notice.
2. Ignorance: There is still a prevalent belief that intercultural knowledge and skills are not really essential to success when collaborating with foreigners.
3. Doubts about training effectiveness: Managers are frequently not convinced that cross-cultural training is really an effective means for gaining control of the complex issues of international cooperation. They prefer the learning-by-doing approach.

ONGOING SUPPORT DURING INTERNATIONAL ASSIGNMENTS

Adopting new thoughts and behaviors requires more time and opportunities to learn than any cross-cultural training program normally can offer. At best, preparation for international assignments can simulate a lengthy process of adjustment, and prepare the individual to learn skills that are necessary to be a "continual learner" while in an international environment. The ultimate success of an expatriate depends on the efforts put forth by the expatriate himself or herself while overseas.

During postings to foreign countries the human resource departments of the German parent companies provide ongoing support to the expatriate and his or her family in different forms. The aims are twofold: (1) Helping the expatriate and family to cope with the adaptation to a foreign environment, and (2) safeguarding the interests of the expatriate in the parent company. Table 4.2 summarizes the extent to which German companies offer different lines of support (Hasbach, 1996).

Although the intensity of support varies, the majority of activities are directed at maintaining a constant and bidirectional flow of information between parent company and expatriate. A widely distributed mentor system ensures that each expatriate has been assigned a senior executive at home who has a "parent" function and takes care of the expatriate's future career development. However, systematic efforts to provide the expatriate with challenging tasks or a meaningful sequence of learning steps are lacking.

Table 4.2
Support Activities of German Parent Companies during Foreign Assignments

Practices	% reporting
Annual home leave	82 %
Mentor system	57 %
Information about parent company activities	70 %
Information about home country	55 %
Performance appraisals	73 %
Visits to parent company	68 %
Technical training	60 %
Language training in host country	39 %

Source: C. P. Hasbach, Die Erfahrungen von Mitarbeitern bei der Wiedereingliederung nach einem Auslandseinsatz (unpublished master's thesis, University of Bayreuth, 1996); based on a survey of 112 German repatriates.

REPATRIATION

For most German expatriates, their return to their home country occurs within four to six years of leaving Germany. Many of the returning expatriates face reentry problems because their expectations concerning career, salary, job, and living conditions are not met upon their return to Germany. Repatriation is the most frequently reported problem with international assignments in German companies (Marx, 1996). Fears concerning reentry are what worry expatriates most. To support the adjustment of returning expatriates, German companies have developed specific repatriation policies and practices. In spite of actual downsizing processes in German companies, 90 percent guarantee job security upon return (Marx, 1996). The obligation to take expatriates back is a minimum and nonnegotiable issue at most German companies. Table 4.3 indicates the use of specific reentry practices as reported by returned expatriates (Hasbach, 1996).

Table 4.3
Repatriation in German Companies

Practices	% reporting
Relocation support	88 %
Preview of financial package upon return	71 %
Information about the company's situation	57 %
Help with finding new position in the company	52 %
Help with finding a new position for the spouse	34 %

Source: C. P. Hasbach, Die Erfahrungen von Mitarbeitern bei der Wiedereingliederung nach einem Auslandseinsatz (unpublished master's thesis, University of Bayreuth, 1996); based on a survey of 112 German repatriates.

The practices reported in Table 4.3 cover the "technical" aspects of repatriation. What is lacking is support for handling what has been termed, "reverse culture shock" (Adler, 1991; Harvey, 1989). On their return, expatriates soon realize that their hopes for advancement in their professional careers, the opportunity to pass on their newly acquired knowledge and experience, social integration with their fellow employees, or finding new jobs for their spouses have been too optimistic. For example, surveys of German repatriates show that about 50 percent of them have not been promoted after returning from an overseas assignment (Müller, 1991; Hasbach, 1996). The confrontation with these unexpected problems can stimulate states of disorientation, anger, stress, and depression, especially when repatriates appraise their situation as being out of control (Black, 1992; Harvey, 1989; Kühlmann & Stahl, 1995; Martin, 1986).

German companies do not offer any counselling or training to help the expatriate and his or her family readapt to work and life "back home." Furthermore, international assignments have not been systematically integrated into overall career planning and succession programs. The returning expatriate is frequently seen as an inconvenient and unwelcome competitor for the few top management positions that have survived the recent downsizing processes in German firms. As a consequence, many repatriates start thinking about getting a job in another company. For the employing company, this means that it runs a high risk of losing their investments in the employee's development via expatriation (Black, Gregersen, Mendenhall, & Stroh, 1999; Gregersen & Black, 1995; Price Waterhouse, 1997; Stroh, 1995; Weber & Festing, 1996). In addition, German MNCs make no systematic use of the international expertise and orientation of the returning expatriate. The former expatriate often represents an overlooked source of international knowledge and personal relationships with foreign partners (Horsch, 1995; Price Waterhouse, 1997; Wirth, 1992).

CENTRALIZATION OF INTERNATIONAL HUMAN RESOURCE MANAGEMENT

The different functions of international HRM are widely centralized in German parent companies (Wunderer, 1992). Usually, the German human resource department holds most of the responsibilities for international HRM activities. A survey of twenty-two German companies with foreign subsidiaries illustrates this ethnocentric orientation very well (Graubmann, 1997).

Between 60 and 80 percent of the respondents reported a concentration of decision-making power at the German headquarters for each of the following international HRM functions: international personnel planning, recruitment and selection, placement, development, and compensation. The decision autonomy of the subsidiaries' human resource departments was limited to human resource issues of lower-level local employees; the structuring of international transfers of German managers was within the responsibility of the German human resource department. The geographical and experiential distance between the expatriate and the human resource managers in the home country made it difficult to plan the learning process step by step, to coach the expatriate when problems arose, and to control for development success. Essentially, the expatriate had to organize his or her own development.

Another disadvantage of centralization is the underrepresentation of foreign managers in the pool of assignment candidates. Given the dearth of German managers who are willing and able to go overseas, German companies increasingly will have to lean on staff from their foreign subsidiaries who possess the potential for international managerial posts.

RECOMMENDATIONS FOR THE DEVELOPMENT OF GLOBAL LEADERS VIA EXPATRIATION

This review highlights the need for stronger links between the management of international postings and their associated development goals. Despite the common intention to use international assignments as a tool for enhancing the global orientation and expertise of a company's actual or future leaders, few German companies actually address this task in a systematic way.

German human resource departments concentrate their activities on international remuneration and tax issues. The practitioner literature abounds with recipes on how to handle these topics. When attending relevant workshops or conferences on international HRM, the structuring of compensation packages for expatriates appears to be the biggest concern of international human resource departments. Admittedly, the area of international compensation is complex and dynamic. Developing an equitable, attractive, and cost-effective remuneration policy requires detailed knowledge of taxation rules, social security laws, cost-of-living indices, housing conditions, currency fluctuations, and so forth, which differ from one country to another and change over time. However, in order to pursue the goal of global leadership development and to maximize the learning impact of international transfers, additional issues have to be addressed. In particular, companies should do the following.

First, specify the criteria that are important for the expatriate to adjust to a foreign environment and to capitalize on his or her sojourn in terms of management development. Technical expertise is important, but not sufficient, to make a foreign assignment a success, particularly when development goals are to be attained.

Second, go beyond the assessment of technical skills and performance in the domestic workplace and include the evaluation of personality characteristics that correlate with the adjustment to different business environments or cultures (e.g., behavioral flexibility, empathy, tolerance for ambiguity), as well as the learning of global leadership competencies (e.g., curiosity, cognitive complexity).

Third, broaden the range of assessment criteria, which implies the use of selection techniques that supplement the widely used "unstructured interview" approach. Assessment centers, situational interviews, and biographical questionnaires could improve international selection decisions. Cross-cultural psychologists have developed specific tools that match the personal characteristics of the candidate with the challenges and demands of an international posting (see Chapter 11).

Fourth, consider the family situation of the expatriate. To date, this issue only plays a minor role in making assignment decisions, but given the increasing member of dual-career couples, MNCs will no longer be able to bypass the spouse issue. Previews of all the work and nonwork aspects of an overseas assignment can create more realistic expectations of what lies ahead for both the expatriate and his or her family. Unless companies provide better assistance in addressing some of the issues associated with the rising number of dual-career couples, many qualified and ambitious candidates will decide against an international assignment.

Fifth, provide cross-cultural training programs as a minimum standard when preparing candidates for a foreign assignment. Training programs will have to provide knowledge of the foreign country and understanding of cultural values and norms, as well as acquisition of behavioral skills that facilitate interaction with host nationals. Attending a cross-cultural training program for a couple of days may be sufficient to learn some facts about a foreign country and its people, but the traditional classroom-type training is an ineffective means for changing skills and attitudes. Development programs with a high impact, such as the Global Leadership Program (Tichy, 1992) are needed. In this program, multinational teams of five to six participants are created, and the program assigns the teams to a developing country that is unfamiliar to the members. The participants have to cooperate on site for two weeks to assess the long-term business prospects of the host country, including entry-strategy recommendations and video documentaries. At the same time, the teams work on their cross-cultural interaction skills.

Sixth, offer support during the assignment that is not restricted simply to relocation services, information exchange, and annual home leaves. Ongoing support also has to guarantee learning opportunities and feedback about the expatriate's leadership development progress. A mentor system can help to integrate the international experience within the expatriate's general career development. The assigned mentors, who have often gone through the same experiences, have multiple tasks in such a program: They coach the expatriate, provide contact with the parent company, locate suitable positions before reentry, give feedback on leadership development progress, and serve as a source of emotional support. The use of former expatriates as mentors will grant a visible recognition of the accomplishments and experiences of repatriated executives and strengthen their commitment to the company.

Seventh, foster strategic human resource planning that includes the repatriation of international assignees. One of the worst experiences of the repatriate is being placed in a "waiting loop" upon return from foreign assignment. Thinking about career options has to start before departure rather than some weeks prior to the termination of the foreign assignment. From the beginning, the expatriate should be included in the corporate succession-planning process. The succession plan should fix the probable length of the assignment, the tasks while abroad, and the prospective job positions on return. During home leaves, existing succession plans have to be updated depending on changing career aspirations of the expatriate and/or new realities in the company's internal labor market. Computer records of upcoming job openings and vacancies as well as candidate-supplied career-path aspirations can lead to a better match between the individual's and the company's goals.

Last, increase cooperation and coordination between headquarters and subsidiaries. A good deal of the international staffing weaknesses of German MNCs are due to poor cooperation and coordination between the human resource functions in the company headquarters and the foreign-based subsidiaries. An improvement calls for a change from an ethnocentric to a geocentric approach of international HRM in German companies. In particular, the responsibilities for international staffing need to be shared and coordinated between the human resource managers from German parent companies and their local subsidiaries (Wunderer, 1992). Taking the goal of global leadership development into consideration, the division of tasks could be as follows: The company headquarters identifies suitable candidates, formulates the specific development goals associated with a foreign assignment, and is in charge of the repatriation. The foreign subsidiary to which the expatriate is assigned has to create challenging learning environments, continuously evaluate the leadership development of the expatriate, and modify the learning process if necessary.

A joint responsibility is recommended for the design, implementation, and control of expatriation programs directed at global leadership development. A management development committee composed of representatives from the headquarters as well as from the subsidiaries is in the best position to decide upon the tradeoffs between investing in performance and in potential, satisfying the operational needs of today and putting into effect the strategic plans of tomorrow. Last but not least, joint management development committees could foster the development of host-country executives through assignments to the company's headquarters.

The description of international HRM practices in German companies reveals many similarities with previous research on expatriation in other countries (Black, Gregersen, Mendenhall, & Stroh, 1999; Kopp, 1994; Scullion, 1994). Thus, a universal thesis can be formulated: Irrespective of their country of origin, MNCs share the same deficits concerning leadership development via expatriation. These findings can be explained by the small number of senior executives who consider international HRM to be an important management function. Despite the unceasing statements by scholars in the field that HRM is a key source of competitive advantage in international business, many practicioners remain unconvinced and are reluctant to allocate more financial resources and manpower to improve policies and practices of international HRM. If Laurent's (1986) comment that international HRM its still in its infancy applies to theory, international HRM practice in Germany is still in its embryonic stage.

NOTE

Most of the surveys the reader is referred to in this chapter were conducted or supervised by Günter K. Stahl. The author gratefully acknowledges his collaboration. The author would also like to thank Mark Mendenhall and Günter K. Stahl for helpful comments on various sections of this chapter.

5

Global Leadership: Women Leaders

Nancy J. Adler

"Women will change the nature of power; power will not change the nature of women."

Bella Abzug, State of the World Forum, 1996

GLOBAL LEADERSHIP AND THE TWENTY-FIRST CENTURY

In his speech accepting the Philadelphia Liberty Medal, Vaclav Havel (1994, A27), President of the Czech Republic, eloquently explained that:

There are good reasons for suggesting that the modern age has ended. Many things indicate that we are going through a transitional period, when it seems that something is on the way out and something else is painfully being born. It is as if something were crumbling, decaying and exhausting itself, while something else, still indistinct, were arising from the rubble.

Havel's appreciation of the transition that the world is now experiencing is certainly important to each of us as human beings. None of us can claim that the twentieth century is exiting on an impressive note, on a note imbued with wisdom. As we ask ourselves which of the twentieth century's legacies we wish to pass on to the children of the twenty-first century, we are humbled into shameful silence. Yes we have advanced science and technology, but at the price of a world torn asunder by a polluted environment, by cities infested with social chaos and physical decay, by an increasingly skewed income distribution that condemns large proportions of the population to poverty (including people living in the world's most affluent societies), and by rampant physical violence continuing to kill people in titulary limited wars and seemingly random acts of violence. No, we do not exit the twentieth century with pride. Unless we can learn to treat each other and our planet in a more civilized way, is it not blasphemy to continue to consider ourselves a civilization (Rechtschaffen, 1996)?[1]

The dynamics of the twenty-first century will not look like those of the twentieth century; to survive as a civilization, twenty-first-century society must not look like the twentieth century. For a positive transition to take place, the world needs a new type of leadership. Where will society find wise leaders to guide it toward a civilization that differs so markedly from that of the twentieth century? While many people continue to review men's historic patterns of success in search of models for twenty-first-century global leadership, few have even begun to appreciate the equivalent patterns of historic and potential contributions of women leaders (Adler, 1996). My personal search for leaders who are outside of traditional twentieth-century paradigms has led me to review the voice that the world's women leaders are bringing to society. This article looks at the nature of global leadership and the role that women will play at the most senior levels of world leadership.

LEADERSHIP: A LONG HISTORY

To lead comes from the latin verb *agere* meaning to set into motion (Jennings, 1960). The Anglo-Saxon origins of the word *to lead* come from *laedere*, meaning people on a journey (Bolman & Deal, 1995). Today's meaning of the word leader therefore has the sense of someone who sets ideas, people, organizations, and societies in motion; someone who takes the worlds of ideas, people, organizations, and societies on a journey. To lead such a journey requires vision, courage, and influence.

According to U.S. Senator Barbara Mikulski, leadership involves "creating a state of mind in others" (Cantor & Bearnay, 1992, 59). Leaders, therefore, are "individuals who significantly influence the thoughts, behaviors, and/or feelings of others" (Gardner, 1995, 6). Beyond strictly focusing on the role of the leader, leadership should also be thought of as interactive, as "an influence relationship among leaders and followers who intend real changes . . . [reflecting] their mutual purposes" (Rost, 1991, 102). In addition, according to Bolman and Deal (1995, 5), true leadership also includes a spiritual dimension:

[T]wo images dominate in concepts of leadership: one of the heroic champion with extraordinary stature and vision, the other of the policy wonk, the skilled analyst who solves pressing problems with information, programs, and policies. Both images miss the essence of leadership. Both emphasize the hands and heads of leaders, neglecting deeper and more enduring elements of courage, spirit and hope.

Thus leadership must be viewed as something more than role and process—something more than the extent to which a particular leader has been influential. To fully appreciate leadership, we must also ask the ends to which a leader's behavior is directed. From this process and outcome perspective, leaders can be viewed as people whose vision, courage, and influence set ideas, people, organizations, and societies in motion toward the betterment of their organization, their community, and the world.

While comprehensive, this definition of leadership cannot be considered historically agreed-upon; indeed, no such agreed-upon definition exists. After reviewing more than 5,000 published works on leadership, neither Stogdill (1974) in the 1970s nor Bass (1990) in the present decade succeeded in identifying a commonly agreed upon definition of leadership. As Bennis and Nanus (1985, 4) concluded:

Decades of academic analysis have given us more than 350 definitions of leadership. Literally thousands of empirical investigations of leaders have been conducted in the last 75 years alone, but no clear and unequivocal understanding exists as to what distinguishes leaders from non-leaders and, perhaps more important, what distinguishes effective leaders from ineffective leaders.

Rather than adding once again to the already over-abundant supply of leadership definitions, this article simply adds two dimensions to the historical definitions of leadership; the first is a global perspective and the second is the inclusion of women leaders and their experience in a field that has heretofore focused almost exclusively on men.[2]

GLOBAL LEADERS: GLOBAL LEADERSHIP

Global leadership involves the ability to inspire and influence the thinking, attitudes, and behavior of people from around the world. Thus from a process and an outcome perspective, global leadership can be described as "a process by which members of . . . [the world community] are empowered to work together synergistically toward a common vision and common goals . . . [resulting in an] improvement in the quality of life" on and for the planet (based on Astin & Leland, 1991, 8; and Hollander, 1985). Global leaders are those people who most strongly influence the process of global leadership.

Whereas there are hundreds of definitions of leadership, there are no global leadership theories. Most leadership theories, although failing to state so explicitly, are domestic theories masquerading as universal theories (Boyacigiller & Adler, 1991, 1996). Most commonly, they have described the behavior of leaders in one particular country, the United States (and, as will be discussed later, of one particular gender, men). This is particularly unfortunate for understanding global leadership since "Americans' extreme individualism combined with their highly participative managerial climate, may render U.S. management practices [including leadership] unique; that is, differentiated from the approaches in most areas of the world" (Dorfman, 1996, 292; also see Dorfman & Ronen, 1991; Dorfman & Howell, 1988; Hofstede, 1991). Recent research on leadership supports this conclusion in finding that the United States is unique in several respects among all of the Eastern and Western cultures that have been studied (Howell et al., 1994). For example, based on 221 definitions of leadership from the twentieth century, Rost (1991) concluded that leadership has most frequently been seen as rational, management-oriented, male, technocratic, quantitative, cost-driven, hierarchical, short-term, pragmatic, and materialistic. Not surprisingly, many of these listed descriptors reflect some of the core values of American culture. For example, relative to people from most other cultures, Americans tend to have a more short-term orientation (e.g., they emphasize this quarter's results and daily reported share prices), a more materialistic orientation (e.g., forty percent of American managers still think that "the bottom line" is *the* criterion for corporate health, whereas no other nation can find even thirty percent of its managers who take this view; see Hampden-Turner, 1993), and a more quantitative orientation (e.g, emphasizing measurable contributions and results rather than relying on less easily quantified qualities such as success in relationship-building).[3]

Of those leadership studies and theories that are not U.S.-based, most still tend to be domestic, with the only difference from the American theories being that their cultural focus reflects the values and context of a country other than the United States; such as descriptions of Israeli leaders in Israel (e.g., Vardi, Shrom, &

Jacobsen, 1980) or Indian leaders in India (e.g., Kakar, 1971). The fundamental global leadership question is not "Do American Leadership Theories Apply Abroad?" (Hofstede, 1980b), nor is it the comparative question of attempting to determine the extent to which behaviors of leaders in one culture replicate those of leaders in other cultures. Both questions frame leadership within a domestic context; the only distinction being that the former focuses on a single country (descriptive domestic theories) whereas the latter focuses on multiple countries (comparative multidomestic theories) (see Boyacigiller & Adler, 1991, 1996).

Global leaders, unlike domestic leaders, address people worldwide. Global leadership theory, unlike its domestic counterpart, is concerned with the interaction of people and ideas among cultures, rather than with either the efficacy of particular leadership styles within the leader's home country or with the comparison of leadership approaches among leaders from various countries—each of whose domain is limited to issues and people within their own cultural environment. A fundamental distinction is that global leadership is neither domestic nor multidomestic; it focuses on cross-cultural interaction rather than on either single-culture description or multi-country comparison. The Secretary General of the United Nations cannot change his message for each of the U.N.'s more than 100 member states. Similarly the CEO of a global company cannot change her message for each of the countries and cultures in which her company operates. As we move toward the twenty-first century, the domain of influence of leadership is shifting from circumscribed geographies to globally encompassing geographies; from part of the world—e.g., a nation or domestic economy—to the whole world. Historically, such transnational leadership "that goes beyond the nation-state and seeks to address all human beings" has been "the most important, but rarest and most elusive, variety of leadership" (Gardner, 1995, 20). However, the essence of such transnational leadership was captured already centuries ago by Diogenes in his assertion to his fellow Athenians, "I am not an Athenian or a Greek but a citizen of the world" (as cited in Gardner, 1995, 51), and again much more recently by Virginia Woolf (1938), one of the twentieth century's thought leaders:

> *As a woman, I have no country.*
> *As a woman, I want no country.*
> *As a woman, the whole world is my country.*

Within this emerging cross-culturally interactive context, global leaders must articulate a vision which, in and of itself, is global;

that is, global leaders articulate the meaning within which others from around the world work and live. According to Britain's Anita Roddick (1991, 226), founder and CEO of the highly successful global firm, The Body Shop:

Leaders in the business world should aspire to be true planetary citizens. They have global responsibilities since their decisions affect not just the world of business, but world problems of poverty, national security and the environment. Many, sad to say, [have] duck[ed] these responsibilities, because their vision is material rather than moral.

Roddick's view of global leaders as "true planetary citizens" echoes Bolman and Deal's (1995, 5) observation that strictly emphasizing the hands and the head of leaders misses the essence of leadership by neglecting the deeper and more enduring elements of courage, spirit, and hope. The vision of a global leader, by definition, must be broader than the particular organization or country that he or she leads.

Beyond having a worthy vision, global leaders must be able to communicate their vision in a compelling manner to people from around the world. According to leadership expert Howard Gardner (1995, 8–9), "Leaders achieve their effectiveness chiefly through the stories they relate," both by communicating the stories and by embodying them. "Nearly all leaders are eloquent in voice," with many being "eloquent in writing as well" (Gardner, 1995, 34). As leaders, "they do not merely have a promising story; they can [also] tell it persuasively" (Gardner, 1995, 34).

Gardner (1995, 11) goes on to distinguish between leaders of a domain and leaders of a society. Leaders of a domain address an audience which "is already sophisticated in the stories, the images, and the other embodiments of that domain. To put it simply, one is communicating with experts"—such as when a medical doctor addresses other physicians. Leaders of a society "must be able to address a public in terms of the commonsense and commonplace notions that an ordinary inhabitant absorbs simply by virtue of living for some years within a society" (Gardner, 1995, 12). According to Ireland's President, Mary Robinson (1996, as cited in Pond, 1996, 59):

A woman leader often has a distinctive approach as the country's chief "storyteller, [personifying] a sense of nationhood and [telling] a story that also [helps] shape people's sense of their own identity." This is leadership by "influencing [and] inspiring" rather than by commanding.

As society goes global, the audience of a leader also goes global. What members of a global audience have in common is only that which is most fundamentally human to each individual. Global leaders, to a much greater extent than their domestic counterparts, must be able to communicate in terms of what is commonsense and commonplace for people worldwide; they must therefore communicate in the most fundamental terms of humanity. Global leaders do not enjoy the simplified reality that their domestic predecessors enjoyed of speaking primarily to people from one culture, one country, one organization, or one discipline.

GLOBAL LEADERS: WOMEN LEADERS

The feminization of leaders and of leadership is a significant development in our understanding and in the governance of global political, economic, and societal structures.[4] As we approach the end of the twentieth century, the number of women in the most senior global leadership positions is increasing and, at the same time, the style of global leadership is increasingly incorporating approaches most frequently labelled as feminine. It appears that "the economic exigenc[ies] of global competition . . . [are making] feminine characteristics admirable in both men and women" (Calas & Smircich, 1993).

This article focuses on women with positional power, women in the most senior leadership roles in major global companies and nations. The focus goes beyond the assumption that scholarship on women leaders must limit itself to women's historically more traditional mode of influence—that of influencing, primarily from behind the scenes, the men who hold society's most elite positions of power while the women themselves hold no positional power. See, for example, contemporary discussions of the influence on their respective presidential husbands of American first ladies, including the more than 50 books published on Hillary Rodham Clinton and the extensive literature on Eleanor Roosevelt (Goodwin, 1995). While the feminist literature has tended to champion the non-hierarchical notion of broadly dispersed leadership—that is, the empowerment of many leaders within society (see Astin & Leland, 1991, among many other)—in contrast to traditional, role-based, hierarchical, and more exclusive notions of leadership, this article attempts to bring the two notions back together. It asks what the nature of elite role leadership, as exhibited by women, will be in the organizationally flattened world of the twenty-first century.

Women Leaders: Numbers Increasing

The "feminization of an occupation or a job refers to women's disproportionate entry into a customarily male occupation" (Fondas, 1997, 258, based on Cohn, 1985, and Reskin & Roos, 1990). Thus the feminization of global leadership would be the disproportionate entry of women into the most senior political and business leadership roles in the world. Is there reason to believe that we will see the feminization of global leadership in the twenty-first century? Yes. While rarely recognized or reported in the media, one inescapable trend is that the number of the most senior global women political leaders—presidents and prime ministers of countries—is rapidly increasing, albeit from a negligible starting point. As shown in Figure 5.1, no women presidents or prime ministers came to office in the 1950s, three came to office in the 1960s, five in the 1970s, eight in the 1980s, and to date in the 1990s twenty-one have already come to office. More than half of all women who have ever served as political leaders—21 of 37—have come into office since 1990. At the current rate of increase, we would expect to have almost twice as many women become president or prime minister in this decade as have ever served before. As shown in Table 5.1, countries as dissimilar as Sri Lanka, Ireland, and Rwanda have had women lead them.[5]

Do we see similar increases in the number of women leading major world businesses as we see among women presidents and prime ministers? Whereas the pattern among global business leaders is not yet clear, initial surveys suggest that there are not very many women CEOs.[6] According to the United Nations' 1995 report, The World's Women, there are no women running the world's largest corporations (as reported in Kelly, 1996, 21). Catalyst reports that only 2.4% of the chairmen and CEOs of *Fortune* 500 firms are women (Wellington, 1996; as reported in Himelstein, 1996). Moreover, only in 1997 did Britain gain its first woman chief executive of a *Financial Times* (FT-SE) 100 firm, Marjorie Scardino at Pearson Plc (Pogrebin, 1996).

Contrary to popular belief, however, women's scarcity in leading major corporations does not mean that they are absent as leaders of global companies. Unlike their male counterparts, most women chief executives have either created their own businesses or assumed the leadership of a family business. A disproportionate number of women have founded and are now leading entrepreneurial enterprises. According to the Small Business Administration, for example, women currently own one-third of all American businesses. These women-owned businesses in the United States employ more people than the entire *Fortune* 500 list of America's largest companies combined (Aburdene & Naisbitt, 1992). As the list of women business leaders in Table 5.2 attests, the reality is that women from around the world are leading major companies. Moreover, contrary to what many people believe, these global women business leaders neither come strictly from the West nor predominantly from the West (see Adler, 1997a).

Figure 5.1
Women Political Leaders: Numbers Increasing

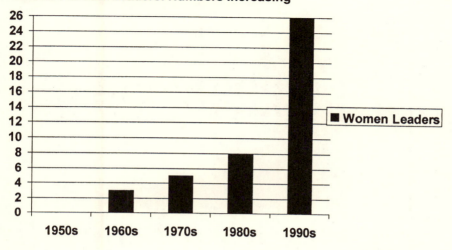

There is, of course, a fallacy in assuming that because global women leaders are still so few in number that they are not important (Bunch, 1991, xi–xii). In fact, as Charlotte Bunch (1991, xii), Director of the Center for Global Issues and Women's Leadership suggests, perhaps the most important question to ask is "why so little attention has been paid to the women who have become [global] leaders and why the styles of leading more often exhibited by women are particularly useful at this critical moment in history."

The Feminization of Global Leadership

In addition to increasing numbers, feminization also refers to "the spread of traits or qualities that are traditionally associated with [women] . . . to . . . people [and processes] not usually described that way" (Fondas, 1997, 258, based on Douglas, 1977, and Ferguson, 1984). Hence, the feminization of global leadership—beyond strictly referring to the increasing numbers of women who are global leaders— refers to the spread of traits and qualities generally associated with women to the process of leading organizations with worldwide influence. Whereas this certainly has not been true of traditional twentieth-century leadership models which have primarily reflected American men and their norms, it appears that twenty-first-century global leadership is increasingly being described in terms that neither reflect the masculine ideal nor the American ethos.

Table 5.1
Women Political Leaders: A Chronology

Country	Name	Office	Date
Sri Lanka	*Sirimavo Bandaranaike	Prime Minister	1960-65;1970-77, 1994-*
India	(Indira Gandhi)	Prime Minister	1966-1977, 1980-1984
Israel	(Golda Meir)	Prime Minister	1969-1975
Argentina	(Maria Estela [Isabel] Martínez de Perón)	President	1974-1976
Central African Rep.	Elizabeth Domitien	Prime Minister	1975-1976
Portugal	Maria de Lourdes Pintasilgo	Prime Minister	1979
Bolivia	Lidia Gueiler Tejada	Interim President	1979-1980
Great Britain	Margaret Thatcher	Prime Minister	1979-1990
Dominica	Mary Eugenia Charles	Prime Minister	1980-1995
Iceland	Vigdis Finnbogadottir	President	1980-1996
Norway	Gro Harlem Brundtland	Prime Minister	1981; 1986-89;1990-1996
Yugoslavia	Milka Planinc	Prime Minister	1982-1986
Malta	Agatha Barbara	President	1982-1987
Netherland-Antilles	Maria Liberia-Peters	Prime Minister	1984; 1989-1994
The Philippines	Corazon Aquino	President	1986-1992
Pakistan	Benazir Bhutto	Prime Minister	1988-1990; 1993-1996
Lithuania	Kazimiera-Danute Prunskiene	Prime Minister	1990-1991
Haiti	Ertha Pascal-Trouillot	President	1990-1991
Burma (Myanmar)	Aung San Suu Kyi	Opposition Leader**	1990.**
Ireland	Mary Robinson	President	1990-1997
Nicaragua	Violeta Barrios de Chamorro	President	1990-1996
Bangladesh	Khaleda Zia	Prime Minister	1991-1996
France	Edith Cresson	Prime Minister	1991-1992
Poland	Hanna Suchocka	Prime Minister	1992-1993
Canada	Kim Campbell	Prime Minister	1993
Burundi	Sylvia Kinigi	Prime Minister	1993-1994
Rwanda	(Agatha Uwilingyimana)	Prime Minister	1993-1994
Turkey	Tansu Çiller	Prime Minister	1993-1996
Bulgaria	Reneta Indzhova	Interim Prime Minister	1994-1995
Sri Lanka	*Chandrika Bandaranaike Kumaratunga	Executive President & former Prime Minister	1994-*

82

Country	Name	Office	Date
Haiti	Claudette Werleigh	Prime Minister	1995-1996
Bangladesh	*Hasina Wajed	Prime Minister	1996-*
Liberia	*Ruth Perry	Chair, Ruling Council	1996-*
Ecuador	Rosalia Artega	President	1997
Bermuda	Pamela Gordon	Premier	1997-1998
Ireland	*Mary McAleese	President	1997-*
New Zealand	Jenny Shipley	Prime Minister	1997-1999
Guyana	Janet Jagan	Prime Minister, President	1997-1999
Bermuda	*Jennifer Smith	Premier	1998-*
Switzerland	Ruth Dreifuss	President	1999
Latvia	*Vaira Vike-Freiberga	President	1999-*
Panama	*Mireya Moscoso	President	1999-*
New Zealand	*Helen Clark	Prime Minister	1999-*

Source: Adapted and updated from Nancy J. Adler (1996), "Global Women Political Leaders, An Invisible History, An Increasingly Important Future," *Leadership Quarterly* 7 (1): 136. © Nancy J. Adler, 1999.

Note: ( ) = No longer living;

* = Currently in office;

** = Party won 1990 election but prevented by military from taking office; Nobel Prize laureate.

Table 5.2
Women Leading Global Companies

Selected women who lead major global companies in countries around the world. Table
states annual revenues, or, in the case of banks, assets.

Argentina

> **Amalia Lacroze de Fortabat, $700 million, President, Grupo Fortabat.** Richest woman
> in Argentina, with nine cement companies, a rail cargo line, eighteen ranches, a news paper,
> four radio stations, part-ownership in a satellite-communications company.

> **Ernestina Herrera de Noble, $1.2 billion, President and editorial director, Grupo
> Clarin.** The largest-circulation Spanish newspaper in the world.

Australia

> **Imelda Roche, $237 million, President, Nutri-Metics International Holdings Pty. Ltd.**
> Skin cream and beauty products sold by 250,000 salespeople in 20 countries.

Brazil

> **Beatriz Larragoiti, $2.9 billion, Vice President and Owner, Sul America S.A.** Insurance
> company with 20% of the Brazilian market.

Canada

> **Maureen Kempston Darkes, $18.3 billion, President and General Manager of General
> Motors of Canada.**

Costa Rica

> **Donatella Zigone Dini, $300 million, Chairman, Zeta Group.** Fifth largest business in
> Central America, conglomerate.

Egypt

> **Nawal Abdel Moneim El Tatawy, $357 million, Chairman, Arab Investment Bank.**

France

> **Colette Lewiner, $800 million, Chairman and CEO, SGN-Eurisys Group.** World's
> largest nuclear fuels reprocessing company with contracts in Japan, Jordan, Pakistan,
> Indonesia, and the United States.

> **Annette Roux, $139 million & $31.9 million, CEO of Beneteau and of Roux S.A.**
> Beneteau is one of world's most respected yacht builders with employees in 28 countries
> and exports accounting for 60% of sales. Roux is one of France's largest hardware
> companies.

> **Anne-Claire Taittinger-Bonnemaison, $100 million & $230 million, CEO, Baccarat
> and Vice President, ELM Leblanc.** Company represents 40% of France's handmade
> crystal production; 70% of sales are exports.

Table 5.2 (*continued*)

Germany

Ellen R. Schneider-Lenné, $458 billion. Member of the board of managing directors, Deutsch Bank AG. Responsible for operations in the United Kingdom.

Hong Kong

Joyce Ma, $112 million, CEO, Joyce Boutique Holdings, Ltd. Designer clothes boutiques throughout Asia in China, Hong Kong, Malaysia, the Philippines, Taiwan, and Thailand, and The Joyce art gallery in Paris.

Sally Aw Sian, $237 million, Chairman, Sing Tao Holdings Limited. Publishes one of Hong Kong's largest Chinese-language daily newspapers, Sing Tao Daily; also publishes overseas from Sydney to San Francisco.

Nina Wang, $1 to $2 billion in assets, Chairlady, Chinachem. Property development, primarily in Hong Kong and China.

India

Tarjani Vakil, $1.1 billion in assets. Chairperson and managing director, Export-Import Bank of India; highest ranking female banking official in Asia; Bank promotes Indian exports and helps Indian companies set up businesses abroad.

Israel

Galia Maor, $35.6 billion. CEO of Bank Leumi le-Israel.

Jamaica

Gloria Delores Knight, 1.86 billion, President and managing director, The Jamaica Mutual Life Assurance Society. Largest financial conglomerate in English-speaking Caribbean.

Japan

Mieko Morishita, $85 million, President, Morishita Jintan Co., Ltd. Leading manufacturer of breath fresheners in Japan, with soft capsule technique in demand both in Japan and abroad.

Sawako Norma, $2 billion, President of Kodansha Ltd. Largest publishing house in Japan. One of companies international divisions publishes general trade books, including English translations of classic Japanese novels.

Harumi Sakamoto, $13 billion, Senior managing director, The Seitu Ltd. A supermarket and shopping centre operator expanding throughout Asia; Sakamoto opened stores in Hong Kong, Indonesia, Japan, and Singapore, and plans to expand to China and Vietnam.

Yoshiko Shinohara, $330 million, President of Tempstaff Co. Ltd. Second largest personnel agency in Japan; benefiting from demand boom for temporary services, including translation.

Table 5.2 (*continued*)

Malaysia

Khatijah Ahmad, $5 billion, Chairman and Managing Director of KAF Group of Companies. Financial services group.

The Netherlands

Sylvia Tóth, $166 million, CEO of Content Beheer. One of the Netherland's top temporary-placement agencies; also conducts training.

Philippines

Elena Lim, $114 million, President of Solid Corporation. Diversified company makes Sony- and Aiwa-brand electronic products exported to Japan, Europe, and the Middle East; is the Philippines' largest exporter of prawns, and produces Kia Pride subcompact cars for the domestic market.

Singapore

Jannie Tay, $289 million, Managing Director of The Hour Glass Limited. High-end retail watches, with boutiques throughout South Asia region from Thailand to Australia.

South Africa

Aïda Geffen, $355 million, Chairman and managing director, Aïda Holdings Limited. Residential commercial real estate firm.

Spain

Mercè Sala i Schnorkowski, $1.1 billion, CEO, Renfe. Spain's national railway system, currently helping to privatize Columbian and Bolivian rail and selling trains to Germany.

Sweden

Antonia Ax:son Johnson, $4.7 billion, Chairman, The Axel Johnson Group and of Axel Johnson AB. Retailing and distribution, more than 200 companies.

Switzerland

Elisabeth Salina Amorini, $2.28 billion, Chairman of the board, managing director, and chairman of the group executive board, Société Générale de Surveillance Holding S.A. The world's largest inspection and quality control organization, testing imports and exports in more than 140 countries.

Taiwan

Emilia Roxas, $5 billion, CEO Asiaworld Internationale Group. Multinational conglomerate.

Thailand

Khunying Niramol Suriyasat, $200 million, Chairperson, Toshiba Thailand Co. High technology. Started first company in 1963; established new companies in 1964, 1969, 1973, and 1976; in 1989 became director of real estate company in joint venture with Mitsui Corporation.

Table 5.2 (*continued*)

United Kingdom

Ann Gloag, $520 million, Executive director, Stagecoach Holdings PLC. Europe's largest bus company, with 7400 additional buses running in Malawi, Hong Kong, Kenya, and New Zealand.

Anita Roddick, $338 million, Founder and chief executive, The Body Shop International Plc. Body creams and lotions, with more than 1300 stores in 45 countries.

Marjorie Scardino, $3.6 billion, Chief executive, Pearson. A publishing and entertainment comglomerate, including the *Financial Times* and *The Economist*.

United States

Sally Frame Kasaks, $658 million, CEO of Ann Taylor Inc. Women's clothing retailer.

Loida Nicolas Lewis, $1.8 billion, Chairman and CEO, TLC Beatrice International

Linda Joy Wachner, $266 million, Chairman, The Warnaco Group, Inc. and of Authentic Fitness Corporation. Owner of both Warnaco, a lingerie maker, and Authentic Fitness Corp.

Zimbabwe

Liz Chitiga, $400 million, General manager and CEO, Minerals Marketing Corporation of Zimbabwe. In foreign-currency terms, the biggest business in Zimbabwe, administers Zimbabwe's sales and exports of minerals.

Source: Based on Caitlin Kelly (1996), "50 World-Class Executives," *Worldbusiness* 2 (2): 20–31.

What is a feminine style of leadership? "Feminine is a word that refers to the characteristics of females" (Fondas, 1997, 260). Many authors argue that "there are character traits, interaction styles, and patterns of reasoning, speaking, and communicating that are culturally ascribed as feminine attributes" (Fondas, 1997, 260). Although theorists debate whether these traits are biologically given or socially constructed, most researchers credit women "with some or all of the following qualities: empathy, helpfulness, caring, and nurturance; interpersonal sensitivity, attentiveness to and acceptance of others, responsiveness to their needs and motivations; an orientation toward the collective interest and toward integrative goals such as group cohesiveness and stability; a preference for open, egalitarian, and cooperative relationships, rather than hierarchical ones; and an interest in actualizing values and relationships of great importance to community (Belenky, Clinchy, Goldberger, & Tarule, 1986; Chodorow, 1978; Dinnerstein, 1976; Eisler, 1987; Ferguson, 1984; Gilligan, 1982; Glennon, 1979; Grace, 1995; Hartsock,

1983; Iannello, 1992; Klein, 1972; McMillan, 1982; Miller, 1976; Scott, 1992; Spender, 1983; Tannen, 1990, 1994)" (as cited in Fondas, 1997, 260). By contrast, as Fondas (1997, 260) summarizes, "traits culturally ascribed to men include an ability to be impersonal, self-interested, efficient, hierarchical, tough minded, and assertive; an interest in taking charge, control, and domination; a capacity to ignore personal, emotional considerations in order to succeed; a proclivity to rely on standardized or 'objective' codes for judgment and evaluation of others; and a heroic orientation toward task accomplishment and a continual effort to act on the world and become something new (cf. Brod & Kaufman, 1994; Gilligan, 1982; Glennon, 1979; Grace, 1995; Kanter, 1977; Seidler, 1994)."

Studies focusing specifically on women managers—as opposed to women in general or senior-level women leaders (on whom there is as yet no body of literature)—document their "orientation toward more participative, interactional, and relational styles of leading" (Fondas, 1997, 259, based on Helgesen, 1990; Lipman-Blumen, 1983; Marshall, 1984; Rosner, 1990). Frequently labelled as the feminine advantage (Chodorow, 1978; Helgesen, 1990; Rosner, 1990, among others), some authors have suggested that all managers today need to incorporate a more feminine leadership style (Fondas, 1997, 259). As Fondas (1997, 259) observes, these findings, "when juxtaposed against calls for companies to improve their competitiveness by transforming themselves into learning, self-managing, empowering, and continuously improving organizations—transformations that rely upon more interactional, relational, and participative management styles—[lead] . . . some writers to conclude that . . . [women] are well-suited for managerial roles in contemporary organizations and that male [managers] need to cultivate feminine leadership traits (Aburdene & Naisbitt, 1992; Godfrey, 1996; Grant, 1988; Peters, 1989)." The current implication is that both female and male leaders also need to cultivate such feminine characteristics in their styles of leadership.

However, leadership approaches that frequently have been labelled as feminine in the North American management literature—including more cooperative, participative, interactional and relational styles—appear to reflect male/female patterns specific to the American culture, rather than broader, universally valid patterns. Relative to American men, male managers in many other parts of the world, including in the fastest growing economies of Asia, exhibit a more supposedly feminine style that do American men. As Cambridge management scholar Charles Hampden-Turner (1993, 1) notes:

America's ultra-masculine corporate value system has been losing touch progressively with the wider world. It needs a change of values, desperately, or it will continue to under-perform, continue to lose touch with the value systems of foreigners, which ironically are much closer to the values in which American women are raised.

American women, who are socialized to display values antithetical yet complementary to American men, have within their culture vitally important cures for American economic decline.

It appears that some of the male/female cultural distinctions documented in the United States among domestic American women and men have been overgeneralized.

For example, as the economy shifts from the twentieth century's emphasis on mass production capitalism to the twenty-first century's emphasis on mass customization—that is, from the twentieth century's machine age emphasis on huge production runs of essentially undifferentiated products to the emerging era of products and services made in short runs and in great variety—the importance of interactional and relational styles increases. Why? Because "the future for developed economies lies in products [and services] uniquely fashioned for special persons" (Hampden-Turner, 1993, 6). Whereas the more typically male (from a North American perspective) universalistic approach of treating everyone the same according to codified rules worked well for mass producing products such as jeans, cokes, and hamburgers sold to a mass domestic market, a more typically feminine (from a North American perspective) particular approach works best for developing products and services—such as software—which must be tailored to the individual client and his or her particular needs. To understand particular markets and particular clients well enough to fashion suitable products and services to their needs, one must develop deep relationships. Not surprisingly, relational skills (labelled by the anthropologists as particularism and by North Americans as typically feminine) outperform the seemingly more objective approach of following the same rules with everyone (labelled as universalism by the anthropologists and as typically male by North Americans). The distinction does not appear to be strictly male/female, but rather a difference between the approach of most American male managers and that of most other managers around the world. Results of research by Trompenaars (1993) and Hampden-Turner (1993) show that American male managers strongly prefer universalism (the less relational style), whereas executives from many very strong economies, such as Hong Kong, Japan, and South Korea, emphasize more relational values which are opposite to those of their American male colleagues (Hampden-Turner, 1993). As Hampden-Turner (1993, 6) summarizes, at the close of the twentieth century:

Most American male executives suddenly find themselves ill-suited to the wider world, trying to codify the uncodifiable, flanked by a huge surplus of lawyers using cumbersome rules where other nations enter trusting relationships with subtle communications.

According to the research, American women display a relational style of communicating that is closer to the style of most non-American managers around the world than to that of most American male managers. Given American women managers' concurrence with the relational styles of their non-American colleagues, it is not surprising that, on average, American women expatriate managers outperform their American male counterparts (Adler, 1994). It is not that the distinction between women and men identified in the American managerial literature is either incorrect or inconsequential, but only that it is incomplete. Without appreciating American male managers as outliers, it is impossible to begin to appreciate what men's and women's approaches can bring to global leadership in the twenty-first century.

GLOBAL WOMEN LEADERS: AN EMERGING PORTRAIT

Beyond knowing that their numbers are increasing and that their approaches to leadership appear to differ from those of men, what do we know about the women who are global leaders that might help us to better plan for the twenty-first century?[7]

Diversity Defines Pattern. The dominant pattern in the women leaders' backgrounds as well as in the countries and companies that select them to lead is diversity. As highlighted in Tables 5.1 and 5.2, the 37 women political leaders and their business counterparts span the globe. They come from both the world's largest and smallest countries, the richest and poorest countries, the most socially and economically advantaged and disadvantaged countries, and from every geographical region. Countries led by women represent six of the major world religions, with four women prime ministers having led predominantly Muslim countries (see Adler, 1996, 1997a).

Many people believe that female-friendly countries and companies select more women leaders. They do not. Seemingly female-friendly countries (for example, those that give equal rights to women) do not elect a disproportionate number of women presidents and prime ministers. Similarly, companies that select women for their most senior leadership positions are not those that implement the most female-friendly policies, such as day-care centres and flextime (Wellington, 1996, as reported in Dobrzynski, 1996). For example, among the 61 *Fortune* 500 companies employing women as chairmen, CEOs, board members, or one of the top five earners, only three are the same companies that *Working Woman* identified as the most favorable for women employees (Dobrzynski, 1996).

The fact that the countries that elect women presidents and prime ministers or have women serving as CEOs of major companies are so diverse suggests that the overall pattern is toward selecting more women as senior leaders, rather than toward a particular group of supposedly female-friendly countries and companies (such as the Scandinavian countries, companies such as Avon Products, or organizations such as Britain's National Health Service) valuing women per se. The dominant pattern is that women are increasingly being selected to serve in senior leadership positions, not that a few countries, companies, or organizations with particularly feminine cultures are choosing to select women to lead them.

People's Aspirations: Hope, Change, and Unity. Why would countries and companies, for the first time in modern history, increasingly choose to select women for senior leadership positions? It appears that people worldwide increasingly want something that women exhibit (e.g., feminine values and behavior) and/or something that they symbolize.

Women leaders' most powerful and most attractive symbolism appears to be change. Women's assumption of the highest levels of leadership brings with it the symbolic possibility of fundamental societal and organizational change. The combination of women being outsiders at senior leadership levels previously completely controlled by men and of beating the odds to become the first woman to lead her country or company produces powerful public imagery about the possibility of broad-based societal and organizational change.

As "firsts," women assuming senior leadership positions literally bring change. When a woman is visibly chosen to become president, prime minister, or CEO when no other woman has ever held such an office and when few people thought that she would be selected, other major organizational and societal changes become believably possible. Mary Robinson's presidential acceptance speech captures the coupling of the unique event of a woman being elected Ireland's first non-male president with the possibility of national change:

I was elected by men and women of all parties and none, by many with great moral courage who stepped out from the faded flags of Civil War and voted for a new Ireland. And above all by the women of Ireland . . . who instead of rocking the cradle rocked the system, and who came out massively to make their mark on the ballot paper, and on a new Ireland (RDS, Dublin, 9 November 1990 as reported in Finlay, 1990, 1).

In addition to symbolizing change, women leaders appear to symbolize unity. For example, both Nicaragua's Chamorro and the Philippines' Aquino became symbols of national unity following their husband's murders. Chamorro even claimed "to have no ideology beyond national 'reconciliation'" (Benn, 1995). Of Chamorro's four adult children, two are prominent Sandanistas while the other two equally prominently oppose the Sandanistas, not an unusual split in war-torn Nicaragua (Saint-Germain, 1993, 80). Chamorro's ability to bring all the members of her family together for Sunday dinner each week achieved near legendary status in Nicaragua (Saint-Germain, 1993, 80). As "the grieving matriarch who can still hold the family together" (Saint-Germain, 1993, 80), Chamorro gives symbolic hope to the nation that it too can find peace based on a unity that brings together all Nicaraguans. That a national symbol for a woman leader is family unity is neither surprising nor coincidental.

Based on similar dynamics in the Philippines, former president Corazon Aquino, as widow of the slain opposition leader, was seen as the only person who could credibly unify the people of the Philippines following Benigno Aquino's death. Although Aquino was widely condemned in the press for naiveté when she invited members of both her own and the opposition party into her cabinet, her choice was a conscious decision to attempt to reunify the deeply divided country.

Given that women leaders symbolize unity, it is perhaps not surprising that a woman business leader, Rebecca Mark, chief executive of Enron Development Corporation, and not a male executive, was the first person to successfully negotiate a major commercial transaction following the Middle East peace accords. Mark brought the Israelis and Jordanians together to build a natural gas power generation station.

When, as Vaclav Havel (1994, A27) says, the world is "going through a transitional period, when something is on the way out and something else is painfully being born," it is not surprising that people worldwide are attracted to women leaders' symbolic message of bringing change, hope, and the possibility for unity.

Driven by Vision, Not by Hierarchical Status. What brings the women themselves into the most senior levels of leadership? Most women leaders are driven by a vision, mission, or cause. They are motivated by a compelling agenda that they want to achieve, not primarily by either a desire for the hierarchical status of being president, prime minister, or CEO, or a desire for power per se. Power and the presidency are means for achieving their mission, not the mission itself.

As children, none of the women leaders dreamed about becoming her country's leader, as have so many male politicians, including America's Bill Clinton and Bob Dole, and Britain's Michael Hesseltine. For example, Golda Meir's mission was to create the state of Israel and to ensure its survival as a Jewish state. Not only did she not dream of becoming prime minister, she rejected the position when it was initially offered to her. Similarly, Anita Roddick (1991, 126), CEO of the Body Shop, describes her contemporary vision as "corporate idealism." Her vision transcends traditional, narrowly defined economic goals; she is neither motivated to be a traditional CEO nor to focus singularly on maximizing either profits or shareholder wealth.

That women have not imagined, let alone dreamed about, leading a country or a major company is not surprising. For all of the women political leaders—except Sri Lanka's current executive president, Chandrika Kumaratunga, who followed her prime minister mother Sirimavo Bandaranaike into office, and Bangladesh's Hasina Wajid—and most of the women corporate leaders, there have been no women predecessors and therefore no women role models. What is important for twenty-first-century leadership is that society, if it is to survive as a civilization, can no longer tolerate nor support the leadership of self-aggrandizement at the expense of the greater, now highly interrelated whole—at the expense of the world's entire population and its physical, spiritual, and natural environment.

Source of Power: Broadly Based. Who supports women in becoming senior leaders? Women leaders tend to develop and to use broadly based popular support, rather than relying primarily on traditional, hierarchical party or structural support. This is particularly apparent among the women who become political leaders who often are not seriously considered as potential candidates by their country's main political parties. They are consequently forced to gain support directly from the people, and thus foreshadow the dynamics of leadership in an organizationally flattened world.

Mary Robinson, for example, campaigned in more small communities in Ireland than any previous presidential candidate before either her party or the opposition would take her seriously. The opposition now admits that they did not seriously consider Robinson's candidacy until it was too late to stop her (Finlay, 1990). Similarly, Corazon Aquino, whose campaign and victory was labelled the People's Revolution, held more than a thousand rallies during her campaign, while incumbent Ferdinand Marcos held only thirty-four (Col, 1993, 25). Likewise, Benazir Bhutto, who succeeded in becoming Pakistan's first woman and youngest-ever prime minister, campaigned in more communities than any politician before her. Her own party only took her seriously when more people showed up upon her return to Pakistan from exile than either they, the opposition, or the international press had ever expected (Weisman, 1986; Anderson, 1993).

In business, the disproportionate number of women who choose to become leaders of entrepreneurial businesses—rather than attempting to climb the corporate ladder and break through the glass ceiling to senior leadership positions in established corporations—echoes the same pattern of broadly based popular support—as opposed to traditional hierarchical support—that women political leaders enjoy. The only difference being that the entrepreneurs' support comes from the marketplace rather than from the electorate. In both cases, the base of support is outside of the traditional power structure and therefore more representative of new and more diverse opinions and ideas. The source of support, and therefore of power, more closely reflects the flattened network of emerging twenty-first-century organizations and society than it does the more centralized and limited power structure of most twentieth-century organizations.

Path to Power: Lateral Transfer. How do the women leaders gain power? Rather than following the traditional path up through the hierarchy of the organization, profession, or political party, most women leaders laterally transfer into high office. For example, Gro Harlem Brundtland was a medical doctor; six years later she became Norway's first woman prime minister. Similarly, Charlotte Beers became both Ogilvy & Mather Worldwide's first woman chief executive as well as their first CEO brought in from outside of the firm (Sackley & Ibarra, 1995). Marjorie Scardino, Pearson's first woman chief executive, is a double outsider. As the first American CEO brought in to lead this traditional British firm, she is a cultural outsider. In addition, because the *Economist*, where Scardino previously served as managing director, is only fifty percent owned by Pearson, she is an organizational outsider. The general public was so surprised by Pearson's selection of Scardino that Pearson's stock dropped initially on the announcement of her appointment (Pogrebin, 1996).

Today's global organizations and society can only benefit from the dynamics of lateral transfers. The twenty-first century needs integration across geographies, sectors of society, and professions. It can no longer tolerate leaders with "chimney stack" careers that, in the past, have resulted in deep expertise in one area, organization, or country without any understanding of the context within which their particular organization or country operates. Transferring across organizations, sectors of society, and areas of the world allows leaders to develop alternative perspectives and an understanding of context that is almost impossible to acquire within a single setting. Due to the historic pattern of promoting men and failing to promote women to the most senior leadership positions from within organizations—most often referred to as the "glass ceiling"—women appear to have inadvertently become the prototypes of a career pattern that is needed more broadly among all twenty-first-century leaders.

Global Leadership: Global Visibility. What difference does it make that a global leader is a woman? For the women who become global leaders, it is always salient that they are women. For example, the single most frequently asked question of former British prime minister Margaret Thatcher (1995) was "What is it like being a woman prime minister?" (to which Thatcher generally responded that she could not answer because she had not tried the alternative).

Women are new to the most senior levels of leadership. As mentioned previously, of the 37 women presidents and prime ministers, only two—in Bangladesh and Sri Lanka—followed another woman into office. All the rest of the women leaders are "firsts." Because women leaders are new, they have the advantage of global visibility. Their unique status as their countries' first woman president or prime minister attracts worldwide media attention, thereby leveraging historically domestic leadership positions into ones with global visibility and the concomitant potential for worldwide influence. For example, following the election of Mary Robinson as Ireland's first woman president:

Newspapers and magazines in virtually every country in the world carried the story. . . . [T]he rest of the world understood Ireland to have made a huge leap forward. . . . Mary Robinson had joined a very small number of women . . . who had been elected to their country's highest office. It was, quite properly, seen as historic (Finlay, 1990, 149–150).

Similarly, President François Mitterand purposely created a worldwide media event by appointing Edith Cresson as France's first woman prime minister. Likewise, in contrast to Benazir Bhutto's male predecessor who not only complained about receiving insufficent worldwide press coverage while abroad but also fired the Pakistani embassy's public relations officer when too few journalists showed up to cover his arrival in London, Pakistan's former Prime Minister Benazir Bhutto always received extensive media coverage no matter where in the world she travelled.

Because of the worldwide media attention given to women leaders, women today are becoming global, rather than domestic, leaders as they assume roles that were primarily domestic when previously held by men. Whether by intention or consequence, the senior women leaders are at the forefront of learning how to move beyond a domestic focus to communicate on the world stage to a global audience.

Whereas many of the dynamics affecting senior women leaders are quite different from those that affect women managers (see Adler, 1997a), it should be noted that international business women also receive more visibility than their male colleagues. Women expatriate managers as well as women on international business trips, for example, report being remembered more easily than their male counterparts (Adler, 1994). Compared with businessmen, global business women gain access more easily to new clients, suppliers, and government officials; receive more time when meeting with international contacts; and are more frequently remembered (Adler, 1994).

THE FUTURE: GLOBAL LEADERS, WOMEN LEADERS

The confluence of twenty-first-century business, political, and societal dynamics gives leaders a chance to create the type of world that they, and we, would like to live in. It demands, as Vaclav Havel (1994, A7) reflected, that leaders find "the key to insure the survival of . . . [our] civilization[,] . . . a civilization that is global and multicultural." The increasing number of women political and business leaders brings with it a set of experiences and perspectives that differ from those of the twentieth century's primarily male leaders. The interplay of women's and men's styles of leadership will define the contours and potential success of twenty-first-century society. The risk is in encapsulating leaders, both women and men, in approaches that worked well in the twentieth century but foretell disaster for the twenty-first century. As Dr. Frene Ginwala, Speaker of the South African National Assembly stated, "the institutions that discriminate are man-shaped and must be made people-shaped. Only then will women be able to function as equals within those institutions." Ginwala's fundamental belief is that "women's struggle is not a struggle to transform the position of women in society but a struggle to transform society itself" (Iqtidar & Webster, 1996, 10). Recognizing the growing number of women leaders is the first step in creating and understanding the type of global leadership that will lead to success in the twenty-first century.

NOTES

1. The opening section of this article is based on Adler's "Societal Leadership: The Wisdom of Peace" (1997d).

2. For contemporary discussions of some of the widely read leadership theories and approaches, see Bennis and Nanus, 1985; Conger, 1989; Conger and Kanungo, 1988; Gardner, 1995; Kotter, 1988; and Rosen, 1996 among many others.

3. For descriptions of American societal and managerial culture contrasted with those of many other countries, see, among others, Hofstede, 1980a; Kluckhohn and Strodtbeck, 1961; Laurent, 1983; Trompenaars, 1993.

4. Based on Fondas's (1997, 257) observation "that the feminization of managers and managerial work is a significant development in management thinking."

5. The Republic of San Marino, a city-state with a population of less than 25,000 people has been led since 1243 by a consul, the Co-Captain Regent, who acts as both head of government and head of state, and is elected for a period of six months. In modern history, four women have held the position of Co-Captain Regent, Maria Lea Pedini-Angelini (1981), Glorianna Ranocchini (1984, 1989–90), Edda Ceccoli (1991–92), and Patricia Busignani (1993). Due to the small size of the country and the frequency of changing leaders, San Marino has not been included in the statistics on global women leaders.

6. Although the results are not yet available, the author is currently involved in a major worldwide survey to identify women who head global businesses with annual revenues in excess of $250 million.

7. For a more indepth discussion of the issues raised in this section, see Adler (1997a).

6

Building Global Leaders: Strategy Similarities and Differences among European, U.S., and Japanese Multinationals

Gary Oddou, Hal B. Gregersen,
J. Stewart Black, and C. Brooklyn Derr

For the last several years the primary markets of most multinational firms have been international ones. Increasingly, U.S., Asian, and European MNCs are looking abroad to expand their market share (Green & Larsen, 1991). While some markets are well developed, others represent new ventures for most firms. This is particularly true with the dissolution of the U.S.S.R., the democratization and capitalization of Eastern Europe, and the opening up of Asian markets, particularly China and Malaysia. The growth and promise of these markets further challenge MNCs to develop an appropriate multinational business strategy (Arnold & Qualch, 1998; Dugan, 1991; Mason, 1991; Sasseen, 1991).

In fact, some believe that the effectiveness of such business strategies will come only as a result of the cultural savvy of the firm's key decision makers (Adler & Bartholomew, 1992; Bennett, 1989; Editor's Viewpoint, 1990; Gregersen, Morrison, & Black, 1998; Kobrin, 1994; Shetty, 1991). This cultural know-how will come as a result of the international experience the firm's key employees gain during the course of their careers. International assignments and travel can result in invaluable knowledge of the social, political, economic, and legal systems of the firm's markets (Bartlett & Ghoshal,

1989; Black, Gregersen, & Mendenhall, 1992a; Franke, Hofstede, & Bond, 1991; Millington & Bayliss, 1990; Stewart, 1990). Given the current and potential importance of international markets to today's firms, the challenge to develop an internationally minded cadre of executives has become clear.

With the proposed unification of Europe, for example, European MNCs and governments have developed specific programs for internationalizing their human resources to the opportunities and challenges within Europe (Bartlett & Ghoshal, 1989; Handy & Barham, 1989). The development of the "Euromanager" has become a clear priority for many European MNCs (Rajan, 1990; Schmidt & Ruiz, 1992).

Although the Europeans are currently focused especially on European markets, they have traditionally been part of the worldwide markets for many years. Firms such as Rhone-Poulenc, ABB, Siemens, Glaxo, Fiat, and many others have had multinational operations for decades.

Like European firms, Japanese and U.S. multinationals have expanded their markets well beyond their borders (Council for International Exchange, 1988). The Japanese have made significant progress in obtaining a large market share of worldwide auto, computer, and consumer electronic markets in a very short time. Although the Japanese initially largely exported, they have increased their direct investment significantly in the United States, Europe, and some parts of Asia. In fact, the Japanese quintupled their investment in Europe from 1984 to 1987 (Hirai, 1989).

U.S. firms have likewise rapidly expanded into international markets or begun to rely more on their foreign markets for important profits. The Council for International Exchange reports that even as early as 1988, 33 percent of U.S. corporate profits were generated by international trade, and that of the largest twenty-three U.S. banks, about half of their total earnings came from earnings overseas. With this kind of market expansion by European, Japanese, and U.S. firms, all face the challenge of determining the best strategies to enter foreign markets. Such challenges mean making appropriate decisions about product development, pricing, distribution, partnerships, recruitment, labor relations, and other areas that reflect international and multinational operations rather than the less-complex domestic operations. The decision makers, then, become a key focus.

What background, experience, expertise, personal characteristics, and training do decision makers bring to the situation? Clearly, the more "internationalized" the manager (i.e., exposure in some form to international business), the more his or her decisions in and about international and multinational markets will probably be appropriate. In essence, the more he or she is aware and knowledgeable about global business issues, the more effective a global leader the executive will be.

The focus of this research, then, was on how firms are internationalizing their human resources—the decision makers—regardless of whether the attempt to internationalize them was planned or not. From a review of the literature, interviews with practitioners, and the authors' own experiences, internationalizing a firm's human resources typically occurs through one or more of the following methods:

1. Expatriating host nationals to foreign operations to fill technical and managerial positions.
2. Bringing foreign nationals to the host organization's operations, mostly to develop and socialize the foreign employee for upper-management positions at the subsidiary, regional, or corporate level.
3. Organizing international or multinational task forces or project teams; these teams are created for a specific business purpose, but with the additional effects of learning to work in a multicultural environment and developing an international perspective.
4. Encouraging extensive international business travel; this is sometimes a response to complement expatriation, but it also has the distinct advantage of providing direct contact with foreigners and their environment instead of using electronic or other means to transmit and gather information.
5. Sponsoring seminars with in-company personnel; this method of internationalizing managers involves gathering appropriate company personnel from around the world or region for a specific business issue or firm concern (e.g., the "Green" movement around the world and how it might affect the firm's products).
6. Sponsoring seminars with noncompany personnel, which essentially does the same thing as 5 but with a different group.
7. Encouraging participation in international networks; such networks could include professional associations, company consortia, and so forth that span country boundaries.

The purpose of this research was to examine and compare methods that Japanese, European, and U.S. MNCs are using that lead to global managerial development.

EUROPEAN FIRMS' STRATEGIES TO INTERNATIONALIZE THEIR HUMAN RESOURCES

Traditionally, European firms have used international assignments as a principal way to maintain control and coordination within their subsidiary networks, but also to provide career development opportunities for selected employees (Barham, 1990; Derr & Oddou, 1991; Oddou, 1991; Scullion, 1994; Tung, 1988b, 1988c). Among European MNCs, the tradition of international assignments is expected to continue (Bartlett & Ghoshal, 1989; Ross, 1996), with an even clearer orientation toward internationalization in general (Vesperini, 1990). Ericsson, the Swedish telecommunications firm, regularly transfers teams of 30 to 100 engineers and managers from one foreign unit to another for one to two years. The French giant Rhone-Poulenc is in the process of formalizing its strategies to use international assignments for specific career development efforts. Volkswagen has begun to strategically assign new employees to international posts to develop an international perspective while they are still in very "formative" career stages.

Due to the high costs and complications resulting from increasing numbers of dual-career couples in Europe, MNCs are expected to balance international assignments with other methods to globalize their key employees. One way to balance such an emphasis is to have foreign nationals assume more responsibility for top posts and to focus on their career development opportunities to prepare them for such top subsidiary and corporate posts.

Common methods of increasing popularity include sponsoring more seminars to assemble their international personnel for perspective exchanges, organizing more international task forces, and otherwise encouraging managers, scientists, and engineers to acquire a broader perspective. European pharmaceuticals, such as Novartis and Glaxo, are centralizing their basic research but decentralizing their applications. Nonetheless, to create a coordinated strategy these firms regularly have scientists from various countries meet to discuss separate developments that potentially affect the others. From these types of meetings, more formalized international project teams often develop.

Recent related research has found that, by and large, European MNCs have similar strategies to those of their U.S. counterparts regarding their human resource development practices (Oddou & Derr, 1992).

JAPANESE FIRMS' STRATEGIES TO INTERNATIONALIZE THEIR HUMAN RESOURCES

As the Japanese move beyond their borders through direct investment, the need to become aware of and work within different countries' cultural systems becomes increasingly important. Research has already shown that much of the Japanese way is not culturally transferable to the markets in which the Japanese operate (Elmuti & Kathalawa, 1991). Specific cultural phenomena such as employee commitment levels, attitudes toward authority, consensus decision making, and Japanese career development practices are not easily applied in other countries. The fact that phenomena are not easily transferable reinforces the practice of developing and focusing on "one's own" (e.g., Japanese) during the international expansion effort instead of integrating with the host culture. In terms of expectations about internationalization strategies at the human resource level, the Japanese seem fairly consistent.

Research shows they manage subsidiaries largely through their own Japanese managers sent from one of the Japanese "family" firms (Negandi, Eshghi, & Yuen, 1985). The "bamboo ceiling" phenomenon for non-Japanese, for example, has already become well known (Schachter, 1988; Taylor, 1990). It is this kind of alleged practice that has influenced consumer behavior in the United States somewhat against Japanese products. Recently, the Japanese have begun to feel the need to increase their international awareness of foreign cultures and decrease their "isolation" from the rest of the world. According to previous research, Japanese expatriates are typically assigned to their international posts for five or so years, longer than either American or European expatriates (Tung, 1988c), and although they do place foreign nationals in top management at foreign sites, they are known to bypass these individuals in terms of giving them real decision-making authority (Negandi et al., 1985).

As a whole, the Japanese seem to integrate with other cultures less than Western cultures do. This tendency to "close off" other societies manifests itself in many ways. For example, the Japanese are known to prefer keeping the authority among those who have known one another, who can trust one another, and who can speak the same language as those in corporate headquarters in Japan (Negandi et al., 1985). In the educational system, many Japanese families remain in Japan while the father is expatriated in order for the children to maintain their Japanese associations and the Japanese integrity of their academic studies (White, 1988).

In short, the Japanese appear in general to be more insular and self-reliant than European or U.S. MNCs in their perspective and practices. This research will test whether this insularity will continue to manifest itself in the human resource practices examined here. The supposition is that this motivation to be a self-contained entity will translate into more human resource strategies that will preserve the "Japaneseness" of the firm, while nonetheless trying to address international market opportunities.

U.S. FIRMS' STRATEGIES TO INTERNATIONALIZE
THEIR HUMAN RESOURCES

It is clear that increasing numbers of firms are entering the international marketplace and that more and more of the profits from U.S. firms' sales are coming from international markets (Council for International Exchange, 1988). Researchers have been arguing that development of managers should include international experiences (Adler & Bartholomew, 1992; Black et al., 1992a; Gutteridge, Leibowitz, & Shore, 1993; Ross, 1996). CEOs and other executives of well-known multinationals are making clear statements about the need for them to increase the international mentality of their management (Bennett, 1989; Derr & Oddou, 1991). In other words, firms do recognize the importance of developing internationally competent human resources (Gregersen & Black, 1995; Tung & Miller, 1990).

U.S. firms have traditionally developed their employees in an international context through expatriation (Gregersen & Black, 1995). U.S. multinationals have relied on expatriates to run their international operations in order to maintain control and coordination between domestic and foreign operations, transfer critical technologies and innovations across borders, and in some cases strategically develop international competencies in future executives (Black et al., 1992a; Cherrington & Middleton, 1995). Expatriate assignments have typically been for shorter periods of time than those of both the Japanese or the Europeans (Tung, 1988c). Although some research suggests that a reduction of expatriates will probably occur because of failure rates and cost (Hamel & Prahalad, 1994; Kobrin, 1988), the increased need for international presence and the increasing number of firms entering the global marketplace suggest that expatriation might rather increase.

However, global expansion and increasing pressures for coordination and innovation are expected to lead U.S. firms to use other methods to internationalize their employees and operations. Training and education have increased among U.S. multinationals (Mervosh & McClenahen, 1997; Tichy, 1992; Tichy, Brimm, Charan, & Takeuchi, 1992). Firms such as GE and Motorola, for example, are well known for their internally funded and operated centers that focus in part on developing international skills in their managers and executives. In addition, Hendry's (1994) research shows that firms will increasingly emphasize networking across countries and global learning in order to cope with the need to compete in the world marketplace.

PROPOSITIONS

Based on the preceding literature review and on logical extensions about similarities and cultural differences in European, Japanese, and U.S. human resource practices and that European, Japanese, and U.S. firms are all increasing their stakes in international business, the following propositions were developed. Where research either has not been conducted or gives no clear direction, the null hypothesis is proposed.

Proposition 1. Japanese and European firms will both show a strong tendency to expatriate their personnel to international posts. U.S. firms will possibly show somewhat less tendency to expatriate personnel.

Proposition 2. The Japanese will tend less to bring foreign nationals into their domestic operations/headquarters as a means of internationalizing their total human resources than the U.S. and European firms. There will be no difference between U.S. and European firms' tendency to bring foreign nationals into their domestic operations.

Proposition 3. The Japanese will tend less to create multinational/international project teams or task forces than will the U.S. and European firms. There will be no difference between U.S. and European firms' tendencies to create multinational/international project teams or task forces.

Proposition 4. The Japanese, U.S., and European firms will tend to participate equally in extensive international business travel.

Proposition 5. The Japanese will have a greater tendency to sponsor seminars with their own company personnel than will their counterpart U.S. and European firms.

Proposition 6. The Japanese will tend less to sponsor seminars with noncompany personnel than will their counterpart U.S. and European firms.

Proposition 7. The Japanese will tend less to encourage participation in international networks than will their counterpart U.S. and European firms.

METHODOLOGY

Sample

First, in order to increase the response rate, follow-up surveys were sent to the samples. To obtain the Japanese sample, 100 questionnaires were sent to Japanese MNCs. Thirty-five useable questionnaires were received, for a final response rate of 35 percent. Similarly, international human resource managers in 100 U.S. multinational firms listed in the *Fortune* 500 were sent surveys. Thirty-six surveys were eventually returned, for a response rate of

36 percent. To obtain the European sample, 100 questionnaires were sent to human resource directors in European MNCs. A surprising sixty-nine useable questionnaires were returned for an effective response rate of 69 percent.

To ensure sample comparability, each sample was measured along a number of dimensions: industries represented, size of corporation, number of major geographical markets entered, and level of perceived competition within those markets. In examining the similarities and differences among the three samples, covariate analyses of these demographic variables used in the ANOVA tests revealed no statistically significant changes in the results and therefore were considered as insignificant mediating variables.

Survey

In addition to demographic information, respondents were asked about the frequency and importance of the seven methods of internationalizing managers, the firm's future trends, the degree of internationalization in the functional areas, and the percentage of foreign nationals in and qualified for local, regional, and corporate top-management positions. These questions were set on a 1–5 point Likert-type scale with the appropriate anchors.

RESULTS

To determine differences in frequency of practice, a one-way analysis of variance was used to find any differences. Respondents were also asked about the perceived importance of each of the seven methods. In all cases except two the perceived importance of each method is consistent with their perceived frequency. As a result, only where the perceived importance of the method differs from the frequency will the "perceived importance" results be mentioned. To examine the results of this survey, let us examine each of the propositions set forth earlier:

Proposition 1. *Japanese and European firms will both show a strong tendency to expatriate their personnel to international posts. U.S. firms will possibly show somewhat less tendency to expatriate personnel.*

As Table 6.1 shows, this proposition was generally supported (p. < 0.01): Japanese x = 4.25, European x = 3.62, and U.S. x = 3.67. U.S. firms clearly show a tendency to expatriate equal to that of the European MNC firms, contrary to what some research suggests to

Table 6.1

Differences in Frequency of Expatriation and Tendency to Bring Foreign Nationals into Domestic Operations in European, Japanese, and U.S. MNCs (Likert Scale: 1 = low tendency to 5 = high tendency)

	European	Japanese	US	p. value
	FREQUENCY OF EXPATRIATION			
Means	3.62 (sd = .99)	4.25 (sd = 1.1)	3.7 (sd. = .97)	0.02
Firms Expecting Increase	49%	46%	40%	
Firms Expecting Decrease	19%	9%	23%	
Firms Expecting No Change	25%	37%	29%	
	FREQUENCY OF INPATRIATION			
Means	2.8 (sd = .98)	2.2 (sd = .98)	3.3 (sd. = .97)	0.001
Firms Expecting Increase	70%	3%	49%	
Firms Expecting Decrease	1%	80%	0%	
Firms Expecting No Change	20%	11%	51%	

be the case. These trends are corroborated by respondents when asked about the future trend of expatriation in their firm. Of the Japanese firms, 46 percent responded that expatriation will increase, while only 8 percent said it will decrease. Paralleling these responses, 49 percent of the European MNCs said this trend will increase, 19 percent said they will expatriate fewer people to subsidiary positions, and 25 percent said the number will remain unchanged. A similar percentage of U.S. firms said expatriation will increase (40%), and a slightly higher number than the Europeans said it will probably decrease (23%). However, significantly more European MNCs said they will be sending fewer expatriates than will Japanese MNCs (p. < 0.003). See Table 6.1 for a summary of the similarities and differences in trends between European, Japanese, and U.S. MNCs.

Proposition 2. *The Japanese will tend less to bring foreign nationals into their domestic operations/headquarters as a means of internationalizing their total human resources than the U.S. and European firms. There will be no difference between U.S. and European firms' tendency to bring foreign nationals into their domestic operations.*

This proposition was also supported. A one-way analysis of variance about the frequency of this practice revealed a significant difference between the two samples: x = 2.1 for the Japanese, and 2.75 and 3.3 for the European and U.S. MNCs, respectively (p. < 0.001), where 1 = not at all frequent and 5 = extremely frequently. A post-hoc Scheffe test showed there was a difference beyond 0.05 level between the Japanese and U.S. responding MNCs and a difference of 0.01 between the Japanese and the European sample. There was no significant difference at the 0.05 level, however, between the U.S. and European MNCs. Further, when asked about the future trend in this area, 80 percent of the Japanese MNCs responded that there will be a decrease in the number of foreigners transferred to Japanese headquarter/domestic positions. Only 3 percent of the thirty-five firms said there would be an increase. This is an interesting finding, however, given that Japanese responded that the importance of bringing foreign nationals into domestic headquarter positions was higher (x = 2.8) than the current frequency of doing so (x = 2.2, p. < 0.002). Yet on the absolute scale of 1 to 5, neither the perceived importance (x = 2.8) or the frequency (x = 2.2) could be considered high (see Table 6.1).

By contrast, 70 percent of the European firms said they will be increasing the number of foreign nationals they bring to major corporate national offices; 49 percent of the U.S. firms said likewise, 51 percent indicating that the number of foreign nationals would remain the same.

Proposition 3. *The Japanese will tend less to create multinational/international project teams or task forces than will the U.S. and European firms. There will be no difference between U.S. and European firms' tendencies to create multinational/international project teams or task forces.*

This proposition was supported (see Table 6.2). On the same scale of frequency as noted, the difference among the firms was significant (p. < 0.001): x = 2.0, Japanese; 2.7, European; 3.0, United States. Again, a post-hoc comparison group test (p. < 0.05) revealed that it is the Japanese firms that differ significantly from the European

Table 6.2
**Differences between European, Japanese, and U.S. MNCs' Tendencies
to Create International Project Teams/Task Forces (Likert Scale: 1 =
low tendency to 5 = high tendency)**

	European	Japanese	US	p. value
Mean Differences	2.79 (sd = 1.2)	1.97 (sd = .86)	3.1 (sd = 1.0)	0.001
Firms Expecting Increase	74%	43%	83%	
Firms Expecting Decrease	3%	1%	0%	
Firms Expecting No Change	15%	34%	17%	

and U.S. MNCs. However, in both areas MNCs will be increasing the number of international task forces/project teams they will organize. In total, 43 percent of the Japanese firms said they will be increasing the number of international task forces/project teams, one (3%) said it would be decreasing, while twelve (34%) said the trend would remain unchanged. This is consistent with their perceived importance of international task forces/project teams (x = 2.4) relative to the current frequency of such teams (x = 1.97, p. < 0.02).

Even more aggressively, fifty-one (74%) of the European firms and twenty-nine (83%) of the U.S. firms plan to increase the international task forces/project teams; two European (3%) and none of the U.S. MNCs plan to decrease the number of international task forces/project teams; ten (15%) European and six (17%) U.S. firms plan to maintain current levels of such teams.

Proposition 4. *The Japanese, U.S., and European firms will tend to participate equally in extensive international business travel.*

This proposition was clearly unsupported based on an ANOVA test (p. < 0.001). On an absolute scale from 1 (rarely) to 5 (extremely frequent), both areas clearly use extensive travel as part of their effort to internationalize (Japanese x = 4.5; European x = 3.6; U.S. x = 3.6). Again, it was the Japanese that were significantly different from the European and U.S. groups (0.01 Scheffe test). Of the Japanese MNCs, 57 percent will increase their employees' international travel in the future, only 3 percent will decrease it, and 37 percent plan to maintain the already high level of travel. This finding contrasts the results on the perceived importance of such a practice (x = 4.1) relative to its frequency (x = 4.5, p. < 0.008). Similarly, twenty-eight (41%) European MNCs plan to increase international travel, five (7%) will decrease it, and thirty (44%) will maintain the current level of international travel. Twenty-one (60%) of the U.S. firms plan to increase international travel, ten (29%) plan to maintain current levels, and only four (11%) plan for a decrease.

Proposition 5. The Japanese will have a greater tendency to sponsor seminars with their own company personnel than their counterpart U.S. and European firms.

This proposition was not supported. In fact, the reverse was true. European firms were much more positive toward this kind of international socialization/education method. Of the Japanese firms, 34 percent said they will increase such seminars, one (3%) plans to decrease, while fifteen (43%) plan to continue in-company international seminars at the current level. By contrast, forty-eight (70%) of the European firms plan to increase this type of seminar, only two (3%) plan to decrease these seminars, and eleven (16%) will keep this effort at the current level. Similarly, the Europeans report a higher frequency of within-company international seminars (x = 3.57) than do the Japanese (x = 2.75) or U.S. firms (x = 2.65, p. < 0.001).

Proposition 6. The Japanese will tend less to sponsor seminars with noncompany personnel than will their counterpart U.S. and European firms.

This proposition was not supported. In fact, once again the reverse was true. On an absolute scale, both areas appear to have a fairly equal commitment to this method. Sixteen (46%) Japanese MNCs responded that they will increase these seminars, one (3%) will decrease, and fifteen (43%) will maintain the current level. Thirty-six (52%) and eleven (31%) of the European and U.S. firms, respectively, report a planned increase in noncompany international seminars; five (7%) and two (6%) of the European and U.S. firms, respectively, report they will decrease the number, and twenty-three (33%) and twenty (63%), respectively, say the number of seminars with noncompany personnel will remain the same. However, a one-way analysis of variance found that the Japanese report a higher frequency of such seminars (x = 2.9) than do the European (x = 2.55) or U.S. MNCs (x = 2.26, p. < 0.02). When rating the importance of such seminars the Europeans rate them somewhat higher (x = 3.28), as do the U.S. firms (x = 3.0), than do the Japanese respondents (x = 2.82, p. < 0.05).

Proposition 7. *The Japanese will tend less to encourage participation in international networks than will their counterpart U.S. and European firms.*

Although the Japanese reported using this method more frequently than the European MNCs, a one-way analysis of variance did not reveal a significant difference between Japanese (x = 3.2), U.S. (x = 3.1), and European MNCs (x = 2.84, p. < 0.11). In addition, when asked about this method's importance, the European and U.S. MNCs rated this as more important (x = 3.5 and 3.4, respectively), than did the Japanese MNCs (x = 2.9, p. < 0.01).

Role of International Assignment in Becoming CEO

In addition, both groups of MNCs were asked if an international assignment was requisite to becoming CEO of the firm. On a scale of 1 (always) to 5 (never), the Europeans (x = 2.5) reported this was more the case than either the Japanese (x= 2.9) or U.S. firms (x = 3.4), although a Scheffe test showed that only the European and U.S. firms differed significantly.

Finally, as another measure of stage and method of internationalization, respondents were asked about the percentage of foreign national management versus corporate national management (i.e., management from the firm's country of origin) qualified for top national, regional, and corporate posts (see Table 6.3). Of the Japa-

Table 6.3
Differences in Percentages of Foreign Born Perceived to Be Qualified to Hold Top National, Regional, and Corporate Posts

	Europe	Japan	US	p. value
Level of Post				
Top National	47%	24%	55%	0.001
Firms Expecting Decrease	22%	5%	34%	0.001
Firms Expecting No Change	13%	0.2%	13%	0.001

nese MNCs, 24 percent reported having foreign nationals qualified for top subsidiary management positions, while the European and U.S. firms reported much higher percentages of qualified foreign nationals (47% and 55%, respectively; Anova, p. < 0.001) Similar results were found by Kopp (1994); post-hoc analysis showed the Japanese firms significantly lower than U.S. and European firms. At the regional level, significant differences were also found despite large variation in within-group responses. Japanese MNCs reported that only 5 percent of their foreign nationals were qualified for top regional positions, whereas 22 percent of the European MNCs and 34 percent of the U.S. firms felt their foreign nationals were so qualified (p. < 0.001). A post-hoc test indicated the significant difference between the Japanese firms and those of the United States and Europe. Finally, the most significant difference was at the corporate senior-management level. Japanese MNCs felt that 0.2 percent of their foreign managers were qualified for top corporate posts, while 13 percent of the European and U.S. firms responded that their foreign nationals were qualified to manage the highest positions in their corporate environments.

CONCLUSIONS

The purpose of this research was to look at the different methods U.S., Japanese, and European MNCs are using that lead toward global management development. Here is an overview of the trends.

In descending order of frequency, the Japanese currently emphasize the following:

- extensive international business travel
- expatriation
- international networks
- seminars with foreign nationals

The European MNCs currently equally emphasize these three global management development methods:

- expatriation
- international seminars with company foreigners
- extensive international business travel

The U.S. MNCs practice primarily the first two items on this list, though the others are also common practices:

- expatriation
- extensive international business travel
- bringing foreign nationals into domestic positions
- building international task forces/project teams
- encouraging international network building

The two practices that all three groups have most in common are expatriation and extensive business travel.

Trends for the Future

According to the Japanese sample, trends in the future will likely continue to be extensive business travel, expatriation, seminars, and encouraging international network building, but they will also create more international task forces/project teams. European MNCs will continue their present practices but plan especially to focus on creating more international task forces/project teams, bringing more foreign nationals into headquarters positions, and encouraging membership in international networks. U.S. MNCs plan to continue their present practices, while emphasizing bringing foreign nationals to domestic positions and developing more international project teams/task forces.

Common Future Practices between Japanese, European, and U.S. MNCs

Based on the mentioned trends, future common trends that can help develop global managers include creating more international task forces and bringing more foreign nationals into their corporate headquarters or other domestic work sites.

Differences among Japanese, European, and U.S. MNCs

We will use the Japanese sample as a reference point for listing differences because the differences among the samples are mostly differences between the Japanese firms and the firms of the other two areas.

1. The Japanese emphasize expatriation more than the European or U.S. companies.
2. The Japanese do not emphasize bringing foreign-born employees into domestic headquarters more than European and U.S. MNCs; U.S. firms report practicing this strategy more than the European firms.

3. The Japanese plan to emphasize international task forces or project teams much more than they currently do.

4. The Japanese clearly emphasize extensive international travel for their executives when compared to firms from Europe and the United States.

5. The Japanese and European MNCs sponsor seminars for their executives with personnel from other firms more than U.S. firms.

6. The Japanese do not sponsor seminars for their managers with company personnel as much as the European and U.S. firms, and European MNCs do so even more than U.S. MNCs.

7. The Japanese do not encourage their human resources to join international networks as much as the European and U.S. MNCs. (Although no two groups differed significantly based on a Scheffe 0.05 test, the one-way ANOVA did show a significant difference overall [p. < 0.04]. The Japanese mean was 2.9, while the U.S. and European means were both 3.4.)

DISCUSSION

Differences in global manager development methods among the three groups arise primarily between the Japanese and both European and U.S. MNCs. For example, the Japanese emphasize expatriation more than the European or U.S. MNCs. This kind of difference might be explained in terms of cultural values. Practices such as expatriation and having one's own executives travel to foreign offices are consistent with the Japanese values of homogeneity, stability, and harmony. Stability, for example, can be created by ethnocentric practices of excluding foreigners, whose culture might disrupt the indigenous one, from important operating positions in a company. The trend to not bring many foreign nationals into domestic operations is consistent with this.

Other clear differences relate to the percentage of foreign nationals actually holding top subsidiary posts and to the percentage of foreign nationals perceived qualified to hold top subsidiary and corporate positions. U.S. MNCs generally report having a higher percentage of foreign born qualified for top national and regional posts than either Europeans or especially the Japanese. Across all three categories of posts, however, the Japanese obviously lag behind the U.S. and European MNCs. This may well be due to the fact that the Japanese have been more insular in the past, either for strategic reasons or because their culture is simply so different from Western cultures that the barriers either way are foreboding.

In general, it appears as though there are some differences in the methods used to help develop global managers and in the percentage of foreign born in positions reflecting a path toward positions of global leadership. There are perhaps more commonalities, however, than differences. All three groups involve their managers in extensive international business travel and expatriation. As increased efforts are made to address the internationalization of markets or the internationalization of business strategies, it is only natural that, despite the costs, MNCs from all countries will continue to emphasize traditional methods of doing international business, such as expatriation and international business travel. Expatriation has been shown to be an important means of strategic control and coordination (Boyacigillar, 1990; Edström & Galbraith, 1977; Kobrin, 1988), and will likely continue to be so.

Regarding the trends for the future, the most cited one among all three groups was creating more international task forces and project teams. Such task forces usually refer to the grouping of several people from foreign countries into a virtual group; that is, they only rarely physically meet together. The rest of the time they communicate by teleconferencing/videoconferencing, telephone, e-mail, and fax. This method combines intercultural exchanges of information, but is also inexpensive.

As mentioned at the beginning of this chapter, it is essential that firms develop an internationally experienced set of executives to be able to respond appropriately to local and global requirements. This means "growing" strategic decision makers in the firm who will lead the organization toward coordinated yet responsive strategies in global markets. Multiple methods can be used to help develop managers in this way, as we have seen in this chapter.

The issue of the effectiveness of the methods must be explored in further research. Certainly, each of these methods has disadvantages and advantages in terms of cost and depth of exposure to foreign cultures. Expatriation is very costly, but it also brings an intense, in-depth cultural experience. Such an experience can create new mental maps for the expatriate. The expatriate can also easily develop a network from exposure over a longer period of time in an expatriate position. This kind of network can be invaluable for a company. On the other hand, a seminar in which people from around the world come within or outside of one's company is more limited in richness of information and potential for developing a solid network of associates. Learning about cultures and how to function in them has a low ceiling with such venues.

In real practice, though, firms have different business needs that require different kinds of human resource practices and operations. Differing types and levels of learning occur as a result. It is probably most important that firms have a good mix of methods to develop their managers to be future global decision makers. It is especially imperative that firms view these different methods as such and strategically use the knowledge gained and recognize the contribution from these various cultural experiences. If firms are going to intelligently compete in this global marketplace, they need to view cultural experiences as an important part of their managers' development.

Part II

PROCESSES CRITICAL
TO GLOBAL LEADERSHIP

7

Expatriation: A Critical Step toward Developing Global Leaders

Zeynep Aycan

Globalization demands that companies invest more in developing and training global leaders. Adler and Bartholomew (1992) assert that global leadership and global management are most needed in the context of transnational organizations. A transnational organization "integrates assets, resources and diverse people in operating units around the world . . . through a flexible management process, in which highly specialized yet closely linked groups of business managers, country or regional managers, and world-wide functional managers form a triad of different perspectives and balance one another" (Bartlett & Ghoshal, 1992, 124). To meet the challenge of managing in this complex system, companies need leaders and managers with a "global mind-set."

Recent studies attempted to conceptualize and operationalize the concept of global mind-set. According to Pucik and Saba (1998), the global mind-set indicates "sharing information, knowledge, and experience across national, functional, and business boundaries and balancing competing country, business, and functional priorities that emerge in the globalization process" (p. 41). Others emphasize the cognitive processes underlying the global mind-set. For instance, Tichy (1992) argues that leaders who have a global mind-set are able to conceptualize and analyze the ways in which geopolitical and cultural forces impact business. Rhinesmith defines the global mind-set as the predisposition to see the world in a particular way, set boundaries, question the rationale behind things that are happening around us, and establish guidelines to show how we should behave. Pucik and Saba (1998) stated that a global mind-set allows people to "drive for the bigger, broader picture, balance paradoxes, trust process over structure, value differences, manage change, and seek life-long learning" (p. 44). To operationalize the construct, Murtha, Lenway, and Bagozzi (1998) recently developed a measure that assessed the extent to which leaders and managers possess a global mind-set.

How can global leaders with a global mind-set be trained and developed? Formal education has its merits in this regard; however, real know-how develops when theory meets practice. Global leadership competencies are developed best if people with such potential are given the opportunity to function beyond national borders. Research (e.g., McCall, Lombardo, & Morrison, 1988; Pucik, 1992; Robinson & Wick, 1992; Tichy, 1989; Yeung & Ready, 1995) strongly supports the idea that experience-based learning (especially in the form of expatriate assignments) contributes substantially to the development of global leaders, and shows that most global managers were expatriates at some point in their career. Compared to global leadership, expatriation takes place in a limited context (i.e., one foreign country at a time). The expatriate is required to become knowledgeable about the host country's cultural, sociopolitical, and business environment, and to become competent in using the host language and managing good interpersonal relations with host nationals. Such responsibilities and roles are magnified for global leaders who must become knowledgeable about the worldwide business environment, and must familiarize themselves with sociopolitical and cultural context of many different countries. In addition, they need to be able to communicate in multiple languages and learn the skills necessary for managing a worldwide web of colleagues (cf., Adler & Bartholomew, 1992). If one looks at the issue from the perspective of transferring knowledge, skills, and abilities from one context to many, then one would consider expatriate assignments as an invaluable exercise and opportunity to accumulate experience toward becoming a global leader. The parallels between expatriation and global leadership enable us to transfer and expand the insights that we gain from the expatriation literature to the study of global leadership and development.

This chapter aims at establishing a link between expatriation and global leadership literatures by applying key issues concerning expatriation to the study of global leadership and development.

First, factors that facilitate expatriation success will be discussed within a conceptual framework, "The Process Model of Expatriate Acculturation" (Aycan, 1997). Following this introduction, the potential contribution of the model to a better understanding of the global leadership development process will be discussed, and the linkages between the model and the emerging variables that seem to constitute global leadership will be examined. The chapter will then conclude with a discussion of the implications of the model for both scholars and practitioners.

THE PROCESS MODEL OF EXPATRIATE ACCULTURATION: A BRIEF OVERVIEW

The Process Model of Expatriate Acculturation was developed by Aycan (1997), and it is complementary in two ways to other conceptual models that had previously been created (e.g., Black, Mendenhall, & Oddou, 1991; Gregersen & Black, 1992; Mendenhall & Oddou, 1985; Naumann, 1992). First, this model examines expatriation as a multifaceted phenomenon influenced by factors on two levels: the individual (e.g., expatriate manager's competencies, motivation, attitudes, etc.) and the organizational (e.g., the parent and local companies' approaches to expatriation in terms of preparation, planning, training, support, etc.). As such, the model focuses on the "success" or "failure" of the expatriation process, rather than the expatriate himself or herself.

Second, the model considers expatriation as a process with different phases. During this process expatriates experience acculturation in phases. In the model, acculturation is defined as the cognitive, affective, and behavioral changes that result from firsthand contact with a new cultural context (Redfield, Linton, & Herskovits, 1936). By making extensive use of the available acculturation literature, this model combines key concepts in the fields of international human resource management and cross-cultural psychology.

The model proposes that expatriate acculturation takes place in five distinct phases (see Figure 7.1). Phase one involves predeparture preparation by the parent company, local unit, and expatriate manager. It is followed by the second phase, which is characterized by the post-arrival initial contact between the expatriate and the new sociocultural environment. In the next phase, acculturation experiences (i.e., conflicts, uncertainties, problems, and acceptance by local nationals) are identified and appraised as being either stressful events or fruitful opportunities for personal and professional growth. Appraisal is followed by coping in the third phase. Psychological (e.g., stress and alienation) and adjustment (e.g., general and work-related) outcomes of appraisal and coping occur in

Figure 7.1
The Process Model of Expatriate Acculturation

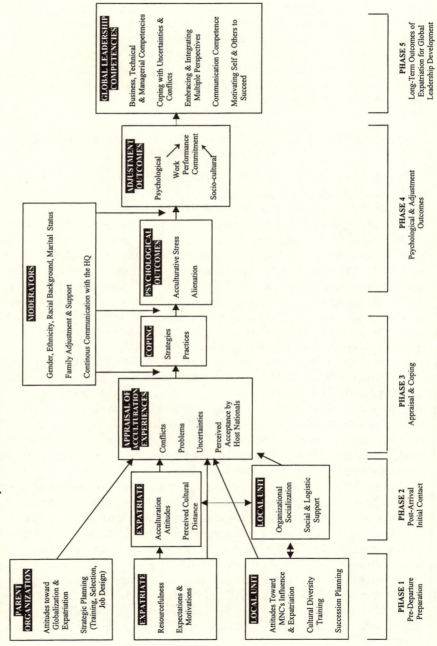

PARENT ORGANIZATION

Attitudes toward Globalization & Expatriation

Strategic Planning (Training, Selection, Job Design)

EXPATRIATE

Resourcefulness

Expectations & Motivations

LOCAL UNIT

Attitudes Toward MNCs Influence & Expatriation

Cultural Diversity Training

Succession Planning

EXPATRIATE

Acculturation Attitudes

Perceived Cultural Distance

LOCAL UNIT

Organizational Socialization

Social & Logistic Support

APPRAISAL OF ACCULTURATION EXPERIENCES

Conflicts

Problems

Uncertainties

Perceived Acceptance by Host Nationals

MODERATORS

Gender, Ethnicity, Racial Background, Marital Status

Family Adjustment & Support

Continous Communication with the HQ

COPING

Strategies

Practices

PSYCHOLOGICAL OUTCOMES

Acculturative Stress

Alienation

ADJUSTMENT OUTCOMES

Psychological

Work Performance Commitment

Socio-cultural

GLOBAL LEADERSHIP COMPETENCIES

Business, Technical & Managerial Competencies

Coping with Uncertainties & Conflicts

Embracing & Integrating Multiple Perspectives

Communication Competence

Motivating Self & Others to Succeed

PHASE 1
Pre-Departure Preparation

PHASE 2
Post-Arrival Initial Contact

PHASE 3
Appraisal & Coping

PHASE 4
Psychological & Adjustment Outcomes

PHASE 5
Long-Term Outcomes of Expatriation for Global Leadership Development

the fourth phase. Before going into the details of the model, the criteria of the model will be discussed.

Domestic or multinational companies expect their employees to stay in the organization and perform well. The same two basic criteria apply to expatriates and domestic employees as indications of success: (1) staying in the organization or completing the full term of the assignment, and (2) performing well on the overseas job. The first question is related to the issue of adjustment, because those expatriates who fail to adjust to the new culture are the ones who prematurely terminate the assignment. Therefore, the two most important criteria for the success of expatriation are adjustment and performance.

Adjustment is conceptualized as changes in the individual in a direction of reduced conflict and increased congruence, or fit, between the new environment and the individual (Berry, 1992). In the context of expatriation, adjustment is conceptualized as the degree of fit between the expatriate manager and the new work and the nonwork environment. Such a fit is marked by reduced conflict and stress and increased satisfaction and performance. In the acculturation literature, three facets of adjustment are identified: psychological adjustment, sociocultural adjustment (Searle & Ward, 1990), and work adjustment (Aycan & Berry, 1996; Hawes & Kealey, 1981; Kealey, 1990). Psychological adjustment refers to maintaining good mental health or psychological well-being. It is marked by a feeling of satisfaction with different aspects of life, and a feeling of relative satisfaction in comparison to others in reference groups, both in the country of origin and in the host society. Sociocultural adjustment refers to one's progress in becoming fully effective in the new society by meeting requirements of daily life and engaging in, and maintaining, positive interpersonal relations with the members of the host society. Finally, work adjustment refers to adequate overseas job performance, which is characterized by the demonstration of behaviors that result in the effective accomplishment of one's required task, and an expression of positive attitudes toward the new work role (Davis & Lofquist, 1984).

From this conceptualization of work adjustment, it becomes apparent that performance is, in fact, an integral part of adjustment. Dimensions of expatriate job performance have been examined in detail by both Ones and Viswesvaran (1997) and Caligiuri (1997). According to these studies, adequate expatriate performance can be identified in three main areas:

• task-related area (e.g., job knowledge and applications, productivity, effort, and quality of the output).

- managerial area (e.g., effective administration, training and development, directiveness).
- interpersonal relations at work (e.g., effective communication, positive interpersonal relations, and leadership).

In addition to job performance, work adjustment includes an affective component toward the new job. Commitment to the local unit has been highlighted in the expatriation literature for its direct link to the individual's intention to stay. Recent research (e.g., Meyer & Allen, 1991) conceptualized commitment as comprised of three components: affective, continuance, and normative. All three forms of commitment are considered to be critical in predicting success in overseas assignments. International assignments are usually perceived as a career advancement involving considerable investment by the firm, including repatriate compensation plans, career pathing, cross-cultural training, and spousal assistance programs. According to the social exchange theory (Homans, 1958), the need for reciprocating such investments is likely to increase such feelings as an obligation toward staying in the job and a desire to perform adequately (i.e., continuance and normative commitment). Support provided by both the parent company and the local unit (e.g., organizational socialization, training, social and logistic support) is likely to lead to a perception that the expatriate's well-being is of concern to the firm, which in turn fosters the affective commitment.

Expatriates perform better and stay committed to their assignment to the extent that they are satisfied with, and feel positive about, their lives in the new cultural context (i.e., psychological adjustment). Interaction with host nationals and participation in social life (i.e., sociocultural adjustment) are also expected to enhance job performance and commitment. Therefore, the model proposes that psychological and sociocultural adjustment are immediate predictors of work adjustment (i.e., good performance and high commitment).

Success or failure in the expatriation process is a collective effort that requires careful planning, organization, and coordination by all three parties involved: the expatriate manager, the parent company, and the local unit. Therefore, the first phase (predeparture preparation) should aim at reducing post-arrival conflicts, problems, and uncertainties, and encouraging acceptance of the expatriate by locals. In this phase, predictors of performance and adjustment include the following:

- the parent company's attitude toward expatriation and strategic preparation.

- a positive and supportive attitude of the local unit toward the MNC's influence and expatriation.
- cultural diversity training and succession planning in the local unit.
- resourcefulness of expatriates (e.g., competencies, resources, skills, personality characteristics, previous experiences).
- predeparture expectations (e.g., expected difficulties and benefits of the assignment).
- motivational states (e.g., willingness and commitment).

In the second phase (post-arrival initial contact) expatriates come into contact with the new culture. Factors that facilitate adjustment and performance in this phase include the following:

- expatriate acculturation attitudes (e.g., integration as opposed to assimilation and separation).
- perceptions (e.g., perceived cultural distance).
- socialization and support in the local unit.

In the third phase (appraisal and coping) expatriates' adjustment is facilitated if they are able to appraise stressful events as challenges and opportunities for personal development (Berry, 1992; Lazarus & Folkman, 1984), and utilize active coping strategies (i.e., changing work environment and seeking information and training).

The fourth phase of expatriation is psychological and adjustment outcomes. In this phase of acculturation, acculturative stress and alienation occur when acculturation experiences are appraised as problematic and have not been successfully coped with. Along with acculturative stress, alienation has a negative impact on all aspects of adjustment, including psychological, sociocultural, and work-related adjustment. Added to the original model is phase 5, which outlines the long-term outcomes of expatriation for global leadership development. In this phase expatriates are expected to develop global leadership competencies, which are detailed in the next section. As can be seen from the model, the link between expatriation and global leadership is indicated with a dashed line to emphasize the fact that although expatriation facilitates the process of becoming a global leader, not all expatriates develop competencies for global leadership.

CONTRIBUTIONS OF EXPATRIATION FOR GLOBAL LEADERSHIP DEVELOPMENT

In this section some of the key issues that are addressed by the Process Model of Expatriate Acculturation will be applied to the field of global leadership development. Global leadership is a developing field and, as such, the question of what constitutes a successful global leader yields a long list of factors, most of which are not adequately conceptualized and operationalized, and are often based on intuition rather than empirical verification (cf. Morrison, in press). Although this chapter does not directly address this question, it is important to understand some of the key characteristics of global leaders in order to discuss how expatriation contributes to the development of such characteristics.

The global leader and manager is expected to play a number of critical roles, such as integrator, coordinator, innovator, coach, and strategy developer (cf. Bartlett & Ghoshal, 1992). In order to fulfill these roles, the global manager must have a number of competencies, as shown in Table 7.1. The ways in which expatriation could help develop these competencies will be discussed in the next sections.

Business, Technical, and Managerial Competencies

Managing business through global lenses requires leaders to be knowledgeable and technically well-equipped in order to assess the present and future opportunities that will help the company gain a competitive advantage in the global market. Global leaders must be aware not only of the company's business strategies, products, and resources, but also of the structure of its domestic and international operations, and of new market opportunities worldwide (cf. Black, Morrison, & Gregersen, 1999; Brake, 1997).

Expatriation certainly helps leaders develop this awareness, as it provides firsthand exposure to the international operations of the organization as well as an opportunity to monitor and scan business opportunities and resources. It also enables expatriates to learn to coordinate and integrate local and global business activities, which is one of the key requirements for becoming a global leader (e.g., Bartlett & Ghoshal, 1992). In addition to these direct benefits, according to the Process Model of Expatriate Acculturation, technical competence and business knowledge help to reduce uncertainties, enhance self-confidence, and generate the courage to execute new behavior. Such skills also facilitate trust and cooperation with international colleagues and partners who respect expertise in business (Zeira & Banai, 1985).

Managerial competencies are one of the key variables in the Process Model of Expatriate Acculturation, and are a necessary complement to business knowledge and technical skills. Kanungo and Misra (1992, 1323) identified various dimensions of managerial competencies. The dimensions help managers to decide what skills

Table 7.1
Key Global Leadership Competencies

Global Leadership Competency	Sources
• In-depth business and technical knowledge, and managerial competency	Brake, 1997; Black, et al., 1999; Bartlett & Ghoshal, 1992; Kotter, 1988
• Ability to cope with uncertainties and conflicts	Brake, 1997; Kets de Vries & Mead, 1992; Kim, 1999; Gertsen, 1991
• Willingness and ability to embrace and integrate multiple perspectives	Barham & Oates, 1991; Black et al., 1999; Gertsen, 1991
• Communication effectiveness	Brake, 1997; Black, et al., 1999; Gertsen, 1991
• Competence in developing and maintaining good interpersonal relations	Brake, 1997; Moran & Reisenberger, 1994
• Willingness and commitment to succeed	
• Ability to motivate and develop people with potential	Bartlett & Ghoshal, 1992; Moran & Reisenberger, 1994; Yeung & Ready, 1995
• Ability and willingness to learn from experience	Spreitzer, McCall & Mahoney, 1997
• Competence in playing the role of a change agent	Barham & Antal, 1994; Brake, 1997; Moran & Reisenberger, 1994

to utilize, and when and how to utilize them in order to engage in cognitive self-controlling adaptive responses. Such competencies are especially critical for global leaders as they facilitate coping and functioning in the face of uncertainty. They conceptualized three dimensions of managerial competencies (Kanungo & Misra, 1992; Kanungo & Menon, 1995): affective, intellectual, and action-oriented competencies. Affective competencies involve controlling aggressive and regressive tendencies, reducing withdrawal and excessive excitement, developing problem orientation, and displaying proactive involvement, enthusiasm, interest in, and commitment to meeting challenges in life. Intellectual competencies involve goal analyses through analytical thinking, diagnostic information generation to assess the situation, planning for alternate courses of action, and self-reflection for strengthening self-efficacy. Finally, action-oriented competencies are comprised of attention to details, persistence in pursuits, concern for time frame, interpersonal sensitivity and empathy, and nondefensive and supportive postures to gain others' acceptance. A resourceful global leader must have all three aspects of managerial competencies, and these can be developed during expatriation.

Managerial competencies develop through both training (e.g., predeparture training in time management, coping, conflict resolution, interpersonal relations, communication, etc.) and firsthand exposure to situations that pose uncertainty, diversity, and challenge (e.g., working in a foreign environment) (cf. Kanungo & Misra, 1992). As such, expatriation experience provides an ideal opportunity for developing managerial competencies. It should be noted that managerial competencies are both the antecedents and consequences of successful expatriation. Expatriates who are equipped with managerial competencies are more likely to succeed in the process. During expatriation, they have the opportunity to further develop such competencies.

Coping with Uncertainties and Conflicts

This is perhaps one of the most important requirements for global leaders. Coordination among different functions and people worldwide is a difficult task that evokes many uncertainties and conflicts. Expatriation offers an invaluable opportunity in which to prepare the global leader to cope with such problems. During expatriation, conflicts arise mainly from the pressure to balance the needs and demands of the parent company and the local unit. The Process Model of Expatriate Acculturation proposes that both the parent company and the local unit maintain attitudes that ignore the influence of multinationals on the local unit. The parent company has three main attitudinal orientations (cf. Adler & Ghadar, 1990; Doz & Prahalad, 1991; Perlmutter, 1969). Ethnocentric orientation of the parent company implies that the local unit is given minimal autonomy, and that decisions are highly centralized at the parent company headquarters. In contrast, MNCs with a polycentric attitude allow greater autonomy in local units (considering the local company as an independent unit), especially in marketing, production, and sourcing as long as cost is minimized and profit is maximized. Finally, MNCs with geocentric attitude integrate values that reflect the home and the host country cultures to reach a truly unified global corporate culture.

In tandem with the parent-company attitudes, the local unit may also have a three-part attitudinal orientation (Aycan, 1997). The subsidiary's attitude concerning foreign influence and expatriation is mainly determined by the characteristics of the country's economic, legal, and sociocultural environment. The local unit's attitude can vary from allowing the parent company to impose its organizational structure and culture (permissive attitude) to rejecting parent-company influence (rigid attitude). In between these extremes the subsidiary may choose to be flexible in order to allow some influence from the parent company—for example, in technical areas—while at the same time keeping other organizational characteristics (e.g., interpersonal relations, managerial style, human resource management practices, etc.) that are consistent with the prevailing local business climate (flexible attitude).

Expatriates encounter conflicts if there is a serious attitudinal clash between the parent company and the local unit (e.g., ethnocentric versus rigid attitude). In addition to such conflicts, ambiguities that are caused by the lack of role clarity and role discretion as well as insufficient resources and information input from both the parent company and the local unit may aggravate an already unstable situation. According to the Process Model of Expatriate Acculturation, coping with conflicts and uncertainties requires effective coping strategies and skills.

Coping strategies have the main goal of reducing the emotional impact of stress through actions and thoughts (Lazarus & Folkman, 1984), and effective coping is particularly important for expatriates and global leaders. Coping strategies have been divided into three groups by Lazarus and Folkman (1984): problem-focused strategies (e.g., working long hours), emotion-focused strategies (e.g., psychological withdrawal), and the search for social support. Diaz-Guerrero (1979) proposed an additional active–passive dimension to add to coping style, where preference for active style reflects a tendency to alter the situation, whereas preference for the passive style reflects self-modification. Feldman and Thomas (1991) found that coping strategies including changing work environment and seeking out information and training are more effective ways of coping than psychological withdrawal. Seeking social support and establishing good interpersonal relationships with international colleagues prove to be highly useful, not only because such contacts facilitate coping, but also because they enable the expatriate or global manager to gain access to local resources, raise awareness of market opportunities, speed up cultural learning, and gain acceptance and cooperation from local colleagues (cf. Black, Morrison, & Gregersen, 1999).

Conflict-resolution skills also contribute to effective coping. Conflict resolution involves understanding others' viewpoints and making an effort to relate to others. It requires a collaborative approach, which in turn increases mutual respect between parties. Research shows that conflict-resolution skills help managers who work across borders to cope more successfully with uncertainties and conflicts (e.g., Abe & Wiseman, 1983; Black, 1990; Hawes & Kealey, 1981). Expatriates as potential global managers often learn to use various negotiation tactics to balance differing attitudes and demands of the parent company and the local unit. Expatriates act as liaisons between the parent company and the local unit (Aycan, 1997), and expatriates may also act as change agents, which is one of the most desirable characteristics of global leaders (cf. Brake, 1997; Moran & Reisenberger, 1994). During expatriation, conflict-resolution skills can be improved mainly through training (during the predeparture or post-arrival period); seeking active feedback from peers, supervisors, and mentors; observing and imitating culturally appropriate reactions and tactics for conflict solving; and active participation in conflict resolution and negotiation situations.

Embracing and Integrating Multiple Perspectives

As discussed in the previous sections, one of the most challenging jobs of global leaders is to balance and integrate multiple perspectives. Multiple perspectives mainly arise as a result of the sometimes conflicting demands of globalization and localization in areas of product design and marketing, human resource management, business ethics, and so on. In order to handle such conflicts, global managers must show both the willingness and the ability to cope with cultural relativity.

In the Process Model of Expatriate Acculturation, it is asserted that the acculturation attitudes of expatriates play an important role in helping the expatriate to successfully manage multiple perspectives. In the acculturation literature, acculturation attitudes are considered to be a critical component of successful adjustment. The Model of Acculturation Attitudes (Berry, 1980) addresses two issues: (1) whether expatriates and global leaders value maintaining their own cultural characteristics, and (2) whether they wish to adopt the host country's cultural characteristics as a means of maintaining interactions with host nationals (see Figure 7.2).

Among the acculturation attitudes, integration yields the best outcomes (e.g., low stress, high satisfaction, and effectiveness in

Figure 7.2
Acculturation Attitudes of Expatriates

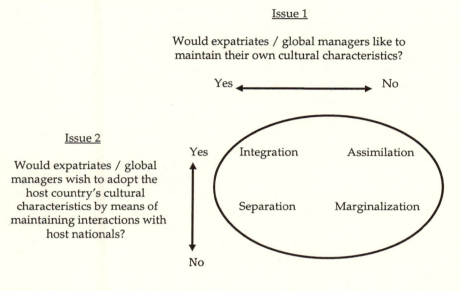

Issue 1

Would expatriates / global managers like to maintain their own cultural characteristics?

Yes ←————————————→ No

Issue 2

Would expatriates / global managers wish to adopt the host country's cultural characteristics by means of maintaining interactions with host nationals?

Yes

| Integration | Assimilation |
| Separation | Marginalization |

No

both work and nonwork contexts). The integrationist attitude not only facilitates cultural learning, but also attracts greater social support from host nationals. As a result, an interactionist attitude further develops through such reinforcements. If one demonstrates an attitude of separation and imposes his or her own values on others, tension, conflict, and stress in interpersonal relations are created, which eventually adversely affects effectiveness. Such adverse impacts may discourage the adoption of an interactionist attitude. Here, a mentor would be of great help in giving the expatriate feedback on his or her attitudes and their results, and guiding him or her toward development of a more balanced and embracing attitude.

Expatriates also develop cultural flexibility skills; cultural flexibility includes a lack of prejudice with respect to others' opinions and behaviors, and a willingness to change one's own behavioral patterns whenever needed (Torbiörn, 1982). Hawes and Kealey (1981) and Ruben and Kealey (1979), for example, found that the most important set of behaviors related to success in international assignments were being flexible, sensitive, respectful, and nonjudgmental. Trying to understand a new culture without being judgmental reduces stress, facilitates culture learning, and enhances the possibility of acceptance by local nationals.

Communication Competence

Effective communication is one of the key requirements for any leader. However, for global leaders effective cross-cultural communication is indispensable (cf. Brake, 1997). Although being multilingual is an important component of cross-cultural communication, fluency does not entirely ensure communication effectiveness. Effective cross-cultural communication includes using culturally appropriate verbal and nonverbal cues, assuming a nonjudgmental posture in talking and listening, ensuring clarity and accuracy of the flow of information, and tolerating misunderstandings and differences in the encoding and decoding of information.

Cross-cultural communication skills often develop during the expatriation process. In the Process Model of Expatriate Acculturation, Aycan (1997) noted that communication skills are among the most critical criteria in selection and performance appraisal. In the model, providing training in cross-cultural communication skills was cited among the key responsibilities of the parent company during the predeparture preparation phase. During the post-arrival phase, expatriates must find the opportunity to familiarize themselves with the daily communication patterns of the local people and the values attached to these patterns. They will also need to learn to be tolerant of misunderstandings, misjudgments, and misperceptions that stem from communication problems. Active listening and effective articulation become more critical than ever in such contexts. The communication skills that are acquired during expatriation are of great use for global leaders.

Motivating Self and Others to Succeed

Actual success in one's job is strongly related to commitment and willingness to succeed. This is especially true for global leaders who, in the face of challenges, uncertainties, and conflicts that are inherent in their jobs, must show stamina in order to continue pursuing their goals. Motivation to succeed is one of the key determinants of expatriate success in the Process Model of Expatriate Acculturation. In the acculturation literature, motivating factors are categorized into two groups: "pull" and "push" factors (Berry, 1992). Both pull and push factors motivate the employee to accept the overseas assignment, but for different reasons: While pull factors are related to the attractiveness of the assignment, push factors relate to the desire to escape from unpleasant conditions in the country of origin.

For expatriates, pull factors can be further categorized according to intrinsic and extrinsic advantages or rewards that are to be gained from the overseas experience. Accordingly, intrinsic rewards of the assignment may include growing personally and spiritually, developing an appreciation of human diversity by exploring different cultures, developing better interpersonal skills, achieving a broader view of life, contributing to the well-being of the country of assignment, and so on. Extrinsic rewards involve monetary and/or career issues, such as enhancing the possibility of promotion, earning money and prestige, developing technical and managerial skills, increasing the chance of finding better employment upon repatriation, and so on. Push factors, on the other hand, may include those forces that motivate the expatriate to accept the assignment as a way of escaping from unpleasant work and/or nonwork circumstances in the home country. Expatriates appraise their acculturation experiences as opportunities for development when motivated by the pull factors, especially if they are intrinsically motivated. Those who are motivated by pull factors are willing to use every opportunity to learn and grow individually and professionally. They are adventurous in nature and change as a result of experience. They learn from every experience, which again, is one of the key characteristics of global leaders (Spreitzer, McCall, & Mahoney, 1997). In order to reinforce the development of intrinsic motivation, expatriates could get in touch with repatriates who could share their experiences about the predeparture motivational state and the ways in which it helped or hurt them during expatriation. The repatriates could also explain the value of nonmonetary rewards that they gained from the international assignments.

Global leaders also have the responsibility of motivating and developing others for success and excellence (Bartlett & Ghoshal, 1992; Brake, 1997; Moran & Reisenberger, 1994). As discussed in the Process Model of Expatriate Acculturation, succession planning and employee development are among the key responsibilities of expatriates. The expatriate could motivate others mainly through becoming a role model and mentor. Practices such as empowerment, participation in decision making, joint goal setting, job enrichment, and training are useful tools to improve motivation among employees. The main contribution of expatriation to global leadership development is to learn to administer such practices in a culturally appropriate way. For instance, participation and joint goal setting may require a paternalistic leadership style in cultures (e.g., Southeast Asia, Asia, Latin America, the Middle East) where patriarchal, patrilocal, and patrilineal relationships prevail within the family and the work unit (Aycan, Kanungo, Mendonca, Yu, Deller, Stahl, Kurshid, in press).

CONCLUSIONS AND IMPLICATIONS

Expatriation is an important step toward becoming a global leader. The discussion so far has aimed at demonstrating that during expatriation managers find the opportunity to acquire and/or master their coping, cross-cultural communication, conflict resolution, negotiation, networking, and coaching skills. They also develop business, technical, and managerial competencies while overseas, where they have to adapt to a variety of roles such as integrator, balancer, change agent, mentor/motivator, and talent developer.

If international assignments are important to global leadership development, then this opportunity should be given early in a manager's life. One way of encouraging this is to include work experience in an international context as a part of the curriculum in graduate and undergraduate business programs. To demonstrate the utility of this approach a pilot longitudinal study was initiated by the author in collaboration with Deniz S. Ones of the University of Minnesota. Results to date are based on a very small sample of expatriate business students. The data presented below are the first of many potential waves of future data collection.

Seven university students who were assigned to various developing countries (e.g., Kenya, Ecuador, India) as part of their internship requirement to work in community development programs participated in this study. A total of fifteen students received the research package before they left for their assignments, and seven of them returned them fully completed. Among these seven participants, there were six female participants.

The research instrument was a questionnaire that was designed to resemble a diary. Included in the questionnaire were various scales and open-ended questions. The measures captured the variables that are included in the Process Model of Expatriate Acculturation. Guided by the model, participants were asked to complete each measure in a designated time period. For example, measures for variables in the predeparture preparation phase were completed a week before the assignment; those for the variables in the post-arrival initial contact phase were completed two weeks after arrival. After completing each questionnaire in a specified time period, participants were instructed to put it in the designated envelope and seal it in order not to return to the questionnaire once it was completed.

The aim of the study was to assess whether early international assignments contributed to the development of global leadership skills. Because of the small sample size, only results from the qualitative data will be presented here. Preliminary qualitative data obtained from open-ended questions suggested that an early expatriation experience is indeed an important preparation for future global leadership. All the participants considered the assignment an integral part of their development, and this was reflected in their comments:

- "My ability of adjustment and tolerance has improved."
- "I learned that clear communication, patience and a sense of humor are essential ingredients for intercultural effectiveness."
- "The assignment made me reevaluate my goals and understand that I had to be more flexible and realistic."
- "This experience has opened my eyes to the variety of people and possibilities in this realm. It provided me with friends and connections elsewhere. It gave me confidence in my ability to do the desired work."
- "My overall experience is one of learning about myself. The difficulties are in fact helping me to learn—how I go about dealing with people here, how they affect me, and so on."
- "My approach to people and events with an open mind and heart was the best substitute for a good pre-departure preparation."
- "I learned how to cope with loneliness and separation from loved ones. I also know now how to turn frustrations into motivational force."
- "I gained independence through this assignment."
- "The overall experience is great! I am learning a lot."
- "This experience was an eye-opener."

The preliminary results demonstrated that an early intercultural experience for business students is a potentially powerful tool for developing future global leaders. They experienced empowerment, independence, and confidence at the end of the assignments, and many of them mentioned that although working with men in overseas assignments was challenging, they considered the assignment to be a valuable opportunity to learn how to overcome this challenge early in their careers.

Early international experience is invaluable (Kets de Vries & Mead, 1992). To complement and facilitate learning through cultural exposure, students and managers could be given training on cross-cultural management, cross-cultural communication, multicultural team building, comparative business studies, global strategy, cross-cultural negotiation, and so on. In addition, training in various topics, such as flexibility, planning and timing, coping, and leadership, will be of great use for self-development.

8

The Quest for Transformation: The Process of Global Leadership Development

Joyce S. Osland

According to many observers and researchers, global competitiveness in the next century will depend upon the quality of leadership steering tomorrow's organizations (Zahra, 1998). The rapid pace of unpredictable change and the complexity of global business dictate a pivotal role for leaders who understand they do not have all the answers and who must be willing to learn alongside their followers (Ireland and Hitt, 1999). Thus, the need to develop global leaders is a priority. There are various ways to develop global leadership: business travel, multicultural teams, training, temporary international assignments, and expatriate assignments. Just as immersion is the most efficient and effective way to learn a foreign language, an expatriate assignment is the best way to develop global leaders. When asked to name the most powerful experience in their lives for developing global leadership capabilities, 80 percent of the leaders surveyed responded that living and working abroad was the single most influential experience in their lives (Gregersen, Morrison, & Black, 1998). The focus of this chapter is to explain the unique contribution of an expatriate assignment to the process of developing global leaders.

While an overseas assignment does not always pay off in terms of career advancement, it can be a valuable opportunity for personal development (Osland, 1995; Oddou & Mendenhall, 1988). Expatriates "take on additional, more important, and different responsibilities in their overseas assignment, and they experience more independence and more potential influence on operations than they had domestically" (Oddou & Mendenhall, 1988, 30). However, in addition to broader job experience, expatriation also results in new mental maps (i.e., a more global, bicultural perspective) and increased skills and competencies. For example, a study of 135 expatriates that measured the "value added" of an overseas assignment to the firm identified these specific competencies that resulted from expatriation (Oddou & Mendenhall, 1988, 30):

1. increased global perspective of their firm's business operations.
2. greater planning ability.
3. increased ability to communicate effectively with people of diverse backgrounds.
4. better able to conceptualize and comprehend business trends and events due to their exposure to contrasting cultural, political, and economic work systems.
5. better motivators as a result of working with culturally diverse personnel overseas.

The last three competencies in the list have been associated with global leadership, as shown in the literature reviewed by Morrison (in press). Unlike the comprehensive list Morrison analyzed, this chapter will address only those competencies that are linked directly to the expatriate experience. These competencies can be organized into six categories:

Business Savvy—the ability to make money in global business; recognizing worldwide market opportunities and understanding competitive conditions (Brake, 1997; Black, Morrison, & Gregersen, 1999).

Continuous Learning—inquisitiveness; the willingness to rethink hypotheses and assumptions (Adler & Bartholomew, 1992; Brake, 1997; Black et al., 1999).[1]

Managing Uncertainty—dealing well with changing conditions and incomplete data (Black et al., 1999).

Cognitive Complexity—the ability to understand complex issues from various perspectives and make sense of paradoxes (Brake, 1997; Black et al., 1999; Petrick, Scherer, Brodzinski, Quinn, & Ainina, 1999).

Behavioral Flexibility—balancing the tensions between globalization and localization, competing values, and business and cultural imperatives;

playing multiple roles (Yeung & Ready, 1995; Black et al., 1999; Petrick et al., 1999).

Cross-Cultural Skills—the ability to establish relationships; connect emotionally; and communicate with, motivate, and manage diverse peoples; cultural understanding (Adler & Bartholomew, 1992; Moran & Riesenberger, 1994; Rhinesmith, 1996; Brake, 1997; Black et al., 1999).

The first item in the list, business savvy, follows naturally from the in-depth exposure that is part and parcel of working in other cultures. The other competencies, however, have to do with the transformational aspect of an overseas assignment. In an effort to capture the essence and the significance of their subjective experience, I interviewed and surveyed thirty-five returned U.S. American expatriates. The following description of expatriate transformation is derived from this study (Osland, 1995).[2]

Listening to expatriate stories made it necessary to look beyond adjustment to the larger transformational process they undergo. The most commonly used words in expatriate descriptions of their lives overseas are "challenge," "adventure," and "learning." Their stories are reminiscent of people who have been deeply touched by midlife crisis, personal growth workshops, personal tragedy, or other unsettling, unique, and psychologically demanding experiences. The difference between these "domestic" challenges and living in another culture is primarily a matter of degree. For better or worse, expatriates are upended by concurrent changes in cultures, job context, and socioeconomic supports. According to one well-accepted theory (Holmes and Rahe, 1967), one's level of stress is related to the number of changes that are occurring concurrently in the different areas of one's life. A move abroad can produce simultaneous changes on virtually all fronts. The cross-cultural context provides numerous stressors, both positive (novelty and adventure) and negative (feeling inadequate, marginalized, perhaps overwhelmed by uncertainty), in an accelerated and accentuated fashion. The cross-cultural setting can be so stressful that it demands that ordinary people rise to extraordinary and even heroic heights, and if they do they usually find they have been transformed in the process and have unearthed strengths in themselves that were never required within their own culture. Expatriates who have overcome innumerable obstacles abroad are like serious athletes or Outward Bound participants who have tested their endurance and live with the confidence that comes from successfully pushing back one's limits. Many expatriates have to plumb the depths of their inner resources, first to survive the differences and changes, then to be effective, and, finally, to develop explanations for the ambiguity of their new experiences. To enable their own personal transformation, they need to resolve, both intellectually and emotionally, the meaning of those experiences.

THE MYTH OF THE HERO'S JOURNEY

A recent study stated that global leaders "are driven by a sense of adventure and a desire to see and experience new things" (Gregersen et al., 1998). Not surprisingly, the metaphor that helps many expatriates make sense of their experience is the myth of the hero's journey (Campbell, 1968). Joseph Campbell, renowned expert on mythology, studied myths from all over the world and identified their common plots and stages. All hero's adventure myths—one of the most common mythical themes—have the same basic plot: *separation* from the world, *initiation* involving penetration to some source of power, and a life-enhancing *return*. For example, "Jason sailed through the Clashing rocks into a sea of marvels, circumvented the dragon that guarded the Golden Fleece, and returned with the fleece and the power to wrest his rightful throne from a usurper" (Campbell, 1968, 30). Mythical heroes either seek to find their destiny outside their known world or inadvertently stumble into another world. In either case, there is an "awakening of the self," as mystics have termed it (Underhill, 1911). Heroes are helped by magical friends who guide them past the dangerous guardians of a different world. Next, they undergo a series of trials that ends with a decisive victory and brings them to the realization of a higher consciousness or a power hidden within themselves. After this transformation, heroes return home from their journey with the power to share with their compatriots the boons (benefits or blessings) they acquired on their adventure, such as the gift of fire or spiritual illumination.

Though it may seem an unlikely comparison at first glance, expatriate businesspeople have much in common with mythical heroes, and their experience overseas has much in common with the stages of the hero's adventure myth (shown in parentheses). Expatriates consider and eventually accept the request to go abroad (The Call to Adventure), leaving behind the domestic office of the organization and the social support of an established life. They embark on the fascinating, adventurous, but initially lonely overseas assignment (Crossing the First Threshold). The location is often shrouded in the ambiguity of unknown languages and customs (The Belly of the Whale). The expatriates' tasks are challenging, often well beyond what they would have been asked to accomplish in their own country in terms of autonomy and in the degree and breadth of responsibility. If they are fortunate, cultural mentors help them understand the other culture and provide the reassurance that they will succeed at their challenges (The Magical Friend). Unfamiliar obstacles of all stripes and colors appear (The Road of Trials). They force the adventuring heroes to question their own identities, their values, and their assumptions about numerous aspects of everyday life previously taken for granted. Some of these obstacles appear in the form of paradoxes the expatriates must learn to resolve, such as how much of their identities they must give up to be accepted by the other culture. When they perform their tasks successfully and learn to adapt to another culture, expatriates experience a solid sense of satisfaction, mastery, and self-efficacy. Among other changes, they return with greater understanding of foreign lands, increased self-confidence and interpersonal skills, and tolerance for differences in people (The Ultimate Boon). Their return home is often marked by a sense of loss at leaving behind the magical charm and fulfillment of the sojourn (The Return). Some companies treat them as heroes and make use of the skills they developed or honed abroad; others do not.

The metaphor of the hero's adventure myth is a framework that helps capture the often heroic essence of the expatriate experience (Osland, 1995). Three stages of the hero's adventure myth, in particular, demonstrate how working overseas contributes to the process of developing global leadership. These stages—Crossing the First Threshold (with its Belly of the Whale substage), The Road of Trials, and The Ultimate Boon—and the global leadership competencies they elicit will be described in the following sections.

CROSSING THE FIRST THRESHOLD

In this stage expatriates are called upon to expand their capacity to learn and to develop their ability to manage uncertainty. When mythical heroes cross the first threshold, they leave behind the known for the unknown. For expatriates this means crossing the cultural and physical boundaries of another culture, which involve learning. Expatriates describe their time abroad as the most accelerated learning period of their lives. The following comments were made by the head of a European auditing department for a multinational manufacturing firm: "I have to learn everything there is to learn over there. I have to learn how to be a manager. I have to learn the European way of living. I have to learn the European company's ways of functioning. Just everything is brand-new. And I am the one who is expected to learn this thing. So I better learn it quickly and figure out the right way to do it quickly."

Expatriates lack a complete understanding about the other culture and how business works, no matter how much homework they have done ahead of time. Despite the tremendous uncertainty this causes, they still have to accomplish their jobs. Expatriates describe the threshold period as a time of strangeness, exhilaration, difficulties, uncertainty, and intense learning. This provides a strong impetus to develop the global leadership competencies of managing uncertainty and continuous learning. For those proactive expatriates who are trying to adapt to another culture and become effective at work, learning is both a necessity and a pleasure. For global leaders who must acquire business savvy as well as innovate and adopt best practices from all over the world, the expatriate experience is a good training ground.

Mythical heroes no longer have the same measure of control over what occurs to them once they leave behind the world they know, because beyond the first threshold lies the "belly of the whale." In this substage of the adventure, heroes are swallowed alive, falling into an abyss of some sort over which they have no control; later on, they are resurrected. This stage is the beginning of the journey inward that results in transformation. For expatriates, the belly of the whale represents throwing themselves into the other culture and opening themselves up to its influence. It depicts the psychological leave-taking of one's own culture. Perhaps for the first time, expatriates are forced to examine their lives, their basic assumptions and values, and the often-taken-for-granted superiority of their own culture (Schultz, 1944). This is the expatriate version of giving up control. When you are introduced in this manner to your own culture, when you open yourself up to learning about another culture, and when you relinquish some of your own freedom in order to respect that culture's norms, it is impossible to foretell how the experience might change you and your view of the world. Once again, learning is a major theme in stories about this stage. "We lived more in those two years than [in any others]. . . . I think in those two years I probably grew the most. You open yourself up more [abroad]. . . . You are just thrown into an environment completely new to you so you have to make friends. . . . [One of the partners] said I went over as a little boy and left as a man."

THE ROAD OF TRIALS

In this stage expatriates continue to deal with uncertainty while being called upon to develop both cognitive and behavioral complexity. For mythical heroes the Road of Trials involves confrontations with numerous obstacles and tests. Mythical heroes slay dragons, elude monsters, and brave the dangers of the underworld in order to pass the test and win the prize they seek. There is no question that expatriates also traverse a road of trials. The most common obstacles are logistical, acculturation, and language difficulties that occur at the beginning of an assignment. They build character and tenacity in expatriates. However, it is another class of obstacles, less commonly articulated, that helps develop global leaders. These are the paradoxes and contradictions inherent in the expatriate context.

Paradox can be defined as "a situation involving the presence of contradictory, mutually exclusive elements that operate equally at the same time" (Quinn & Cameron, 1988). The nature of a cross-cultural setting produces paradoxes for expatriates that are obstacles either to their effectiveness at work or to their coexistence with the other culture. The following are some examples:[3]

Possessing a great deal of power as a result of your role but downplaying it in order to gain necessary input and cooperation.

Generally thinking well of the host-country nationals while at the same time being very savvy about being taken advantage of by them.

Feeling caught between contradictory demands of headquarters on the one hand and the host-country nationals and the local situation on the other.

Seeing as valid the general stereotype about the culture but also realizing that many host-country nationals do not fit that stereotype.

Giving up some of your native culture's values in order to be accepted or successful in the other culture, while at the same time finding some of your core values becoming even stronger as a result of exposure to another culture.

As a result of being abroad a long time, feeling at ease anywhere but belonging nowhere.

Becoming more and more "worldminded" as a result of exposure to different values and conflicting loyalties, but becoming more idiosyncratic as to how you put together your own value system and view on life.

Trying to represent your company as best you can in order to succeed but also realizing that the "ideal" values you act out abroad may not exist back at headquarters.

Being freed from many of your own cultural rules and even from some of the host culture's norms, but not being free at all from certain host-country customs that you must observe in order to be effective.

Two conclusions can be made about the perception of expatriate paradoxes. First, the more involved expatriates are with the foreign culture, the more likely they are to perceive paradoxes. In other words, a certain threshold level of acculturation is necessary before expatriates become aware of these paradoxes. Second, the paradoxes were only problematic when first confronted; once resolved, they no longer constituted an obstacle. Mastering them or learning to live with them seemed to require an even higher level of acculturation than simple awareness of their presence. Expatriates resolve paradoxes by learning to take a contingency approach, once they have developed the cognitive maps that include both contradictory truths as well as the cues that tell them which truth is most closely aligned with effectiveness. For example, expatriate managers learn to judge a situation and figure out when they need to manifest their power and when they need to empower others, determined by what would be most effective in the particular situation.

The expatriates in this study were asked to describe a critical incident involving a paradox they handled overseas. From the following list of the common approaches they used, one can see that learning to deal with paradox is a good developmental exercise for global leaders.

They looked for reasons to explain the situation so they could understand why the other culture behaved as it did—so they could understand the "foreign" side of the paradox.

They determined what their role was in the particular situation and gauged whether they could influence or change it and whether or not they had the right, as an expatriate, to do so.

They weighed the contingencies of the situation: What would happen if they chose to act on either side of the paradox?

They discerned the critical factors (norms or actions) that were absolutely essential for effectiveness or success.

They "picked their battles" in conflicts between headquarters and the local company and avoided those conflicts they could not win.

They accepted what they could not change.

They learned from the experience and applied it to the next paradoxical situation.

Wrestling with paradox and contradiction develops three global leadership competencies: managing uncertainty, cognitive complexity, and behavioral complexity. It builds the cognitive complexity that characterizes top managers (Streufert & Swezey, 1986). Cognitive complexity is defined as the extent to which people are multidimensional in their thinking and the number of different relationships they can make between different dimensions or concepts. People with high cognitive complexity possess a variety of maps in their cognitive bank and have the flexibility to shuffle them around, seeking the most appropriate one in a given situation. This description also applies to expatriates who have learned to deal with paradox, which involves perceiving more than one truth or one mind-set. Until paradoxes are resolved, expatriates must manage the uncertainty they engender. Paradoxes also force expatriates to analyze situations closely and develop the behavioral complexity needed to respond appropriately and effectively in different ways in different situations. Petrick and colleagues (1999) maintain that successful global CEOs must balance four competing criteria: profitability and productivity; continuity and efficiency; commitment and morale; and adaptability and innovation. Dealing with expatriate paradoxes is good training for balancing these particular competing values as well as the tension between globalization and localization.

THE ULTIMATE BOON

This stage describes the personal transformation of expatriates, which lies at the heart of the process of global leadership development and explains how expatriates are likely to acquire the competencies addressed in this chapter. In myths, penetrating to a source of power involves a transformation to a higher consciousness by means of a death and rebirth. The death symbolizes the submission of the ego, giving oneself over to a higher good or "putting aside" a former life and way of looking at the world. The rebirth lies in seeing the world through different eyes or taking on a different role. The heroes' consciousness is transformed either by the trials themselves or by illuminating revelations.

Three aspects of mythical transformation help to elucidate the expatriate experience: (1) the need for sacrifice, (2) the move from dependence to independence, and (3) the heroes' discovery of a universal power within them.

The Need for Sacrifice

Campbell (1968) describes the hero as a person of self-achieved submission who "must put aside his pride, his virtue, beauty, and life, and bow or submit to the absolutely intolerable" (p. 108). Although such extravagant demands are seldom required of them, expatriates are no strangers to sacrifice. Their stories are full of references to doing difficult things "for the good of the company" or for their family. Many of them make sacrifices to accomplish arduous tasks abroad and to be effective and accepted in the other culture. Furthermore, expatriates may sacrifice some of their values, normal ways of behavior and perception, their extended family, and, in certain instances, their comfort.

The Move from Dependence to Independence

The move from dependence to independence is a common mythological theme that also involves a form of sacrifice. It means leaving behind a former way of life, a former consciousness. This transformation is the basis for many initiation rites found throughout the world. Most cultures use such rites to formally mark the end of childhood (dependence) and the beginning of adulthood (independence). Expatriates often experience a sense of dependency during the beginning months of their assignment. They have left behind many of their cultural and personal anchors. In many respects, they are starting over again, like a child, learning a new culture and a new language. Once the code of the new culture has been broken, with or without the help of a cultural mentor, they can function independently once more. This move from dependence to independence is a proud moment and one that many expatriates can pinpoint as the specific time when they began to feel comfortable in the other culture or effective on the job.

Discovery of a Universal Power Within

Mythical heroes, like expatriates, find that the adventure evokes qualities of their characters they did not know they possessed. Heroes learn that the power or ability to accomplish something lay within them all the time. As Campbell (1968) states, "The perilous journey is not labor of attainment but reattainment, not discovery but rediscovery. . . . Godly powers were within the heart of the hero all the time. . . . The hero is symbolical of that divine creative and redemptive image which is hidden within us all, only waiting to be known and rendered into life" (p. 39).

Most modern societies have fewer rites of passage and opportunities to test oneself. For many expatriates, life in their own country is not as challenging as it is overseas, because they are not called upon to use all their talents or to rise to the occasion in the way that is demanded by an international assignment. Although one can certainly be challenged within one's own culture, the sheer novelty and uncertainty of entering another culture can throw expatriates off balance. As a result, they often become aware of hidden resources and skills unneeded within their own culture but essential for coping abroad.

In addition to a different level of consciousness about themselves, expatriates may acquire a new way of perceiving the world. Because the balance of their lives is disrupted and their normal routines are left at home, expatriates are usually more open to new experiences and new perceptions. Expatriates say that they sometimes become callused in their own culture by predictability, routine, and even materialism. Finding novelty at home requires a special effort. Once the familiar frame is broken by entering a new culture, people are freed to look at their surroundings with a more childlike appreciation. Thus, it is not a surprise that novelty and learning emerged as major themes in expatriate interviews and are among the things they missed most upon returning home.

In myth, consciousness is transformed by exposure to trials or illuminating revelations. For expatriates, consciousness is transformed by exposure to cultural differences, to trials, and to paradox, sometimes with the help of a magical friend (cultural mentor) who provides explanations. Making sense of different cultures and their beliefs is a challenge. In the process, the expatriates' own views change and they acquire a different consciousness, a bicultural or multicultural perspective—in effect, a global mind-set. This is the change in consciousness most frequently described by expatriates: the acquisition of a more cognitively complex perspective that also includes an appreciation of paradox. Becoming a citizen of the world, acknowledging the similarities and differences among cultures, and learning to see one's own culture through the eyes of another are other examples of this new consciousness.

THE NATURE OF THE EXPATRIATE TRANSFORMATION

The basic theme of the hero's adventure is a separation from the world, a penetration to some source of power, and a life-enhancing return. The source of power for the expatriate is a bicultural perspective, increased self-awareness, and the knowledge that he or she had the inner resources to master a difficult situation. These are some of the ways that expatriates change overseas. The nature of the changes depends on the individual expatriate and the type of adventure sought. Nevertheless, the transformation process expatriates describe seems fairly universal and is closely related to that found in myth.

For mythical heroes, the process of transformation involves a dying and a birth. But whether small or great, and no matter what the stage or grade of life, the call rings up the curtain, always, on a mystery of transfiguration, a rite or moment of spiritual passage, which, when complete, amounts to a dying and a birth. The familiar life horizon has been outgrown; the old concepts, ideals, and emotional patterns no longer fit; the time for the passing of a threshold is at hand (Campbell, 1968, 51).

LETTING GO AND TAKING ON

A similar process occurs with expatriates. The death and rebirth of the transformation process they describe takes the form of "letting go" (death) and a "taking on" (rebirth). The various factors involved in this process are presented in the following list:

Letting Go	*Taking On*
Cultural certainty	Internalized perceptions of the other culture
Unquestioned acceptance of basic assumptions	Internalized values of the other culture
Personal frames of reference	New or broader schemas so that differences are accepted without a need to compare
Unexamined life	Constructed life
Accustomed role or status	Role assigned by the other culture or one's job
Social reinforcement knowledge	Accepting and learning the other culture's norms and behavior
Accustomed habits and activities	Substituting functional equivalents
Known routines	Addiction to novelty and learning

During their sojourn, expatriates relinquish (1) cultural certainty, (2) unquestioned acceptance of basic assumptions, (3) personal frames of reference, (4) the unexamined life, (5) accustomed role and status, (6) knowledge of social reinforcement, (7) accustomed habits and activities, and (8) known routines. The first four factors are either cognitive or attitudinal; they relate to the mental maps that undergo extensive redefinition as a result of a cross-cultural experience. The other factors are concerned with social relationships and outside activities.

Letting Go of Cultural Certainty:
Internalizing Perceptions of the Other Culture

Cultural certainty is the implicit faith and pride people have in their own country. For example, many Americans have an image of the United States as a superpower that generously comes to the aid of other nations. An assignment to Europe usually results in a crash course in international politics and the awareness that the U.S. image abroad is not always favorable. Expatriates may find themselves on the firing line, forced to defend their country's foreign policy and domestic conditions, which, to their chagrin, are not always defensible. Furthermore, expatriates discover that other countries have some advantages that are lacking at home. Those who live abroad come to realize that their particular cultural software is not the only one that functions, nor is it necessarily the best one. This process of relinquishing cultural certainty may be hastened by exposure to critical views of their own country. They may also take on some of the views the other culture holds about their own culture, so they return with a more cognitively complex view of their country. This usually means they have a clearer idea of their homeland's positive and negative points; despite being forced to see its flaws, they often become more patriotic abroad.

Letting Go of Unquestioned Acceptance of Basic Assumptions: Internalizing the Values of the Other Culture

This category, like the preceding one, forces expatriates to consider factors that were previously taken for granted. Schein (1988) wrote about the basic assumptions that form a hard-to-excavate layer of cultural notions—the implicit cognitive maps that people inherit from their cultures. Coming into contact with other cultures makes these assumptions visible and forces expatriates to question their validity. At the same time, they may be taking on values of the other cultures. This is a natural part of the assimilation process (Berry, 1983). Consciously or unconsciously, expatriates adopt and internalize values of the other culture.

One of the paradoxes expatriates confront is simultaneously relinquishing and strengthening their values. In the process of shedding some of their peripheral cultural beliefs and values that are less acceptable to the other culture, some of their core values (for example, patriotism, religious values, individual freedom) assume even greater importance. As one expatriate said, "I became more American while I was there. Even though I accepted the way things are there, it made me realize how American I really am."

Letting Go of Frames of Reference: Adopting New and Broader Schemas

When people first go abroad, they are intrigued by the differences they observe; as time goes on, it is the similarities that capture their attention. But in the beginning they inevitably compare what they see to what they know at home, which is their frame of reference. Over time they relinquish this frame of reference as a basis for judging the other culture. Well-adapted expatriates learn to accept the other culture as it is, without feeling a need to compare it to home-country standards. In the language of social cognition theory (Fiske & Taylor, 1984), people organize their perceptions into schemas, or mental maps of various concepts, events, or types of stimuli. Once established, schemas determine what people pay attention to and remember. Expatriates, however, let go of their frames of reference and take on new and broader schemas in other cultures.

Letting Go of the Unexamined Life: Constructing a Life

As Socrates noted, the unexamined life is not worth living. For many expatriates, the experience of living overseas triggers an examination of their life. The surprises, changes, and contrasts (Louis, 1980) confronted in a new culture lead to introspection. Spouses in particular have to construct a new life for themselves (Adler, 1986), and, in doing so, evaluate their lives to determine what should and should not be included. Several expatriates echoed this observation: "My wife had nothing. I mean, she woke up and had no structure to her day. She really had to construct her life, and fortunately [she] did it." Expatriates also live under a time sentence that pushes them to take advantage of whatever a foreign country has to offer or to get certain goals accomplished at work. Thus, many expatriates let go of an unexamined life and take on a carefully considered, constructed life.

Letting Go of Accustomed Role and Status: Taking on the Roles Assigned by the Other Culture or One's Job

An expatriate assignment usually involves some type of role change, either at work or in one's personal life. Such changes may involve higher or lower status, although the former is most likely for businesspeople. All expatriates, however, assume the role of stranger, an unknown commodity, once they leave the borders of their own country. If they cannot speak the local language, they may even be treated as morons, a humbling shock to one's self-concept. An even greater shock is to find oneself stereotyped in an unflattering role. Being forced to relinquish accustomed roles and take on assigned roles can be threatening to one's sense of self. Maintaining one's own identity and not buying into someone else's mistaken perception, be it overly positive or overly negative, is a challenge.

Letting Go of Accustomed Habits and Activities: Substituting Functional Equivalents

Rather than bemoaning the loss of one's usual activities, successfully acculturated expatriates "take on" replacements and substitutions that serve the same function. This requires flexibility and openness, for example, to learning local sports, musical instruments, and dances, and acquiring a taste for local foods. The willingness to substitute local activities that serve the same function prevents expatriates from missing home as much and brings them into closer contact with the local people.

Letting Go of Known Routines: Becoming Energized by Novelty and Learning

When expatriates accept the call to adventure, they leave behind their known world. They relinquish the security and comfort of living in an environment where there are relatively few surprises or paradoxes. Well-acculturated expatriates gladly trade their known routines for the exhilaration of experiencing different cultures and different situations. They grow to thrive on the learning and novelty that are a major part of an overseas experience for those who are willing to see it. Some expatriates travel constantly to perpetuate the novelty and learning. As one expatriate described it, living abroad is like returning to childhood when every day brings novel adventures and something new. The challenge and excitement that comes from the opportunity for lifelong learning is one of the principal attractions of expatriate life. Each country is a new chance to learn, whether it is the first or the tenth overseas assignment.

THE IMPETUS BEHIND TRANSFORMATION

What is the impetus behind the transformational process that occurs with most expatriates? Very simply, it is their desire to become acculturated, to fit into another culture, and to be effective at work. They talk about transformation in terms of letting go of things, which sometimes involved sacrifices or adjustments that not all expatriates were willing to make. Their stories are full of comparisons with unsuccessful expatriates who were not flexible enough or not committed enough to let go. Many carry a clear picture in their minds of the Ugly American (or Ugly Whatever) they do not want to be. Such efforts represent yet another sacrifice expatriates make to be successful overseas. It is not a simple matter to give up things as fundamental as cultural certainty, basic cultural assumptions, or accustomed roles. It takes courage to examine oneself and one's culture in this way and to step outside the bounds of conformity. But only by sacrificing these things can the expatriate be "reborn" in Campbell's (1968) terms and move to a higher consciousness—a bicultural perspective. Expatriate transformation promotes self-knowledge. As one expatriate stated with obvious satisfaction, "I have a better idea of how I tick."

EXPATRIATE BOONS

Expatriate stories about their personal transformations abroad provide evidence that they develop the business savvy, cognitive complexity, and cross-cultural skills needed by global leaders. Virtually all expatriates acknowledge that they have changed overseas in a positive way. However, one could argue that this merely reflects a tendency to make post-hoc rationalizations about a challenging experience, which is one of several caveats to consider when returned expatriates provide self-report data on their overseas experiences. Another caveat is the possibility of selective recall; some individuals may recall primarily positive aspects while others more readily recall negative aspects. Furthermore, interviews about past experiences may include retrospective sensemaking (Weick, 1995), which would be less likely in data collected while expatriates are overseas in "the thick of it." However, many expatriates commented that no one was willing to listen to their stories and thoughts about living abroad, so it appeared that some interviewees were making sense of their experience as they talked. This appears to confirm Harrison and Hopkin's (1967) observation that Peace Corps volunteers returned with war stories or anecdotes but not with conceptual maps that organized their stories. The longer-term expatriates I interviewed seemed to have processed and made more sense of their experiences. Self-report data, in general, may be subject to "shifts in opinion, self-evaluation, self-deception, manipulation of self-presentation, embarrassment, and outright dishonesty" (Denzin & Lincoln, 1994, 389). On the other hand, the benefit of listening to expatriate stories is a more unfettered view of what the subjective experience means to them in their own words and in its totality—hopefully, a closer approximation of their reality. The expatriates in this sample were similar to each other in terms of the basic transformational themes that emerged from the interviews and the letting go/taking on process they described. But the specific details of their transformations were unique because the journey inward that characterizes the hero's adventure naturally produces unique lessons.

Despite the caveats mentioned in the preceding paragraph, all but one expatriate in the sample quickly and easily identified perceived changes in themselves, which constitute the personal boons they bring home: (1) positive changes in self, (2) changed attitudes, (3) improved work skills, and (4) increased knowledge.

Positive changes in self. Among the positive changes expatriates reported are increased tolerance, patience, confidence, respectfulness, maturity, open-mindedness, competitiveness, adaptability, independence, and sensitivity, and decreased impulsiveness. Even expatriates who did not completely enjoy the experience felt that it was a form of personal development. All described it as an experience that helped them to mature and build their character.

Changed attitudes. Some of the commonly reported changed attitudes that expatriates bring home are (1) a broader perspective on the world, (2) greater appreciation of cultural differences, (3) increased realization of how fortunate Americans are, (4) different attitudes toward work, and (5) a feeling that life is more interesting now than before. These changed attitudes are often an indication of greater cognitive complexity.

Improved work skills. A particularly important boon for companies are the improved work skills expatriates bring home. These include (1) improved communication skills in general and increased listening skills in particular, (2) an improved management style, (3) a better understanding of power, (4) the ability to do higher-quality work, and (5) broadened exposure to business. Improved interpersonal skills are mentioned most frequently. These changes relate to the global leadership competencies of business savvy and cross-cultural skills.

Increased knowledge. As noted before, expatriates see their time abroad as a period of accelerated learning. Much of that learning naturally centers around other countries—their language, history, culture, politics, economics, and art. In many respects, an overseas assignment is analogous to a good liberal arts education.

DISCUSSION

The purpose of this chapter is to explain how an expatriate assignment contributes to transforming people into global leaders by developing a specific set of competencies: business savvy, continuous learning, ability to manage uncertainty, cognitive complexity, behavioral flexibility, and cross-cultural skills. The hero's adventure myth, a metaphor that helps many expatriates make sense of their overseas experiences, highlights the transformation that often occurs in the cross-cultural context. Peter Adler (1975) also focused on the transformational nature of living in another culture; his model consists of five stages: contact, disintegration, reintegration, autonomy, and independence. Expatriate research, however, has generally focused not on transformation, but on adjustment. Although literature reviews of adjustment stages have yielded inconclusive and mixed support (Church, 1982; Black & Mendenhall, 1991), much of the literature assumes that there is a predictable, linear cycle of overseas adjustment that follows the U-shaped curve first identified by Lsygaard (1955). Gullahorn and Gullahorn (1963) added the sojourners' adjustment to the return home, extending the U curve to a W curve. The stages in the W-curve model are honeymoon, culture shock, adjustment, mastery, and reverse culture shock upon repatriation. After the initial euphoria, sojourner adjustment decreases during the six- to twelve-month period due to culture shock. Adjustment rises after this period, peaks at mastery, and then decreases again when the expatriate returns home.

When we compare the U curve to the hero's adventure framework, there are some surface similarities. Crossing the First Threshold contains some aspects of the honeymoon period (the accelerated learning and excitement of the unknown). The Belly of the Whale and the Road of Trials stages have some parallels with culture shock. The Ultimate Boon stage certainly contains aspects of adjustment; for example, when expatriates take on values and frames of reference of the other culture. This stage also emphasizes mastery, as does the U-curve model, although the definition of mastery is broader in the hero's adventure model.

These similarities aside, there are significant differences between the two models. The hero's adventure metaphor makes no pretense of assigning time markers to each stage, because personal transformation is an unpredictable and nonlinear process. Critics of the U-curve model have also argued that its assumption of a smooth, linear adaptive process does not reflect reality (Pedersen, 1995). With regard to culture shock, Pedersen wrote, "Transformation occurs through a series of degeneration and regeneration events or crises in a nonregular and erratic movement of change. Part of this process is conscious and other parts more unconscious as the visitor seeks greater success in the host environment" (p. 4).

Unlike the U-curve model, the hero's adventure model is an example of grounded theory building that tried to capture the subjective expatriate experience. The theme of transformation that emerged subsumes the concept of adjustment; adjustment is a part of what expatriates experience but it is not the whole picture. It allows for more idiosyncratic perspectives within a broader conceptual framework.

Another difference between the models is the use of myth and metaphor to understand human behavior. Like metaphors, myths allow us to step back from the stimuli and minutiae of our lives in

order to reinterpret our experiences from a higher level of abstrac-
tion and generalization. Myths are like universal poetry that illumi-
nates basic human truths and provides guidance. Both metaphors
and myths capture the essence; the hero's adventure myth captures
the often heroic and transformational essence of living overseas. Thus,
the underlying assumption of the hero's adventure model is one of
personal transformational journeys. Another assumption is that the
cross-cultural experience is positive (after the challenges are mas-
tered) for expatriates who have embarked on a hero's adventure.

Although this resonance is true for many expatriates and although the cross-cultural context is particularly fertile ground for
personal development and transformation, not all expatriates take
advantage of the opportunity for personal growth, nor do they adjust to the other culture. As Campbell (1968) warns, the hero gets
the particular adventure for which he or she is ready. There are
several reasons that explain individual differences with regard to
transformation and adjustment:

- People do not react the same way to an overseas experience, nor does
  the same person necessarily always react the same way to overseas
  challenges.
- Some expatriates fail to adjust or integrate themselves into another
  culture due to their personality type. For example, rigid personalities
  often perceive a cross-cultural experience as a threat, and they lack the
  flexibility to make the necessary cognitive and behavioral adjustments.
  The ambiguity encountered abroad is problematic for people who see
  the world only in terms of black and white. People with unstable personalities or serious personal problems generally have to devote their
  energies inward toward coping rather than outward toward the other
  culture. In contrast, flexible, open-minded, stable, curious, adventurous personalities are more likely to enter other cultures successfully.
- People are at various stages of intercultural sensitivity. Bennett (1993)
  identified a developmental model, a continuum of increasing sophisti-
  cation in dealing with cultural differences, which moves from ethnocen-
  trism through stages of greater recognition and acceptance of difference.
  People who are willing to progress along this continuum are more likely
  to experience transformation in an overseas assignment. People at more
  advanced stages of intercultural sensitivity are more likely to adjust
  successfully.
- People go abroad for a variety of reasons and these reasons affect their
  willingness to adjust, integrate, and open themselves to another culture. Some expatriates accept an assignment for extrinsic reasons—
  hardship pay, a reportedly glamorous lifestyle, résumé building—that
  have nothing to do with a quest for adventure or a desire to learn about
  another culture. Others go abroad as a last-chance option before termi-

nation or an escape from personal, family, or even legal problems. Some expatriates end up overseas only because they are afraid to turn down the assignment.

- Expatriates vary in the degree to which they are seeking personal development or seeking to experience another culture. This category relates most closely to Campbell's (1968) statement about heroes who get the adventure for which they are ready. As a result, the degree of cultural involvement also varies.

- Attitude seems to play an important role in both transformation and adjustment. It determines whether people are vanquished or energized by difficult challenges. Attitude also determines whether people make positive or negative attributions or interpretations about cultural behaviors they may not completely understand. Whether or not people are willing to make the necessary sacrifices to acculturate is also partly determined by attitude.

- Similarly, the expatriate's motivation to succeed at work and to become acculturated strongly influences cultural involvement, which in turn affects both transformation and adjustment.

- The particular job can affect the willingness to adjust and the necessity for transformation. Some jobs (manufacturing, R&D) require less cultural involvement than others (service, management). Other jobs are "mission impossibles," which are so difficult that expatriates lose the motivation to be successful at work or adapt to the local culture.

- Another external factor that affects transformation and adjustment is the location of the assignment. Hostile host-country nationals or extremely adverse conditions may also affect the motivation to immerse oneself in the local culture.

Thus, there are personal and external factors that affect individual transformation and adjustment. The more expatriates involve themselves in other cultures (the deeper they throw themselves into the "Belly of the Whale") the more likely they are to experience the personal development needed to become global leaders.

NOTES

1. Black and colleagues (1999) refer to learning, what they call "inquisitiveness," as a driver, a state of mind, rather than a competency. However, other authors have defined continuous learning as a competency.

2. Although this study included only Americans, expatriates from other nationalities have provided anecdotal evidence that their own expatriate experience is similar.

3. These paradoxes were developed with Asbjorn Osland.

9

Leading Global Teams: Overcoming the Challenge of the Power Paradox

Martha L. Maznevski and Lena Zander

The ability to lead global teams is a critical element in every global leader's skill portfolio. As the environment becomes more complex and dynamic, business challenges begin to incorporate more dimensions, and interdependence among units and organizations grows. It is simply impossible for one person to have access to all pertinent knowledge and resources, and to bring them together in value-added combinations. The team, therefore, is one of the most ubiquitous structural vehicles for making and implementing decisions in today's global companies. Global teams—teams that span national and geographic borders—are composed of people drawn from a range of functional, business, and geographic backgrounds, combining their expertise to address the organization's challenges. The challenge for global leaders is to help these teams achieve high-quality performance, given the teams' complex composition and mandates. Because of the important role played by these teams, global leaders' effectiveness will depend in a very real way on how well they lead their global teams. However, beyond illustrating this point convincingly and thoroughly, very few authors have explored how global teams should actually be led.

The objectives of this chapter are to identify what we do know about leading global teams, and to make some initial progress at exploring and addressing what we suggest is a pivotal dynamic for their leaders. By reviewing research on global teams and global leadership, we demonstrate that the most difficult challenge for leaders of global teams is presented by their multicultural nature. From a closer examination of this research and our own experiences conducting field research, we show how most dilemmas raised by cultural differences can be resolved. In this discussion, however, we identify one dilemma that seems to resist resolution. We call this dynamic the power paradox: a situation in which the leader and one or more members differ strongly from each other in their preferences for the ideal distribution of power in decision making and action in such a way that the preferences are mutually incompatible. We review and analyze previous research from this new perspective in an attempt to disentangle the power paradox and isolate its most problematic elements. Finally, we offer suggestions for a future research agenda and some tentative advice for human resource professionals and global leaders themselves.

REVIEW OF PAST RESEARCH

Although there has been only limited research published specifically on how to lead global teams, research in three related areas can provide insight into the phenomenon. The first area concerns the nature of culture and its influence on social dynamics, the second addresses the interaction of cultures in multicultural teams, and the third compares leadership in different countries and cultural contexts.

Culture and Leading Global Teams

Culture incorporates a society's (or social group's) commonly shared deep-level values and norms concerning how it will function interdependently (Adler, 1997c; Hofstede, 1980a; Kluckhohn & Strodtbeck, 1961; Lane, DiStefano, & Maznevski, 1997). Culture is reinforced, shared, communicated, and passed on to new members through implicit reward of attitudes and behaviors, and through shaping by societal institutions such as schools, legal infrastructure, and mass media (Hofstede, 1980a; Schein, 1984). The society or social group can be a family, profession, religion, country, or any other group that defines itself socially. It is explicitly interdependent, establishing and transmitting assumptions and norms regarding its members' interaction and interdependence. An individual may belong to several cultures, such as a religious, professional, and organizational culture, each nested within a larger societal culture and some intersecting each other (Erez & Earley, 1993). In international business research, the most often-examined group is the nation. This is not unreasonable: It is at the national level that the legal, political, and economic contexts of international business are most salient, and the institutions that carry and shape culture are often national in scope. However, it is always critical to ask whether another group's culture is more relevant to a specific question than the nation's culture, and it is equally important to remember that specific individuals may not feel or behave in accordance with their identified culture.

The cultural perspective is particularly salient in illuminating the challenges of implementing business strategies internationally. When members of different national cultures come together, their basic templates for conducting interdependent action often differ greatly (Adler, 1997c; Hofstede, 1980a; Lane et al., 1997; Trompenaars, 1993). These differences can damage business relationships, as one person interprets another's words or behavior in a way in which it was not intended and, more important, neither person recognizes that the misinterpretation has occurred. Furthermore, business performance yields better results when management practices are congruent with national culture (Earley, 1994; Newman & Nollen, 1996; Wright & Mischel, 1987). Anyone operating in or leading global teams must clearly take into account the team members' cultural backgrounds in order to be effective.

Multicultural Teams

Research findings relevant to understanding multicultural teams come from two sets of research. The first stream compares group dynamics across cultures and draws implications for multicultural settings. The second stream, which began much more recently and incorporates the first, studies multicultural situations directly and attempts to discern interaction patterns related to effectiveness. We will focus here on the second set of research, which is most directly applicable to the leading of global teams.

Studies in the field of multicultural-team effectiveness usually compare the performance of culturally diverse groups with that of culturally homogeneous groups. A general finding is that multicultural groups offer high potential for performance on complex decision-making tasks, but that they often fail to realize that potential (Adler, 1997c). In addition to culture influencing behavioral norms, it also provides a perceptual filter through which a person interprets information needed to make decisions (e.g., Abramson, Lane, Nagai, & Takagi, 1993; Adler & Ghadar, 1989; Erez & Earley, 1993; Hofstede, 1980a; Lane et al., 1997; Laurent, 1983, 1986; Stening, 1979; Sullivan & Nonaka, 1988). These differences in perspective offer potential for multicultural teams to perform well. When compared with culturally homogeneous teams, multicultural teams have been shown to have higher creativity (Ling, 1990), and to develop more and better solution alternatives to a problem and criteria for evaluating those alternatives (Kumar, Subramanian, & Nonis, 1991; McLeod & Lobel, 1992; Watson, Kumar, & Michaelsen, 1993). However, as already introduced, cultural values also influence members' preferences for social interaction norms (e.g., Bettenhausen & Murnighan, 1991; Earley, 1993; Levine & Moreland, 1990). Because of this influence, multicultural groups have difficulty executing processes related to task integration, such as structuring a problem (Fiedler, 1966), developing a task strategy (Anderson, 1983), resolving conflicts constructively (Kirchmeyer & Cohen, 1992), and creating cohesion (Kumar, et al., 1991; Watson et al., 1993). This difficulty with integration processes hinders their performance.

Two sets of empirical studies have shown that when multicultural groups engage in effective integration processes, they perform at least as well as, and sometimes better than, homogeneous teams. Watson and colleagues (Kumar, et al., 1991; Watson et al., 1993) found that cohesion and integration were related to effectiveness for all groups, but that multicultural groups took much longer to achieve these conditions and had to manage the processes explicitly in order to do so. Once they did, they performed equally as well as the homogeneous teams on overall solution quality, and better on generating alternatives and range of perspectives shown. The researchers speculated that given more time, the multicultural teams would have begun to outperform the homogeneous ones on overall solution quality. Maznevski and colleagues (Lane et al., 1997; Maznevski, 1994; Maznevski & DiStefano, 1996) also demonstrated that improved integration processes (communication, conflict resolution, and constructive problem solving) were associated with better group outcomes, and observed that multicultural groups tended to have more difficulty achieving a high level of process effectiveness than culturally homogeneous groups did.

Of particular relevance to the current topic is the finding that the most effective multicultural teams develop a combination of (1) common norms followed by everyone and (2) a norm of adapting to individuals' own preferences for behavior (Lane et al., 1997; Maznevski, 1994). The latter strategy is possible because the various sets of norms are not as often incompatible as they are simply different. For example, a team might have some members in whose cultures it is acceptable to voice opinions freely in front of a group, and others from cultures in which this is highly unacceptable. This difference may cause conflict or misunderstandings within the team, and it is usually counterproductive to suggest that everyone adopt a common norm concerning vocal participation in group meetings. However, interaction can be sequenced so that both sets of norms coexist, and the team can build mechanisms allowing everyone to contribute in the way he or she feels most comfortable. For example, one team with this profile began taking extensive e-mail polls and holding frequent informal meetings among subgroups of members outside of "official" group meetings to obtain the opinions of members who preferred a more private mode. They also assigned specific members the responsibility for bringing these opinions into open discussions. Teams with different cultural profiles can find ways of managing participation and resolving differences in modes that integrate everyone's contribution.

To summarize, the research on multicultural teams suggests that members of a global team are likely to differ in how they perceive information and in their assumptions about the appropriate norms guiding team interaction. A critical aspect of the global leader's task, therefore, is to facilitate integration and help the team develop both common norms and a norm of adaptation to individuals' cultural values.

Comparative Leadership

A large part of earlier leadership research focused on identifying one excellent management or leadership style (see Bass, 1990, for a review of more than 7,500 studies of leadership since the beginning of this century). A majority of these studies were carried out in one country and the results were assumed to be universally applicable. However, with the arrival of the comparative multicountry leadership studies, researchers identified differences in leaders' attitudes and personal traits across countries, as well as differences in styles of leadership, in particular with regard to what is considered as appropriate leader–subordinate behavior. It was often assumed that these systematic differences were related to culture, but this relationship was only discussed vaguely with reference to history, tradition, and the like, and was not translated to rigorous hypotheses or empirical testing.

In many of the earlier comparative studies, managers were asked how they manage or should manage their employees, and in a few of the studies employees' leadership preferences were mapped (e.g., Ah Chong & Thomas, 1997; Al-Jafary & Hollingsworth, 1983; Badawy, 1980; Bass, Burger, Doktor, & Barrett, 1979; Bottger, Hallein, & Yetton, 1985; Haire, Ghiselli, & Porter, 1966; Heller & Wilpert, 1981; IDE, 1976; Peterson, Smith, & Tayeb, 1993; Redding & Richardson, 1986; Schaupp, 1978; Smith, Misumi, Tayeb, Peterson, & Bond, 1989; Tannenbaum, Kavcic, Rosner, Vianello, & Wieser, 1974; Tayeb, 1995). These studies were conducted in the Americas, Asia, Australia-Pacific, Europe, and the Middle East. The results consistently displayed differences in managerial attitudes as well as employee preferences regarding leadership across countries. Most often, these differences were assumed to depend broadly on cultural differences, but, as noted earlier, this relationship was not further analyzed.

Given the importance to international business of clearly understanding the nature of cross-cultural leadership, Zander (1997) conducted a large-scale study to analyze the relationship between cultural dimensions and employees' preferences regarding interpersonal leadership in eighteen countries. First, in line with earlier research, she demonstrated that employees' preferences regarding leadership varied across countries. In addition, she incorporated research on cultural dimensions, which had presented strong but largely untested hypotheses regarding the relationship between culture and leadership preferences (Hofstede, 1980a; Lane et al., 1997; Laurent, 1983; Schwartz, 1994; Trompenaars, 1993). She demonstrated that the relationship with culture was very clear, with strong correlations between the interpersonal leadership behaviors preferred by employees in a particular country and the same country's cultural values as assessed in other research. She concluded that not only do managers display and exercise different managerial styles as shown in earlier research, but employees also differ in their preferences regarding leadership across countries. In the context of multicultural teams this implies that not only will the team leader's behavior vary across different cultural settings, but the team members will bring with them into the team different expectations about the role of the team leader. These expectations are clearly related to fundamental cultural values. Furthermore, as demonstrated by Newman and Nollen (1996), there is evidence that leadership is effective when it is congruent with cultural values, advocating local adaptation. These findings are parallel to those emanating from research on multicultural teams concluding that preferences for interaction behavior differ by culture, and that the best multicultural teams find ways to accommodate these differences.

THE POWER PARADOX

Leaders of global teams share a number of challenges with leaders of domestic teams. However, we suggest that a global team leader's greatest challenge will be unique, and will be a function of the multicultural nature of these teams. As we have demonstrated, research findings consistently suggest that an effective global leader should lead each follower in a global team in a manner consistent with the follower's cultural expectations (local individual adaptation), while simultaneously helping the members themselves develop a set of norms that allow for differences in social-interaction preferences.

At first glance, this may seem next to impossible. However, by combining global business knowledge and skills creatively (Black, Morrison, & Gregersen, 1999), the team's leader can resolve most of these situations and lead the team to achieve new heights of performance. In our experience conducting field research and management education and working with multicultural student groups over time, we have seen many instances of teams resolving these differences constructively. One of the most important points to recognize is that each team's solution will be unique to the team's profile and situation. However, some differences among members raise dilemmas that are seemingly impossible for the leader to resolve. Over several years and multiple contexts, we have begun to see a pattern in these exceptionally difficult cases. They are characterized by mutually inconsistent differences among members in terms of assumptions about distribution of power and responsibility. The following two quotations from leaders of multicultural teams reflect this dilemma:

Leading this team has been a challenge. I gather information from everyone, make decisions about where to cut costs, then let them all know how to implement it in their areas. But some team members just disregard my instructions and do it their own way. They don't seem to appreciate that I'm trying to coordinate moves across the whole globe, and I need to make these decisions for everyone. (Leader of a global resources company's strategic cost-cutting multicultural team.)

We've introduced empowerment very heavily in Shanghai. People are expected to make and implement decisions for their area on their own, and they have the authority and responsibility to do so. The European and North American management team members have slid into this mode easily, but I still get the feeling that the Chinese members are making decisions because I told them to. When the presidency revolves to the Chinese partners next year, I suspect we'll see an end to empowerment. That will be fine for the

Chinese members, who assume it should be that way anyway, but it will cause a lot of problems among the Western team members who have come to expect to make decisions. (President of a joint venture in Shanghai.)

In both of these situations the leader led according to one or another set of norms regarding power distribution, a set that conflicted with the assumptions of some team members. However, in each case any other approach to power and responsibility would conflict with the preferred mode of other members. Each of these situations caused a great deal of strife and conflict in teams that had otherwise developed synergistic approaches to managing their cultural differences.

On closer examination, we can discern why differences in assumptions about power create a logical paradox within the team. The cultural dimension of relationships among people (Kluckhohn & Strodtbeck, 1961) incorporates the three subdimensions of individualism (each person's main responsibility is to and for one's self and one's immediate family), collectivism (each person's main responsibility is to and for a larger group, such as an extended family or workgroup), and hierarchy (power and responsibility are naturally arranged in a hierarchy, such that those higher in the hierarchy have power over and responsibility for those lower in the hierarchy) (see also Hofstede's [1980a] individualism and power distance dimensions; Triandis's [1988] individualism and collectivism). Unlike other dimensions of culture (Hofstede, 1980a; Kluckhohn & Strodtbeck, 1961; Trompenaars, 1993), power and responsibility assumptions carry with them corollary assumptions about the power and responsibility that others should have; that is, they directly address the nature of interdependence within the group. While the assumptions are held by individuals, their main object is the organizational system itself and their secondary object is the individuals' places within that system. Only systems that are consistent with the individual's own view of how power should be distributed are acceptable to the individual. Since cultural dimensions related to power and responsibility prescribe mutually inconsistent organizational systems of power distribution, differences among individuals on this dimension create a power paradox. My culture may lead me to assume that the leader should treat both you and me (and all other team members) as subordinates in a hierarchy of decision-making power, while your culture may lead you to assume that the leader should treat both you and me (and all other team members) as equals to himself or herself. In this situation, the leader cannot use either of the mechanisms for creating synergistic processes in multicultural teams. The leader cannot develop a common norm that we both agree upon, nor can the leader lead us in different ways without violating the power and responsibility norms of both our cultures. The leader is caught in a power paradox.

In addition to explaining the logic of the power paradox, we can also explain why it causes such deep conflict and even anguish within teams. Issues of relationships among people (individualism, collectivism, and hierarchy) are very closely related to our concept of self: "The enduring attachments and commitments to the self help define who we are" (Sandel, 1982, cited in Erez & Earley, 1993, 26). Assumptions about power and responsibility are related to our self-concept in many ways, each probably reinforcing the others. Erez and Earley (1993) identify three aspects of the self: the public or independent self, or one's perception of others' views of oneself; the private self, or one's perception of what makes one unique; and the collective or interdependent self (social identity), or one's perception of one's own role with respect to others in a group. The cultural dimension of relationships among people is strongly associated with both the public and collective self, and may also be associated with the private self. These views of the self are motivated through three mechanisms: self-enhancement, self-efficacy, and self-consistency (Erez & Earley, 1993). Because all these self-regulatory processes depend in large part on evaluation of self as seen by others, in comparison to others, and in response to others, one's assumptions about relationships among people will affect how they are executed.

Moreover, from the perspective of the leader, power and responsibility are two key elements of leadership. To the leader, differences in assumptions about relationships among people strike not only at sense of self as a team member, but also at sense of self as the person in the particular team role that determines the distribution of power and responsibility. Given the importance of issues concerning relationships among people to team members' and leaders' concept of self, it is hardly surprising that situations of mutual incompatibility are so difficult to manage.

Having identified the power paradox in multicultural teams and explained why it arises and causes seemingly insurmountable difficulties, it is important now to disentangle it. Although the most troublesome conflicts in multicultural teams surround this issue, do all multicultural teams with differences among members on the dimension of relationships among people experience the power paradox? If not, why not? Can we circumscribe the subset of situations in which it does arise and/or causes the greatest problems?

At this point our arguments turn from reviewing past research to explain a phenomenon we observed to suggesting broad propositions based on a reanalysis of previous studies. In this discussion we explore two lines of thought. The first is based on social and cognitive psychology and concerns the salience of the cultural difference as a function of the larger context. The second takes a closer look at the leadership task itself, subdividing it and demonstrating that the power paradox may be associated with only one element of leadership.

Salience of Power and Responsibility and the Larger Group Context

It is possible that in spite of the central place of relationships among people in the concept of self, the power paradox lies relatively dormant in some groups. When might this be the case? Two possibilities are addressed here: the relative importance of other dimensions of culture in an interdependent setting, and the nature of faultlines within the group.

A particular set of values or cognitive structures affects perception, interpretation, and behavior to the extent that it is salient to the situation (Erez & Earley, 1993; Lord & Foti, 1986). It has often been surmised that some dimensions of cultural values or orientations are more central to a particular culture than other dimensions are. If this were the case, then individuals in interdependent settings (i.e., those for which cultural values provide the most direct guidance) would notice and respond to the aspects of the situation that were most salient from their culture's perspective, perhaps independent of the role a particular dimension plays in their own self-concept. To explore the potential viability of this idea, we reexamined data on cultural dimensions in five countries, as presented by Maznevski, DiStefano, Gomez, Noorderhaven, and Wu (1997). In this study, eleven cultural dimensions are grouped into four basic orientations, with Relationships among People as one of the orientations, and individualism, collectivism, and hierarchy as dimensions of this orientation.[1] In this study, the more strongly a respondent felt about a particular cultural dimension (either strongly agreeing or strongly disagreeing), the more that respondent's score differed either positively or negatively from a standard mean of 0. By aggregating responses within cultural groups and comparing absolute scores of each dimension across cultural groups, we obtained a proxy of each dimension's salience to the culture.

This procedure resulted in interesting patterns among the five country cultures of the Maznevski and colleagues (1997) study: Canada, Mexico, The Netherlands, Taiwan, and the United States. When looking only at the Relationships among People orientation, the five countries split into two groups, with Canada and the United States scoring significantly higher on individualism and lower on hierarchy than Mexico, The Netherlands, and Taiwan. This would predict difficulties among team members or between a leader and team members who are from these two cultural groupings. However, when incorporating other dimensions and looking at absolute scores, respondents from each country, on average, felt most strongly about different cultural issues (i.e., had the strongest absolute scores for different orientations). This would suggest that the differences in the Relationships among People dimension might not always be salient to all members, and therefore might not inevitably cause the power paradox effects to emerge.

Proposition 1. *The power paradox is more likely to evoke negative consequences in a multicultural team to the extent that Relationships among People cultural dimensions are central to team members' cultures.*

In a similar line of thought, Lau and Murnighan (1998) proposed the concept of faultlines to describe group schisms based on characteristics of members. They define a faultline as a demographic attribute that divides a team into subgroups homogeneous on the attribute. For example, a gender faultline would divide a mixed gender team into separate subgroups of men and women. The subgroups formed by faultlines have the potential to engage in coalitional conflict that could be extremely difficult to resolve. The authors discuss situations that would lead to weaker and stronger faultlines, and propose a set of elements influencing whether or not the faultlines lead to destructive conflict. They suggest that stronger faultlines are formed to the extent that multiple demographic characteristics align with each other, such as age, occupation, and gender. Faultlines are proposed to be activated to the extent that they are salient. They will be most salient at the beginning of a group's interaction, when members do not know each other as individuals, and to the extent that the faultlines are related to the task. Finally, teams with subgroups that are the same size are expected to engage in more intense bipolar conflict, while in a team with unbalanced subgroups the larger subgroup is expected to dominate the smaller one(s).

Although Lau and Murnighan (1998) limited their discussion to easily identifiable demographic attributes, it is not difficult to extend their analysis to deeper-level cultural dimensions. In their terms, the power paradox can be rephrased as a faultline on issues of power and responsibility. We would expect this power faultline to be activated—that is, to cause dissention—when it is salient, and to be salient when the task concerns or is related to issues of power and responsibility. Since these issues are important in the undertaking of almost any team task, it is not surprising that the power paradox is raised so frequently. Lau and Murnighan's analysis is also helpful in suggesting when the effects of the power paradox might be strongest. A strong faultline along power dimensions would exist if other cultural dimensions or demographic dimensions were aligned with the Relationships among People dimension. For example, if all those members who believed power should be distributed hierarchically also preferred to control and change the environment and plan activities carefully and rationally, while all those who believed power should be distributed equally also preferred to approach the environment with a broad systems integration approach and to engage in activities without becoming involved in too much planning (Lane et al., 1997), then the faultline would be especially strong and we would expect strong conflict to emerge.

Proposition 2. *The power paradox is more likely to evoke negative consequences in a multicultural team to the extent that (1) other cultural and/or demographic differences are aligned with differences on individualism, collectivism, and hierarchy; (2) team members do not know each other well personally; (3) issues of Relationships among People are related to the task; and (4) differences on Relationships among People divide the team into equal-size subgroups.*

Decoupling the Leadership Task: Empowering versus Directing

Two elements of leadership, empowering and directing, are frequently identified as representing mutually exclusive management styles. An empowering leader delegates responsibility, and allows and encourages subordinates to participate in decision making and strategy formulation, take initiatives, and give advice to managers. The opposite of empowering is most often seen as directing. A directing leader continually supervises his or her subordinates and reviews their work. Managers are expected either to empower or to direct their employees (see Bass, 1990, for an extensive review). Since leaders tend to be either empowering or directive, the corollary assumption has been that employees want either to be empowered or directed, and not both. In Zander's (1997) study it is evident that this was not the case. There were no significant correlations between employees' preferences regarding directing versus empowering. Instead, empowering and directing were two separate dimensions displaying different patterns of employee expectations across the eighteen countries included in the study. Some individual employees held the assumption that empowering is the opposite of directing, but not a majority of them. Members of a team who see empowering and directing as completely separate dimensions (no correlation) may accept a norm of individual adaptation; that is, the leader leading with either empowering or directing behaviors toward different members as their preferences dictate. But members who see both behaviors as either desirable or undesirable (positive correlation) or who prefer one but not the other (negative correlation) may reject individual adaptation. Therefore, it may not be differences on strength of preference for empowering or directing alone that raises the power paradox, but instead differences on type of relationship assumed between empowering and directing.

Proposition 3a. *Negative consequences of the power paradox will not be associated with differences in team members' preferences for either empowering or directing by themselves.*

Proposition 3b. *The power paradox is more likely to evoke negative consequences in the team to the extent that team members differ from each other in relationship between preference for being empowered and preference for supervision.*

Employees' preferences regarding empowering were identified as closely related to cultural values. However, not all of the correlations were consistent with the assumptions and hypotheses of previous research. Intriguingly, the results of Zander's (1997) analysis of the relationship between followers' preference regarding empowering and cultural dimensions suggest another way to approach disentangling the power paradox. Previous research has generally assumed that propensity to accept empowerment is inversely related to acceptance of hierarchy. For example, Lane and colleagues (1997) suggested that the degree of hierarchical differentiation would be related to the forms of decision making used in an organization, and Hofstede argued that the degree of employment participation in decision making is highly dependent on how equally power is distributed. In direct contradiction to these hypotheses from previous research, in Zander's (1997) study the preferred degree of hierarchical and power differentiation in the culture was not strongly related to employees' preferences for empowering. Moreover, preference for empowering was not related to the other configurations of power and responsibility distribution—individualism or collectivism. Instead, preferences for empowering were closely associated with assumptions concerning how authority is assigned or obtained, whatever the degree of hierarchical differentiation or distribution of power and responsibility.

More specifically, Zander's (1997) study incorporated the results of two researchers' dimensions of culture emphasizing the nature of authority allocation. First, across eight European countries and the United States, Laurent (1983) measured whether authority is based on the position a person holds or related to the person who holds the position. Among the countries that overlapped with Zander's study, employees had lower preferences for empowering in the countries where authority was seen as personal than they did in the countries where it was seen as instrumental, or based on the position. Second, across fifty countries Trompenaars (1993) measured whether authority was obtained through achievement rather than ascriptive criteria such as seniority or family ties. Consistent with his hypothesis, Zander found that employees in the achievement-oriented countries had higher preference for empowering than those who worked in ascriptive-oriented countries. Zander concluded that employees' preferences for empowering were not related to the degree of hierarchical differentiation in the cultural environment where the employees worked, but how authority was allocated. While the correlations between directing and cultural dimensions were not as consistent, Zander's results suggest we cannot conclude that directing is most preferred in cultures where power should be distributed hierarchically, as previously assumed.

In global teams, then, manifestations of the power paradox may become most evident when people disagree not only about how power should be distributed, but also about how power is legitimately attained, with the latter not necessarily following from the former. Because preferences for the method of power allocation are more closely related to specific types of leadership behaviors, the effects of the "double difference" of power distribution and power allocation may be particularly evident in a team's response to its leader's behavioral style. Research suggests that the cultural values guiding authority allocation are equally as deep set and fundamental as those guiding hierarchical preferences (Laurent, 1986; Trompenaars, 1993), and there is no clear-cut response to the challenges arising from this dilemma. It could be possible, though, that values guiding processes, such as authority allocation, are less closely related to a concept of self and more susceptible to dynamic integration team practices than the more static hierarchical differentiation values.

Proposition 4. The power paradox is most likely to evoke negative consequences in the team to the extent that team members also differ in their assumptions of how power and authority are legitimately allocated.

DISCUSSION: RESOLVING THE POWER PARADOX

The power paradox is a critical stumbling block in our path to develop a strong understanding of effective global team leadership. The problems it creates in the teams it affects are not trivial. Consider these quotations from two members of the same multicultural team, a global resource company's strategic cost-cutting team charged with a mandate of reducing millions of dollars of costs from a critical value chain:

Member 1: I can't believe how upset he [the leader] gets when we just do our job! And half the members of our team just sit around and wait for his decisions, instead of taking action themselves. How is the company ever going to get anywhere with people like that?

Member 2: Our team's effectiveness is really hindered by some of the members who continue to go ahead on their own without knowing what is happening in other areas and without waiting to see how our leader wants us to coordinate the moves. Some people just have no respect for authority and the best way to make decisions.

This team's performance was disappointing, which surprised the leader and managers. According to members, though, the results were expected given that "half the members didn't know how to do their jobs within the team." We have seen many global team leaders manage their teams' processes very effectively, only to be completely perplexed by this challenge.

We cannot resolve the power paradox in this chapter, but our discussion of the phenomenon in the context of global team leadership is an attempt to illuminate some important ideas and point toward directions for examining the phenomenon. The following are three main points from our discussion.

First, leaders of multicultural teams must address two separate sets of power-related dynamics, one regarding the relationship between the leader and the team members, and a second regarding the relationships among team members. In some cultures it is assumed that the leader is responsible for decision making, and differences among members on this assumption directly affect the relationship between the leader and those team members whose beliefs are different from the leader's. Resolving this issue is qualitatively different from coaching team members to resolve perceived power imbalances among themselves. Future research on leading global teams should identify and examine both sets of dynamics.

A second point is the strategy of diminishing the negative consequences of the paradox by decreasing its salience. Assessing the viability of this strategy requires identifying the demographic and cultural characteristics of individual team members to understand potential faultlines, areas of similarity and difference, and patterns of prioritization, then observing the team over time to examine how the various differences are made more or less salient and how the salience of a particular dimension influences the team's outcomes. This perspective would also benefit from an understanding of which cultural dimensions are most amenable to change or integration with other perspectives, and which are most static and inherently unchangeable.

A final point is the possibility of decoupling aspects of power dynamics previously assumed to be inseparable. For example, counter to hypotheses generated by previous research, Zander's (1997) study showed that preference for hierarchy is not correlated with preference for empowerment, and that directing is not necessarily the opposite of empowering. Based on our discussion of these findings, we encourage researchers exploring the nature of power dynamics in multicultural teams to measure different aspects of preferences for power distribution and authority allocation rather than assume they are all correlated, allowing us to gain further insights into the relationships among the different dimensions.

Research on all these questions, addressing the propositions we raise as well as others, would provide great benefit to our understanding of global team effectiveness. Because of the tentative nature of our discussion and the current state of research on this topic, we also suggest that exploratory case-based research on the power dynamics of leading multicultural teams would be appropriate. A well-conducted grounded-theory study might cast more light on the nature of the power paradox, and also has the potential to identify other issues that are not suggested by previous literature.

IMPLICATIONS FOR GLOBAL LEADERS AND HUMAN RESOURCE PROFESSIONALS

Two lessons for global leaders and human resource professionals emerge as important from this preliminary look at the challenges of leading multicultural teams. The first can simply be summarized as "know the multicultural team process" and the second as "manage the multicultural team process." Research has already shown us that the difference between a successful, efficient, productive, and creative multicultural team and one that is quite the opposite is how the process is managed. In this chapter we discussed why the multicultural-team process is different from that of a homogeneous team and we pointed to some particularly difficult challenges facing the multicultural-team leader, especially what we call the power paradox.

To know the multicultural-team process involves knowing not only the different team members but also being cognizant of the process issues that could arise so as not to be surprised by them. The leader should know that if differences exist, things may get difficult. It is particularly important to be aware that the beginning of a project is fundamental for creating the basis for a positive process. This is even more true in multicultural teams than in monocultural ones, since there is a need for members to become acquainted with each other not only as team members, but also as individuals with different cultural backgrounds, preferences, and assumptions.

To manage the multicultural-team process involves a series of important steps. Informal time spent face to face, especially in the first stages of the project, has been found to be exceptionally valuable in understanding member's preferences and assumptions, facilitating both leader-to-member as well as member-to-member communication throughout the rest of the project. As demonstrated here, this initial face-to-face time may be especially critical if there are differences among members on preferences for power and responsibility relationships, since the leader can use this time to explore other similarities that can be leveraged and other ways to manage the power paradox. Throughout the team's time together, the leader should be creative about looking for ways around the power paradox, as we have discussed in this chapter. A key intervention for managing the multicultural-team process is for the leader to act as a "cultural interpreter." However, the more the other members also assume this role the fewer cultural misunderstandings will occur and the more the team can focus on its task at hand. A cultural interpreter identifies situations in which two or more members have different frames of reference, preferences, and assumptions guiding their contributions, but the differences go unrecognized and the assumed similarity leads to misunderstandings. Thus, a good interpreter intervenes explicitly by making the team members aware of underlying reasons leading to the communication problems before the team moves on in its discussions. In some cases intervention through conflict resolution from the team leader or perhaps a human resource professional may be very important to the team, especially if other differences align with the power-related differences. The team may need help sorting out how to be constructive instead of resorting to process-destructive behaviors.

Finally, to know and to manage the process in a multicultural team requires the same basic skills that are necessary for leaders to be effective in global companies in general. A company where cultural differences are seen as assets rather than liabilities, and where global has ceased to mean ethnocentric dominance and instead aims at multicultural synergy, will bring the best ideas to the market and maintain competitive advantages. These companies will be led by leaders who can effectively and creatively manage the paradoxes inherent in multicultural teams.

NOTE

1. Space precludes reporting on the study in any detail here; however, copies of the paper can be obtained from the first author of this chapter.

10

Synergy Effects in Multinational Work Groups: What We Know and What We Don't Know

Siegfried Stumpf and Ulrich Zeutschel

A very important characteristic of our modern world is that business activities are becoming more and more international and global (Adler, 1997c). Many enterprises maintain business relations all over the world: Manufacturing plants are placed in foreign countries, new markets abroad are opened up, and alliances are formed with companies from other countries, such as the mergers of Chrysler and Daimler-Benz or of Deutsche Bank and Bankers Trust. Also, due to work migration and closer national ties, such as between European countries, the staff even in corporate head offices is more and more often composed of people coming from different nations and ethnic backgrounds. The trends of internationalization and globalization influence organizational processes in many ways. Due to these changes, leaders in organizations will be confronted with new requirements and they will have to develop new competencies in order to be effective (cf. Brake, 1997). According to Adler and Bartholomew (1992), future global leaders must be transnationally competent by having the following skills: (1) understanding the worldwide business environment from a global perspective; (2) being able to learn about many foreign cultures' perspectives, tastes, trends, technologies, and approaches to conducting business; (3) being capable of adapting to living in many foreign cultures; (4) being able to work with people from many cultures simultaneously; (5) being capable of creating a culturally synergistic organizational environment; (6) being able to interact with foreign colleagues as equals; and (7) being capable of using cross-cultural interaction skills on a daily basis.

One of the new requirements for organizations and leaders is that as a consequence of internationalization and globalization, multinational work groups are becoming the rule rather than the exception in many enterprises. For global leaders, multinational teams are important in two respects: First, they are a challenge because making such teams effective or even synergistic is anything but an easy undertaking. Second, multinational teams are an excellent opportunity for leaders to acquire the skills regarded as characteristic for future global leaders.

This chapter aims at giving a survey of our knowledge concerning the effectiveness of multinational work groups. A research project performed at the University of Regensburg is described. Then, recommendations for managing multinational work groups are given, whereby implications for developing global leaders are discussed. Finally, perspectives for future research are outlined.

WHAT IS SO SPECIAL ABOUT MULTINATIONAL WORK GROUPS?

According to Sundstrom, De Meuse, and Futrell (1990) work groups constitute an essential feature of modern organizations and can be defined as "interdependent collections of individuals who share responsibility for specific outcomes for their organizations" (p. 120). What are the implications of increasingly multinational work groups for organizations? First of all, it simply means that work groups become more diverse or heterogeneous with regard to the group members' nationality. Diversity and heterogeneity, however, are central characteristics of all groups: It is virtually impossible to find a completely homogeneous group, because no team member is identical with his or her teammates. There are innumerable ways in which group members may differ from one another. McGrath, Berdahl, and Arrow (1995) name five clusters of group members' attributes with particular importance for heterogeneity issues in work groups: demographic attributes (i.e., nationality, ethnicity), expertise (i.e., task-related knowledge and abilities), values, habits, and status. According to the integrative multicultural approach proposed by McGrath and colleagues, demographic attributes such as nationality play a key role in the functioning of work groups: "When group members are diverse on certain demographic attributes, they can be regarded as having diverse cultural identities. Those cultural identities reflect differential sociohistorical experiences" (p. 30). Hence, following McGrath and colleagues it is likely that these identities are associated with actual differences in expertise, values, habits, and status; moreover, it is probable that group members recognize these cultural identities and generate certain expectations concerning the other members' expertise, values, habits, and status. If work groups in an organization are composed of group members from different nationalities and cultural backgrounds, this may have consequences for workgroup effectiveness.

Based on an exhaustive review of research on group productivity, Steiner (1972) proposed his well-known equation concerning group effectiveness: actual productivity = potential productivity − process losses. The potential productivity of a group depends on its resources and their relations to the task requirements. Process losses are caused by inadequate coordination or by deficits in motivation. If the diversity in a group is increased due to multinational composition of group members, this has advantages as well as disadvantages for the group. Adler (1997c, 131) proposed three general principles concerning the consequences of multinationality in groups:

1. The potential productivity of the group increases because there are more perspectives, experiences, and ideas in the group.

2. There is a risk of increased process losses, because diversity may bring about attitudinal problems such as dislike and mistrust, as well as perceptual problems due to stereotyping and communication difficulties. The resulting lack of cohesion may impede consensual decision making and concerted action.

3. Whether the increase in potential productivity is realized or whether the group suffers rising process losses is dependent on the way in which the diversity is managed. "Highly productive and less productive teams differ in how they manage their diversity, not, as is commonly believed, in the presence or absence of diversity" (Adler, 1997c, 138).

WHAT DO WE MEAN BY "SYNERGY"?

Consulting the *Fremdwörterduden* (Drosdowski, Grebe, Köster, Müller, & Scholze-Stubenrecht, 1982), the German reference book for foreign terms, we find two meanings of the word "synergy":

1. Energy, used for maintaining the group and for fulfilling the group's task.

2. Interaction of substances or factors which promote each other.

The former meaning originates from group psychology and is connected to the work of Cattell (1948), who postulated that synergy in the sense of the group's total energy can be divided into one component for maintaining the group ("maintainance-energy") and another component for fulfilling the group's tasks ("task-energy"). The latter meaning seems to be referred to in most applications of the term "synergy" and is directly related to its Greek origins: The prefix "syn" means "together with, jointly, simultaneously" (Drosdowski, Grebe, Köster, Müller, & Scholze-Stubenrecht, 1963); the term "energy" goes back to the Greek adjective "en-ergós" (acting upon) derived from the Greek noun "érgon" (work, activity) (Drosdowski et al., 1963). Thus, the core meaning of the term "synergy" may be described as "acting jointly," or "acting together."

The notion of synergy is often linked to attributes that more precisely describe the results of mutual enhancement between two or more elements (Scherm, 1998, S. 64):

- Originality, creativity, novelty—the interaction between several elements leads to original, new, and creative solutions.
- More than the sum of the parts—the interaction between the elements results in something that according to the Gestalt formula is more than the sum of its parts.
- Superiority—the interaction between several elements leads to solutions that are better than solutions effected by any one element alone or by any noninteractive combination of those elements.

In most definitions of "intercultural synergy" one or more of these attributes can be found. Thomas (1993) defines this concept as "the combination of cultural diverse elements like orientation patterns, values, norms, behaviors etc. in such a way, that a structure results which is of higher quality than the sum of elements. The total result is then of higher quality than each single element and also than the sum of elements" (p. 408). In this definition the principle of "more than the sum of the parts" is inherent. Adler (e.g., 1997c) proposes a concept of synergy that puts particular emphasis on the aspect of originality and the creation of new solutions compatible to all cultures involved. Maznevski (1994) refers to the attributes "more than the sum of the parts" and "superiority" when stating that intercultural synergy is given if "the integrated product is something greater than the sum of its parts. . . . By integrating the diverse strengths of the various people on a team, solutions and strategies can be developed that produce greater results than the simple addition of each contribution alone" (pp. 537–538).

In the social psychological tradition of small-group research the idea of synergy is linked to the work of Collins and Guetzkow (1964) and their concept of "assembly effect bonus," which became very influential in past group research and is still frequently used today when questions of group effectiveness are addressed. This concept has so much in common with the attributes of synergy that it seems appropriate that other authors such as Hall and Watson (1970) refer to it as "synergy-bonus." According to Collins and Guetzkow (1964, 58), the following definition can be given: A group has reached synergy if its level of productivity (1) exceeds the potential of the most capable group member, and (2) exceeds any combination of the efforts of the group members working separately.

In the appendix to this chapter the meaning of this definition is illustrated by an example demonstrating that we need a lot of information about individual and group patterns before we can decide whether a group has reached synergy. Moreover, the example indicates that condition 2 is very strong and not easily fulfilled.

WHAT DOES RESEARCH ON SYNERGY, DIVERSITY AND GROUP EFFECTIVENESS TELL US?

Let us first have a look at research results concerning synergy effects in groups in general. Referring to the definition of synergy given by Collins and Guetzkow (1964), the following can be stated:

1. A large number of research studies show that groups often do not fulfill even condition 1 and fall behind the performance of their most capable members (Steiner, 1972, 19ff).

2. Some studies demonstrate that groups can fulfill condition 1 and therefore perform better than their best member. The following percentages of group superiority over the best group member are reported: In a study of Hall and Watson (1970), depending on the experimental condition up to 75 percent of the groups performed better than the best group member; in Hall and Williams (1970) up to 50 percent of the groups; in Nemiroff and King (1975) up to 72 percent of the groups; in Nemiroff, Pasmore, and Ford (1976) up to 50 percent of the groups; in Watson, Michaelsen, and Sharp (1991) up to 74 percent of the groups; and in Michaelsen, Watson, and Black (1989) 97 percent of the groups.

3. Research results that clearly show that groups fulfill condition 2 are very rare. In Michaelsen and colleagues (1989) the authors claimed that their groups reached synergy, but reanalyses by Tindale and Larson (1992a, 1992b) indicated that this was not the case. Research results supporting the fulfillment of condition 2 originate from studies that demonstrated motivational enhancement due to group composition, which in turn led to performance improvements (Stroebe, Diehl, & Abakoumkin, 1996). Differences in the capabilities of the group members may stimulate a more capable group member to increase his or her efforts (cf. the research on social compensation by Williams &

Karau, 1991), or may cause a less capable group member to improve his or her performance (cf. research on the Köhler effect by Witte, 1989). On the other hand, equally distributed capabilities may lead to motivational gains due to social competition. All of these effects, however, are dependent on very special circumstances, such as the type and significance of the group task.

Consequently, the social psychological quest for synergy has been rather unsuccessful up to now. Looking at the research results one gets the impression that much is gained if groups succeed in minimizing their process losses, and that process gains like synergy are nothing but a wonderful dream. This conclusion concerning synergy in groups is akin to some views about the possibility of creating synergies in the economic realm. Despite the fact that many enterprises are "desperately seeking synergy" (Goold & Campbell, 1998) by performing mergers with other companies or by initiating in-plant synergy drives, the results are very often disappointing: "Many synergy efforts end up destroying value rather than creating it. . . . Rather than assuming that synergy exists, can be achieved, and will be beneficial, corporate executives need to take a more balanced, even skeptical view" (p. 132). In newspaper editorials as well, a skeptical view becomes more and more prevalent (e.g., Die Zeit, 1999).

The topic of synergy in groups is often discussed in social psychology with regard to studying group-composition effects. Important issues in this research field are the value of diversity in groups, as well as the consequences of heterogeneity and homogeneity in groups (Moreland, Levine, & Wingert, 1996). Knowledge concerning these questions could help us to create the "ideal group," a matter of tremendous practical interest. The state of the art in research on group composition effects may be summarized as follows:

1. Empirical findings concerning the relationship between diversity and group effectiveness are inconsistent. Some investigations detected a positive relation, while others found a negative relation or no relation at all (cf. the overview articles from Guzzo & Dickson, 1996; Moreland et al., 1996; Maznevski, 1994).

2. The reliability with which available models and theories can explain the effects of diversity is far too low, considering the importance of the topic. Guzzo and Dickson (1996) state, "The extent to which team effectiveness is affected by the heterogenity among members is a complicated matter" (p. 311) and "the processes (cognitive, social) through which heterogeneous group compositions have their effect on team performance are far from fully specified" (p. 312).

3. It can be assumed that heterogeneity has multiple simultaneous effects on group effectiveness. Some of these effects (e.g., a broader variety of solutions effected by heterogeneity) may be goal promoting, while

others such as reduced group cohesion may work against it. The overall effect of heterogeneity in a group is difficult to predict from present research results.

4. The inconsistency of research results could be due to the following intervening variables (cf. Moreland et al., 1996, 17):

   • The type of heterogeneity. Heterogeneity is not a uniform concept, but may exist in different qualities and quantities.

   • The type of task. How is the task of the group actually constituted? Different tasks may lead to different findings concerning the effects of heterogeneity. Unfortunately, at present "for most types of tasks, there is simply too little evidence to draw any conclusions about the effects of diversity on team performance" (Jackson, 1996, 67).

   • The extent of group integration. Heterogeneity in a group may lead to disintegration of the group or, in extreme cases, even to its falling apart. Despite all heterogeneity, the group needs to function as an integrated unit, which is promoted by so-called integration mechanisms (cf. Maznewski, 1994). Such integration mechanisms could be an adequate role structure, an integrating group leader (cf. Maier, 1967), or, particularly, the ability of the group members to communicate with each other (Maznewski, 1994). It can be assumed that in heterogeneous groups such as multinational teams this integration does not come about instantly or automatically, but will require substantial time and support (cf. the study of Watson, Kumar, & Michaelsen, 1993).

These statements seem to be valid for both group-composition research in general and research on multinationally composed groups in particular. At present we know that it is at least very difficult to attain synergy in groups, and that perhaps synergy is nothing but a chimera. Our knowledge concerning the effectiveness of both heterogeneous work groups in general and multinational groups in particular is still rather fragmentary. Clearly, more empirical research and theoretical integration are needed in order to predict effects of heterogeneity on group effectiveness with some reliability, to compose groups for optimal performance, and to facilitate their effectiveness. In the last section we will give some recommendations on future research for closing these gaps in our knowledge.

THE REGENSBURG RESEACH PROJECT ON INTERCULTURAL SYNERGY IN BINATIONAL WORK GROUPS

The Synergy Project, conducted from April 1995 to April 1998 with a grant from the Volkswagen Foundation, was aimed at investigating the conditions, modes, and means of facilitating effective cooperation of professionals from different cultural backgrounds in work groups and project teams. Its particular focus, intercultural synergy effects, was addressed by these principal research questions: Which culture-specific interaction patterns and problem-solving styles can be identified with respect to national subgroups? Which potentials for mutual supplementation and enhancement are inherent in these patterns and styles? How are these potentials actualized in bicultural cooperation? Which process features are associated with successful bicultural cooperation? What recommendations can be given for fostering successful cooperation in multicultural teams?

In the exploratory phase, a total of nineteen extensive interviews were conducted with senior staff members in international personnel and team development and with experienced leaders and coordinators of international teams and task forces in large corporations and nongovernmental organizations, as well as with independent trainers and consultants. Observations about corporate settings and organizational boundary conditions of international teams were gathered in a small number of field studies in multinational teams in the area of product development.

The main study consisted of systematic observation and comprehensive data collection in several series of mono- and binational problem-solving groups formed specifically for the purpose of this investigation. Teams of three to four persons worked on a computer-assisted business simulation that required them to gather information from various departments of a small garment-manufacturing company, and to take the necessary business decisions as a team. Target criteria for task performance were the company's assets, personnel satisfaction, and employment capacity at the conclusion of the simulated time period of twelve to fifteen months.

The total study sample consisted of twenty-seven teams of German, U.S., and Indonesian university students from a variety of disciplines. The results reported here pertain to ten groups comprising twenty Germans and eighteen Americans from the universities of Hamburg and Regensburg. These groups were studied in a two-phase design: In two "training" sessions of three hours each participants familiarized themselves with the simulation in monocultural teams. In the second phase they were assigned to binational "expert" teams and worked on the same simulation in two additional sessions.

All sessions were completely videorecorded for further analysis and were concluded with a written survey on work satisfaction and mutual perception of group participants, followed by a group discussion about the cooperation process, which was structured by evaluation questions from an external moderator. Individual and group evaluations plus unstructured observations by the experimenter and the moderator were supplemented with process data from the simulation itself, such as information retrieval and decision input, business parameters, and duration of simulated months. Videographs from selected group sessions were analyzed in detail with the help of a coding system for problem-solving interactions developed specifically for this purpose (Simon, 1997). Individual contributions to the group discussion were categorized according to the problem-solving phase they addressed (goal clarification, process clarification, problem analysis, production phase, process control) and to their respective function (e.g., analyzing the situation, proposing an idea or action, commenting, specifying a proposal, asking a factual question, finalizing a decision, coordinating the discussion). Category frequencies were analyzed in their distribution across the five problem-solving phases for each team and session, and in the form of communication profiles of individual team members within certain problem-solving phases. Also, group indices were computed from category frequencies as operationalizations of interaction characteristics, such as the degree of controversy or the ratio of proactive contributions. Interaction features associated with effective bicultural cooperation were identified through an extreme group comparison of the two most-successful versus the two least-successful German/U.S. teams in terms of task performance and individual work satisfaction.

Findings and Discussion: Culture-Specific Interaction Patterns

Differences in problem-solving and interaction styles became apparent in contrasting the monocultural training groups of German and U.S. participants. They were categorized into four areas: (1) task completion, (2) group climate and relations, (3) group structure, and (4) group process. Within each area general orientations could be identified as summaries of individual contrasts between the national groups.

Task Completion

Specific contrasts in this domain could be summarized by insight orientation versus action orientation. German teams were clearly guided by the former, trying to assess and control as many task-related factors as possible and to identify their underlying cause–effect relationships in order to construct an abstract representation of the problem in the form of a model or paradigm. U.S. teams limited the number of problem factors they dealt with, formulating middle-range theories about the problem and testing their predictions by a trial-and-error strategy. With regard to evaluation of task completion, Germans focused primarily on deficits and shortcomings, while U.S. teams registered and "celebrated" accomplishments more readily.

The latter contrast is also indicative of the German teams' primary emphasis on task completion, often at the expense of group climate and harmonious relations among team members, while U.S. teams strove to achieve a deliberate balance between the two areas, often with the help of an internal facilitator.

Group Climate and Relations

The underlying dimension ranged from polarization to harmonization. In German groups, conflicts were approached directly, with a confrontative and even an extrapunitive attitude. The conflict style of U.S. teams fell somewhere in the middle between polarization and harmonization. They showed a readiness for compromise, while Germans clearly enjoyed arguing out differences in opinion.

Group Structure

Differences observed in this area could be summarized by demarcation on one hand and open access on the other; however, the specific contrasts observed are not clear cut across this dimension for the national groups represented. Both German and U.S. teams emphasized equal rights of all team members (i.e., horizontal structure), and showed a clear division of tasks. However, German team members favored individual decisions at the operative level within their respective area of responsibility (a demarcation strategy in line with clear division of tasks), while U.S. teams more often discussed operative decisions among their members. This appeared to be motivated by a desire to share information rather than responsibility and was thus also compatible with a division of tasks.

Group Process

As opposed to a polychronic style (Hall, 1983), both German and U.S. teams employed monochronic strategies by planning and implementing operations consecutively. German teams in general were striving for long-term regulation of group processes, with a strong emphasis on continuity and implementation of fixed procedures, while U.S. teams evaluated group processes more regularly and adjusted procedures and task roles accordingly.

Effective Process Regulation in Bicultural Cooperation

For the German and U.S. problem-solving teams, detailed inter-action analyses were carried out for the two most successful teams, numbers 12 and 18, and the two least successful teams, numbers 11 and 17 (in terms of performance in the business-simulation task and the team members' average ratings of work satisfaction), from coded videographs of the first 60 minutes of their initial work session and of the entire 120 minutes of their second session. Differences between successful and unsuccessful teams were found in three areas: (1) process clarification and control, (2) degree of controversy, and (3) interaction capacity and initiative. They are summarized in Table 10.1.

Process Clarification and Control

The proportion of process-related contributions was larger in the first session for both successful teams (28% and 17%) than for unsuccessful teams (17% and 16%). Particularly in the second session, successful teams followed through on a larger proportion of proposals about group procedure by reaching a positive or negative decision rather than letting the proposal go without discussion (63% and 65%, as compared to only 58% and 27% for the unsuccessful groups). Also, there was a higher increase in the ratio of implemented proposals about group procedure between the first and the second session in the successful teams (32% and 21%) than in the unsuccessful teams (15% and 9%). Successful teams thus seemed to benefit from more extensive process clarification in the beginning by more efficient and goal-directed work routines in the second session. As Frese and Zapf (1994) point out, planning of procedures constitutes a vital feature of effective problem solving.

Degree of Controversy

The percentage of proposals that are followed by counterproposals serves as an indication of controversial discussion, which was consistently more pronounced in the successful teams (9% and 7%) than in the unsuccessful groups (6% and 3%) in the first session. A similar difference was found in the second session (19% and 8% versus 8% and 2%). According to a study by Hoffman, Harburg, and Maier (1962), questioning of proposals fosters creative problem solutions. The higher degree of controversy, in combination with development of more efficient work routines, may thus have accounted for superior task performance in the successful teams.

Table 10.1

Differences in Group Processes between Unsuccessful and Successful Teams

Index	Least successful teams		Most successful teams	
	Team 11	Team 17	Team 12	Team 18
Process-related interactions, first session	17%	16%	17%	28%
Reaching decisions on proposals about group procedure, second session	58%	27%	63%	65%
Increase in implemented proposals between first and second session	15%	9%	32%	21%
Proposals followed by counter-proposals, first session	6%	3%	9%	7%
Proposals followed by counter-proposals, second session	8%	2%	19%	8%
Increase in frequency of contributions between first and second session	1.03	0.66	1.28	1.23
Pro-active contributions, second session	9%	9%	16%	17%

Note: The figures in the first six rows represent percentages for the occurrence of specific interactive behaviors. The figures in the last row result from dividing the number of contributions in the second session by the number of contributions in the first session.

Interaction Capacity and Initiative

The frequency of contributions increased in the second session in the successful teams by a factor of 1.28 and 1.23, respectively, while it remained constant (1.03) or even decreased (0.66) in the unsuccessful groups. At the same time, the proportion of proactive contributions (i.e., proposals, counterproposals, and specifications of more general proposals), was generally higher in the successful teams, particularly in the second session (16% and 17%), than in the unsuccessful teams (9%).

CONCLUSIONS

Synergetic Potential of Adaptive Differences

The contrasting styles of problem solving and group interaction identified among the monocultural "training" groups represent differing positions on underlying preadaptive polarities (Demorgon & Molz, 1996), such as deduction/induction, divergence/convergence, commitment/flexibility, and planned/spontaneous action. In bicultural encounters, the differing positions present a definite challenge as a lack of shared orientation, but may be reconciled by "adaptive oscillation" between the contrasting styles or behavioral patterns resulting in a broader action repertoire. As bicultural cooperation continues and a team-specific "third culture" evolves (Casmir, 1999), the different styles may be integrated or even transcended into an innovative behavioral pattern.

Observations in the German and U.S. training groups as well as in the bicultural expert teams suggest the following areas of potentially synergetic cooperation:

1. The analytic efforts toward understanding of complex causal relationships on the part of German participants may effectively combine with the U.S. action orientation in testing and implementing problem-solving steps.

2. The greater readiness of U.S. team members to accept proposals and to quickly negotiate compromises may be a productive complement to the German inclination for critical analysis and detailed argumentation.

3. The striving for safe and optimal decisions with long-term validity on the German side may be supplemented toward greater efficiency by the U.S. strategy of improvisation and systematic short-term evaluation.

4. The U.S. cultural standards of considerate, constructive criticism and conscious acknowledgment of productive contributions and attained "milestones" may enter a beneficial alliance with the German propensity for frank and direct emphasis on critical shortcomings—although the merging of these styles will not be easily accomplished due to clearly divergent value perspectives.

Synergy Is Not for Free

The actualization of synergetic potential inherent in culture-specific differences does not depend so much on the good will of members of multinational teams, but on careful attention to group processes. In the absence of a common frame of reference and shared work routines and interaction habits, it becomes necessary to take the time and energy for acknowledging and assessing differences between cultural subgroups in the team, and to develop and continuously evaluate new work procedures and interaction patterns. The interaction characteristics of successful bicultural teams in the present study demonstrate the importance of process clarification and goal-oriented planning, as well as of constructive controversy in group discussion. Attention to group process rather than to task content is a primary function of team facilitation, either by a member of the team or by an external moderator. In this respect, we already found marked differences between German teams and U.S. teams in the training phase of our study: Influential members of German teams tended to concentrate on task leadership (i.e., content-related contributions), while their counterparts of U.S. teams tended to act as team facilitators, emphasizing process-related activities, such as keeping track of the time, mediating differences in opinion, or fostering balanced participation by all team members. Not surprisingly, the facilitator's role in the binational teams was typically taken by a U.S. team member, and was particularly strong in the more successful teams.

Recommendations for the Management of Multinational Work Groups

Research studies like the one described in this chapter show that multinational teams offer many chances and potentials, but an effective combination of all that diversity is not easily achieved. The benefits of heterogeneity in groups will not be realized unless corporate executives, group leaders, and team members contribute to the success of team cooperation. In any case, synergy is not for free! The following recommendations aim at supporting the management of multinational work groups in particular, whereby some implications for developing global leaders are outlined. In addition, recommendations for work groups in general should be considered (cf. Hackman, 1998).

Adequate Leadership Development

The success of diverse work groups will depend on skills and support of both the higher management in the organization and especially the team leaders (cf. Jackson, 1996). According to Maier (1967) a group leader is crucial for the quality of organization and integration in the group and therefore serves as the group's central nervous system. In the case of a multinational team, transnationally competent leaders are needed. In general, these leaders should have the skills enumerated in the first section of this chapter. Especially with regard to groups, they have to be sensitive and adaptive to cultural diversity and be able to integrate and effectively communicate contrasting and diverse information (cf. Ayman, Kreiker, & Masztal, 1994); they should also be capable of applying conflict-resolution techniques compatible with the different cultural styles represented in the group and should be able to foster the group's development. Consequently, global-team leaders must possess extensive intercultural knowledge and competences. Our findings with regard to process reflection suggest that they should define themselves more as process monitors and facilitators or mediators, rather than as task (content) specialists. The following instruments and activities support the development of transnationally competent team leaders:

Systems for Identifying Global Leaders

The first step in developing global leaders is to identify global leadership potentials. This identification should be performed in a systematic way and supported by reliable and valid instruments. For example, questionnaire tools for measuring transnational competencies in general and abilities to learn from experiences in particular can be used (Spreitzer, McCall, & Mahoney, 1997). Moreover, intercultural assessment centers are a promising method for identifying required potentials, because this method allows candidates to be confronted with critical intercultural situations and for their behaviors to be systematically observed and assessed (Kühlmann & Stahl, 1996).

On-the-Job Development

With regard to transnational leadership competencies, it can be assumed that experience is the best teacher (cf. McCall, Lombardo, & Morrison, 1988; Yeung & Ready, 1995). Consequently, the most important way to become a global-team leader is to perform leadership activities in multinational teams. Leading a multinational team cannot be learned in the classroom. Future global leaders have to face the challenge of leading a multinational team and they have to learn by their experiences. This learning-by-doing approach should be accompanied by supporting activities like consultation and training.

Consultation

Leaders from time to time need help when being confronted with new and unfamiliar problems. Coaches from inside or outside the organization could help them to find solutions for these problems and to explore and test new ways of behavior. Moreover, a trustful and stable relationship with a mentor can be supporting.

Off-the-Job Training

In order to prepare leaders for the specific problems in multinational work groups and to treat particular leadership problems in such groups, off-the job training is of importance (for a review on intercultural training, see Black & Mendenhall, 1990). A variety of training techniques could be used, which can be categorized along the dimensions "culture general versus culture specific" and "didactic/expository versus experiential/discovery" (Gudykunst, Guzley, & Hammer, 1996). Training should be preceded by an analysis of the participants' training needs and succeeded by an evaluation of the training effect.

Adequate Team Composition

An important precondition for staffing an effective work group is a detailed analysis of the task requirements. If group cooperation is a means for completing a certain task, then the major consideration for group composition should not be a preconceived blend of certain nations or cultures, but a careful match between members' task-related knowledge and skills on the one hand and task requirements on the other hand.

Promotion of Cultural Sensitivity

Preparatory training should be provided to sensitize all future team members to general aspects of intercultural cooperation (e.g., by a culture-assimilator approach; see Albert, 1983), and to supply them with the most essential background information on the different cultures represented in the team. Such training could build the foundation for further insights about which cultural standards are typical for one's own culture and for the other cultural groups involved, what the commonalities and differences between the different cultures are, and what all this means for intercultural encounters.

Team-Building Procedures

A team has to become a well-integrated and effectively functioning social system. In order to reach that goal, the initial phase of team building is very important, particularly in a multinational team with very little shared orientations and procedures. Getting off to a good start facilitates productive group dynamics in the long run. Therefore, opportunities should be created for team members to become acquainted with each other, allowing sufficient time to explore each other's personal and cultural backgrounds, specific expertise, experiences, and interests. In this way, similarities and differences between the team members can be discovered—similarities to strengthen group cohesion and differences as potential for mutual enhancement. Furthermore, kick-off meetings should explicitly aim at group integration by clarifying common goals, discussing and working out rules and norms for cooperating, and addressing questions such as which working language maximizes participation for all members, or which roles should be instituted in the group. These team-building procedures should be carried out in a systematic way and external support by a competent facilitator should be available.

Feedback and Reflexivity

Feedback on group processes and group performance is helpful for effective cooperation (cf. Watson et al., 1993). Data concerning group processes can be gathered, analyzed, and then presented to the group. Feedback concerning group performance should be given by the group's superior. In order to guide multicultural teams through their difficult formative phase, even minor successes should be consciously noted and celebrated. In a systematic project-management approach, milestones should therefore not be set too far apart. The group should from time to time reflect on its goals, strategies, and processes in order to adapt them to internal or external requirements if necessary (cf. West, 1996). Moreover, a team should reflect on its own "third" culture, and the group members' implicit intercultural knowledge should be made visible and available for all group members (Moosmüller, 1997b). In order to foster process reflection and adaptation even under conditions of permanent time pressure, team leaders should actively initiate and moderate meetings set aside for process evaluation. External coaching, consulting, or facilitation may be helpful in the beginning to establish methods and feedback formats that are compatible with the different cultural styles represented on the team.

RECOMMENDATIONS FOR FURTHER RESEARCH
ON MULTINATIONAL TEAMS

As has been shown, at present our knowledge concerning the functioning of multinational teams is still too fragmentary. In order to deepen our understanding the following proposals seem useful.

For development of models with sufficient explanatory power, specific requirements of the group's task and the specific cultural commonalities and differences of the group members should be analyzed in more detail and described more precisely in empirical investigations. These factors constitute important input variables for group effectiveness, and without further knowledge on how these factors are realized, an appropriate and deep understanding of the results will not be possible. Also in this regard more precise and testable theories concerning the relationship between task characteristics, diversity factors, and effectiveness would be useful: Catch-all research questions such as "Are heterogeneous groups better than homogeneous groups?" will necessarily produce inconsistent results. More-specific hypotheses need to be developed about which kinds of heterogeneity promote group effectiveness with regard to type of task; a similar strategy was proposed by Driskell, Hogan, and Salas (1987) for studying the effects of personality traits on group performance.

Group effectiveness is not simply a relation between input and output factors, but strongly depends on the group's internal processes (Hackman & Morris, 1975). Therefore, group processes constitute a very important field of research. With regard to heterogeneous teams, it may be assumed that group performance is particularly dependent on the way in which the heterogeneity is managed and integrated (Adler, 1997c; Maznevski, 1994). More research focusing on these managing and integration practices is needed: "The process of integration itself, although so vital to the performance of diverse management teams, has not yet been the focus of group research. To enable management teams to use their diversity productively, it is crucial that integration now be examined closely" (Maznevski, 1994, 538).

Groups in general and diverse groups in particular may need plenty of time to arrive at highly effective group processes. Most small-group research is conducted in the laboratory with groups existing only for very short periods. It would be fruitful to devise more longitudinal studies on actual groups existing for longer time periods and having more time for managing and integrating their heterogeneity effectively.

The effects of detailed feedback on group processes and performance should be investigated more extensively. Also, more studies should be undertaken on reflection processes in groups (cf. West, 1996) and on the ways these processes should be instituted in heterogeneous groups in order to be effective. Feedback and reflection processes might well be some of the most important means to improve the effectiveness of multinational work groups.

APPENDIX

Let us demonstrate what the synergy definition of Collins and Guetzkow (1964) means by giving an example. Imagine that we have a group G with three individuals i_1, i_2, and i_3. The group has to master a divisible task consisting of ten subtasks a_1 to a_{10} that are not interdependent. In order to assess the individual capabilities of the group members, each group member first tries to solve the complete task by working separately. In a consecutive session the group members work together as a team on the entire task. For each subtask correct and incorrect solutions exist. Let us assume the following results: i_1 has solved three subtasks (30%), i_2 four subtasks (40%), i_3 two subtasks (20%), and by working as a team the group has solved seven subtasks (70%). In comparison with individual performances, group performance is much higher. However, can we speak of synergy in this case? In order to answer this question we have to check conditions 1 and 2 in the definition of Collins and Guetzkow. Condition 1 is fulfilled because the group performs better than the best individual i_2. In order to check condition 2, we need more information concerning the concrete pattern of group and individual solutions. Let us assume that these solution patterns look as presented in Table 10.2.

Table 10.2
Solution Pattern for the Group and for Individual Group Members

	a_1	a_2	a_3	a_4	a_5	a_6	a_7	a_8	a_9	a_{10}	Sum
G	1	1	1	0	1	1	0	1	1	0	7
i_1	1	1	1	0	0	0	0	0	0	0	3
i_2	0	0	0	1	1	1	1	0	0	0	4
i_3	0	0	0	0	0	0	0	1	1	0	2

Note: 0 = task not solved; 1 = task solved.

Table 10.3
Synthetic Solution Vector

	a_1	a_2	a_3	a_4	a_5	a_6	a_7	a_8	a_9	a_{10}	sum
SYNT	1	1	1	1	1	1	1	1	1	0	9

Note: 0 = task not solved; 1 = task solved.

Condition 2 stipulates that group performance is superior to any combination of individual performances. That is the case if group performance is higher than the best combination of individual performances. This best combination results if we take for each subtask the best individual performance. In this way we get a so-called synthetic solution vector SYNT which looks as presented in Table 10.3.

In a column of SYNT there is the number 1 (correct solution) if and only if at least one group member solved the subtask by working alone. So we see that the group G performs worse than the best combination of individual performances (sum G = 7 < sum SYNT = 9). Therefore despite the superiority of group performance over the best individual performance, condition 2 is not fulfilled and thus, despite the good performance of the group, there is no synergy in this case. If we compare the vectors G and SYNT, we see that on two subtasks, a_4 and a_7, the group chooses the wrong solution despite the fact that there is one group member who is capable of solving the task. In both subtasks the group suffers a process loss because its potential productivity given the individual resources of its members is smaller than its actual productivity. The example also shows that it is a necessary but not sufficient condition for synergy that the group attains a process gain by solving at least one subtask that none of its members is capable of solving individually.

Part III

EXTENDING FUNCTIONAL PRACTICES IN GLOBAL LEADERSHIP DEVELOPMENT

11

Using Assessment Centers as Tools for Global Leadership Development: An Exploratory Study

Günter K. Stahl

In order to succeed in today's highly competitive and rapidly changing global business world, executives must possess additional capabilities to those required in a less complex domestic environment.
They need global leadership competencies (Adler & Bartholomew,
1992; Brake, 1997; Dalton, 1998; Gregersen, Morrison, & Black,
1998; Kets de Vries & Mead, 1992; Mendenhall, 1999; Stroh &
Caligiuri, 1998; Tichy, Brimm, Charan, & Takeuchi, 1992; Tung &
Miller, 1990; Yeung & Ready, 1995). Most important, as multinational corporations are facing the competing—but in fact complementary—demands of centralization versus decentralization, of
worldwide integration, and, at the same time, adaptation to local
cultural environments, executives must have the ability to function in both a global and a local culture; they must balance the
often conflicting demands between corporate headquarters and local stakeholders; they must understand the worldwide business
environment from a global perspective and reconcile the dilemmas
that cultural variety imposes upon management (Black, Gregersen,
Mendenhall, & Stroh, 1999; Doz & Prahalad, 1986; Evans, Lank, &
Farquhar, 1990; Rahim, 1983; Ronen, 1986; Trompenaars, 1994).

People are not born global leaders, they must be developed. However, the development of global leadership capabilities is not an easy task. Findings of empirical studies indicate that multinational corporations often fail to develop the knowledge and skills necessary for managers to succeed in a global business world (Gregersen et al., 1998; Tung, 1981; Tung & Miller, 1990). Based on the results of a recent survey of U.S. *Fortune* 500 firms, Gregersen and colleagues (1998) found that most companies lack the quantity and quality of global leaders they need: 85 percent do not think they have an adequate number of globally competent executives, and 67 percent believe that their existing leaders need additional knowledge and skills before they meet needed capabilities. In spite of this, a stunning 92 percent of the firms report that they do not have comprehensive systems for developing global executives. Several studies have also found that European and Japanese companies frequently fail to bridge the gap between existing management resources and those necessary for meeting the challenges of a global business world (e.g., Edström & Lorange, 1984; Forster, 1997; Kopp, 1994; Oddou, Gregersen, Black, & Derr, 2000; Stahl, 1998b).

Global leadership skills are most effectively developed through international job assignments (Black, Gregersen et al., 1999; Evans et al., 1990; Oddou, Mendenhall, & Bonner Ritchie, in press; Tung & Miller, 1990). However, it is evident that not everyone has the ability to become a global leader, and international development assignments are costly. Multinational corporations need to carefully assess whether they have enough young managers with the required leadership talent, and select those for development who have the potential to become global leaders. The capacity of managers for an international assignment has to be appraised in order to plan their careers and customize training programs. Moreover, global leadership development must be viewed as an ongoing process rather than a one-time event, which means that the learning progress of young managers must be monitored throughout the early stages of their careers. Thus, the assessment of global leadership potential is a critical part of the development process for both the individual and the company (Gregersen et al., 1998; Trompenaars, 1994; Van Houten, 1990).

This chapter will argue for the use of assessment centers as an effective tool for the evaluation and development of global leadership skills. The findings of a series of studies designed to examine how behavioral-assessment techniques can be utilized to help appraise and develop global leadership competencies will be presented. First, the results of a research project aimed at identifying core competencies that are critical to the success of managers in international assignments will be discussed. Second, how behavioral-assessment techniques can be designed to measure and develop such competencies will be described. Third, evidence from an exploratory study indicating that assessment centers can effectively assist HR professionals in the identification, career planning, and development of global leaders will be presented.

PROJECT 1:
IDENTIFICATION OF INTERCULTURAL SKILLS AS AN ELEMENT OF GLOBAL LEADERSHIP COMPETENCE

Obviously, an international executive must possess all the characteristics of a good local manager. However, he or she needs additional capabilities to reconcile the dilemmas that cultural variety imposes upon management (Gregersen et al., 1998; Spreitzer, McCall, & Mahoney, 1997; Trompenaars, 1994). In particular, as more and more executives are temporarily posted on international assignments, abilities that facilitate cross-cultural adjustment and effectiveness become critical. While international assignment responsibilities are not the same as the requirements of global leadership, the characteristics that are crucial to a manager's success in a foreign culture are an important—if not the most important—part of global leadership competencies (Mendenhall, 1999, 2000). Without the ability to adjust to a foreign environment and to establish trusting relationships with local employees, customers, and other host-country stakeholders, managers will not be able to achieve the various goals associated with their international assignments (see, e.g., Mendenhall & Oddou, 1985; Rahim, 1983; Ronen, 1986; Tung, 1987). This is particularly true for positions requiring extensive contact with the local community, such as chief executive officers or marketing managers of foreign operations (Tung, 1981).

Which factors, then, are critical for a manager's effectiveness abroad? Scholars in the field of expatriate acculturation and productivity have identified a general set of "intercultural competencies" that include interpersonal and communication skills, adaptability, and certain perceptual predispositions (see Dinges & Baldwin, 1996; Kealey, 1996; Kealey & Ruben, 1983; Mendenhall, 2000; Mendenhall & Oddou, 1985; Ones & Viswesvaran, 1997; Ronen, 1989; Ward, 1996 for reviews). Kealey and Ruben (1983), after reviewing the literature on intercultural effectiveness, summarized the "ideal" expatriate as being

an individual who is truly *open* to and *interested* in other people and their ideas, *capable of building relationships of trust* among people. He or she is *sensitive to the feelings and thoughts of another*, expresses *respect* and positive regard for others, and is *nonjudgmental*. Finally, he or she tends to be *self-confident*, is able to take *initiative*, is *calm* in situations of frustration or ambiguity, and is *not rigid*. The individual also is a *technically or professionally competent* person. (pp. 165–166)

Most of these factors have been corroborated by recent empirical research investigating the adjustment and effectiveness of business executives on international assignments (e.g., Black, 1990; Clarke & Hammer, 1995; Dunbar, 1992).

These studies have significantly increased our understanding of the factors that determine a manager's success in a foreign culture. However, since most of the research focused on U.S. managers working in specific regions or countries of assignment, it is not clear if findings from these studies are generalizable across different countries of origin and different countries of assignment. In addition, authors have addressed concerns about much of the extant research on the personality determinants of expatriate success (Deller, 1997; Dinges & Baldwin, 1996; Ones & Viswesvaran, 1997). In particular, Dinges and Baldwin (1996) criticize the focus on "the elusive general 'traits' presumed to be the critical underlying predispositions for intercultural competence" (p. 120), and strongly recommend for future studies more "behaviorally oriented measures based on the task environment in which intercultural competence is to be assessed" (p. 121).

In an initial effort toward closing this gap, Kühlmann and Stahl (1996, 1998) empirically investigated the behavioral tendencies, attitudes, and skills that are critical to the success of managers in international assignments in a sample of German expatriates. Over the course of three years, in-depth interviews were conducted with 246 German managers who were either on assignment abroad or were recently repatriated into the home organization. As a method of data collection, a modified form of the "critical incident technique" (Flanagan, 1954) was employed, which aimed at identifying critical encounters between expatriate managers and host nationals (local employees, customers, suppliers, etc.). After the interviews were fully transcribed, expatriates' behavior was analyzed as to positive and negative outcomes; from the analysis of effective and ineffective expatriate behavior in various cross-cultural business situations, successful and less successful problem-solving strategies were derived, as well as underlying attitudes and skills.

Based on the results of this analysis, seven factors were identified that appear to be critical to success in international work assignments. The findings indicate that managers posted abroad must possess a more than average amount of the following "intercultural competencies":

- Tolerance for ambiguity—the ability to function effectively in a foreign environment where the expatriate experiences ambiguity, complexity, and uncertainty.
- Behavioral flexibility—the capacity to vary one's behavior according to the immediate requirements of the situation and the demands of the foreign culture.
- Goal orientation—the ability and desire to achieve one's task goals despite barriers, opposition, or discouragement.
- Sociability and interest in other people—a willingness to establish and maintain meaningful social relationships, combined with a genuine interest in other people.
- Empathy—the capacity to accurately sense other peoples' thoughts, feelings, and motives, and to respond to them appropriately.
- Nonjudgmentalness—the willingness to critically reexamine one's own values and beliefs, and to avoid judging other people against one's own norms.
- Meta-communication skills—the capacity to clarify culturally different perceptions and to sensibly "guide" the intercultural communication process.

Examples of behavioral indicators of these constructs are presented in Table 11.1. Five of the seven core competencies in this profile correspond to key factors in the cross-cultural adjustment process that Mendenhall and Oddou (1985) have identified in their review on expatriate acculturation and effectiveness. Instead of meta-communication skills, Mendenhall and Oddou emphasized the importance of nonverbal communication skills and willingness to communicate with host-country nationals. Goal orientation, the second factor that is not a part of their model, has been identified by Kealey (1996) and Ronen (1989) as a critical determinant of cross-cultural effectiveness. In summary, the findings from this sample of German expatriate managers are consistent with previous research indicating that interpersonal and communication skills are most critical to the success of managers on an international assignment (e.g., Black, 1990; Clarke & Hammer, 1995; Kealey, 1989, 1996; Kealey & Ruben, 1983; Mendenhall, 2000; Mendenhall & Oddou, 1985; Ronen, 1989).

It is important to note that this profile of intercultural competence is not comprehensive. Rather, it contains a number of core factors that are critical to the success of managers in various cross-cultural business situations, in many different countries of assign-

Table 11.1
Determinants of Success in International Assignments

Profile of the successful international manager

Attitudes and skills	Behavioral indicators
Tolerance for ambiguity	Feels comfortable in ambiguous or highly complex situations; doesn't push for a particular solution; reacts patiently toward foreign business partners; stays calm in difficult situations; etc.
Behavioral flexibility	Rapidly changes behavior if given appropriate feedback; finds creative problem solutions; compromises; shows readiness to revise former decisions; statements match gesticulations; etc.
Goal orientation	Actively takes part in meetings; doesn't withdraw if faced with difficulties; tries to overcome language barriers; pays attention to time restrictions; struggles to overcome obstacles; etc.
Sociability	Initiates contact with foreign partner; makes new appointments; asks about the partner's personal background; is talkative; smiles at partner; exchanges "conversational currency"; etc.
Empathy	Considers the local partner's situation; shows appropriate discretion; argues from the position of the host national; picks up on the partner's contribution sympathetically; etc.
Nonjudgmentalness	Expresses approval of the host culture; avoids stereotypes; avoids making jokes about host nationals; discusses the uniqueness of the host country in a factual manner; etc.
Meta-communication skills	Tries to dissolve ambiguities and misunderstandings; provides appropriate feedback; asks if he or she has been understood; negotiates rules of play for the conversation; summarizes contributions; etc.

ment, and on many position levels. These factors likely represent the minimum requirements for an international assignment; in other words, unless a manager possesses a certain baseline level of behavioral flexibility, empathy, nonjudgmentalness, and so forth, he or she will not be able to function effectively in a foreign culture. However, it is doubtful that a "one-world manager" or "universal communicator" exists who, due to his or her brilliant intercultural competencies, is equally well respected, understood, and effective in all countries. To accurately predict a manager's success in an international assignment it seems necessary to modify or weight the general profile of skills, attitudes, and personality traits according to the demands of the particular position and the host country, and then match the person to the job (Kealey, 1996; Ronen, 1986; Tung, 1981).

PROJECT 2:
DEVELOPMENT AND EVALUATION OF THE
INTERCULTURAL ASSESSMENT CENTER

In the introductory section of this chapter it was argued that appraisal of international management talent is a critical part of global leadership development (e.g., Gregersen et al., 1998; Trompenaars, 1994). However, the assessment of intercultural skills as an important element of global leadership competence is not an easy task. According to Kealey (1996), "Researchers know much about the criteria associated with cross-cultural success, [but] their knowledge and skill on how to validly and reliably assess people on these criteria remain weak" (p. 97). It is therefore not surprising to find that most multinational corporations lack effective methods for selecting managers for international assignments (Deller, 1997; Gertsen, 1990; Miller, 1973; Stahl, 1998b; Tung, 1981).

Among the various methodologies available for appraisal and selection of managers, the most promising avenue for improving international screening processes lies in the development of behavioral assessment techniques. According to Mendenhall, Dunbar, and Oddou (1987), the fact that overseas acculturation and productivity are multidimensional phenomena should be reflected in the strategy of the international screening and selection process. Therefore, assessment centers that measure a variety of skills by utilizing a battery of tests and simulations would seem to be ideal for evaluating intercultural competencies. Other scholars also argue strongly for the development of behavioral-assessment techniques, because instruments such as unstructured interviews or psychological inventories have proved to be of little use in evaluating the skills necessary for success on an international assignment (Black, Gregersen, & Mendenhall, 1992a; Gertsen, 1990). Kealey (1996) summarized well the benefits of behavioral-assessment techniques when he noted, "The best predictor of behavior is behavior. What people say and what people do are often inconsistent" (p. 97).

With these potential advantages of the assessment-center methodology in mind, Kühlmann and Stahl (1996, 1998) designed a number of behavioral-assessment techniques to evaluate competencies that are critical to the success of managers in international business assignments. The primary goal of this exploratory research was to test whether assessment-center techniques, such as role plays, case studies, and group discussions, can be employed to validly and reliably measure intercultural skills. Another goal was to evaluate the utility of assessment centers within the broader context of leadership development, in particular its utility as a tool for the identification and development of international management talent.

In a first step, scripted accounts of cross-cultural business situations were collected from the interview data of the sample of German expatriate managers already described in this chapter. Based on these accounts, critical incidents and attendant coping responses of managers in international assignments were identified. These descriptions of critical encounters with foreign employees, customers, suppliers, and so forth provided the "raw material" for the design of behavioral-assessment techniques. Finally, a number of cross-cultural role plays, case studies, group discussions, and negotiating simulations were developed that focused on critical business encounters in many different countries of assignment. The various exercises were combined to form the Intercultural Assessment Center (IAC). The short version of the IAC, which requires one day, is illustrated in Figure 11.1.

Note that most of the tests and simulations employed in the IAC not only provide diagnostic information about the particular strengths and weaknesses of a candidate regarding an international assignment, but can serve as effective training tools as well. There is a growing number of scholars in the field of cross-cultural training and global leadership development who argue that, in addition to purely didactical or analytical approaches, a comprehensive training program should also include elements that foster experiential learning (e.g., Baumgarten, 1995; Mendenhall et al., 1987; Yeung & Ready, 1995). Exercises such as cross-cultural role plays, group discussions, and negotiating simulations enable managers to test and modify their behavior in a wide range of international business situations. Research has shown that these methodologies can be effective in sensitizing individuals to cultural issues, in improving work performance abroad, and in helping employees to develop global mind-sets (Bhagat & Prien, 1996; Black & Mendenhall, 1990; Deshpande & Viswesvaran, 1992; Earley, 1987; Kealey & Protheroe, 1996). Assessment centers can thus be a promising tool for the evaluation and development of global leadership competencies, especially if combined with detailed performance feedbacks.

The IAC has repeatedly been used by HR professionals of German multinational corporations to evaluate the capacity of young

Figure 11.1
Criteria and Exercises in the Intercultural Assessment Center

Exercises \ Determinants of intercultural effectiveness	Tolerance for ambiguity	Goal orientation	Sociability	Empathy	Nonjudgmentalness	Behavioral flexibility	Meta-communication skills
Individual Exercises							
Presentation	X	X	X	X	X	X	
Impression Management Exercise	X					X	
Cross-cultural Roleplays	X			X	X	X	X
Analysis of Film Sequences				X	X		
Isomorphic Attribution Exercise				X	X		
Intercultural Competence Questionnaire (ICQ)	X	X	X	X	X	X	X
Group Exercises							
Group Discussion "International Assignment"	X	X	X	X	X	X	X
International Negotiating Simulation	X	X	X	X	X	X	X

Source: T. M. Kühlmann and G. K. Stahl, Fachkompetenz allein genügt nicht—Interkulturelle Assessment Center unterstützen die gezielte Personalauswahl, *Personalführung Plus*, 96 (1996): 22–24; T. M. Kühlmann and G. K. Stahl, Diagnose interkultureller Kompetenz: Entwicklung und Evaluierung eines Assessment Centers, in *Interkulturelle Personalorganisation*, ed. C. Barmeyer and J. Bolten (Berlin: Verlag Wissenschaft & Praxis, 1998).

managers for international assignments. After a self-presentation that dealt with their motivation to go abroad and with factors that might facilitate or hinder an expatriate assignment, candidates in the IAC were exposed to the various tests and simulations. Throughout the assessment center, the candidates' performance was monitored by trained observers. Once the assessment center ended, the observer ratings were quickly analysed via a computer program. On the following day, candidates received detailed feedback regarding their particular strengths and weaknesses for an international assignment, as well as suggestions for further training.

Preliminary evidence indicated that the tests and simulations employed in the IAC can help determine which candidates are best suited for an international assignment. One source of evidence comes from peer ratings collected at the end of the assessment center. Each candidate was asked to rank all other participants according to their supposed adjustment and productivity in an international work assignment. After analyzing the peer ratings of forty-two managers who participated in the IAC, it was found that candidates scoring high on the criteria of intercultural competence were appraised by their peers as being more adaptable to a foreign environment and more effective when posted abroad. The Spearman rank correlation between the results of candidates in the IAC and their supposed adjustment in a foreign assignment was $r_s = 0.43$ ($n = 42$, $p < 0.01$), and the correlation between assessment-center results and peer ratings of their cross-cultural productivity was $r_s = 0.33$ ($n = 42$, $p < 0.05$). Thus, judgments about the candidates' aptitude for an international assignment, as demonstrated in the IAC, were corroborated by appraisals of their intercultural skills made by colleagues.

PROJECT 3:
USING ASSESSMENT CENTERS AS TOOLS FOR GLOBAL LEADERSHIP DEVELOPMENT— RESULTS OF AN EXPLORATORY STUDY

Another source of evidence for the effectiveness of the IAC as an assessment and development instrument comes from a pilot study that was conducted in a large German multinational corporation, DaimlerChrysler Aerospace. This Munich-based producer of aircraft, satellites, and defense systems has implemented the IAC as part of its international management-development system.

Aspiring young managers with a proven record in a domestic position were nominated for the company's international management-development program by their supervisors. After their nomination, candidates first participated in an extended version of the IAC, which required two days. At the end of the assessment center, participants received detailed feedback about their particular strengths and weaknesses regarding an international assignment, as monitored by trained observers in the IAC. The results of this assessment process were then linked with international training and development measures. Based on the identified "gaps" in the skills required for effective performance in international assign-ments, decision makers in the HR department were able to cus-tomize their management-development measures to meet the specific needs of participants. The resulting program, named QUICK, included a variety of international management-develop-ment tools:

- Intensive foreign-language training.
- Cross-cultural communication workshops.
- Self-awareness and sensitivity training.
- Seminars on change management.
- Multicultural-team leadership training.
- Assignment to project teams and task forces abroad.

QUICK thus involved both classroom training and experience-based learning projects. Seminars were taught by academics, in-house trainers, and external consultants. In addition, participants organized voluntary meetings in order to discuss company-related topics through-out the eighteen-month program. These social gatherings created a common language and cohesion among managers from different func-tions, most of whom had never met before. After the program had ended, the managers participated in a second version of the IAC that measured the same criteria with different, yet structurally similar, exercises to evaluate their newly acquired skills.

Using a sample of twenty-two managers, a longitudinal design was employed to evaluate candidates' learning progress during the QUICK-program. Figure 11.2 presents the mean scores of candi-dates on the measured criteria of intercultural competence before and after the program ended. The findings indicate that candidates scored considerably higher on most assessment-center criteria af-ter QUICK had ended. Unfortunately, it was not possible to em-ploy a more rigid control-group design in this exploratory study. We did, however, control for the possibility that the second version of the IAC was "easier" than the original one, thereby inflating the results. This was done by assigning a subgroup of candidates (n = 11) to the original version of the IAC first, and then evaluating their learning progress in a parallel version after the program had ended; with the other subgroup (n = 11), the process was reversed.

There are several possible explanations for these findings: There may have been learning effects; candidates may have done better in the second assessment center simply because of the fact that they knew each other more intimately than at the time of the first assessment; and, of course, the international management-devel-

Figure 11.2
Intercultural Assessment Center Results Before and After an
International Management-Development Program (n = 22)

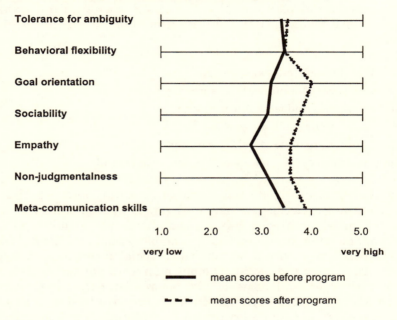

opment program may have been effective in enhancing candidates' intercultural skills. None of these explanations can be ruled out, and it is likely that all these factors contributed to the results. Nevertheless, since all of these factors would predict higher scores on the assessment-center criteria after participating in an international management-development program, the findings tentatively support the effectiveness of the IAC as a tool to assess managers' intercultural skills and to evaluate the effectiveness of international management-development measures.

IMPLICATIONS FOR RESEARCH AND PRACTICE

In recent years specific instruments have been designed to evaluate and develop the skills that are critical to success in international assignments (Black, Gregersen et al., 1999; Deller, 1997; Kealey, 1996; Kühlmann & Stahl, 1998; Ronen, 1986; Spreitzer et al., 1997; Stahl, 1998a). The Intercultural Assessment Center employs a number of role plays, case studies, group discussions, and international negotiating simulations to evaluate managers' intercultural competencies. DaimlerChrysler Aerospace, a large German multinational corporation with ventures in many European countries, has implemented the *IAC* as part of its international management development program. In this chapter, preliminary evidence was presented indicating that assessment centers can effectively assist HR professionals in the identification, career planning, and development of international managers. Although the predictive validity of the IAC has yet to be confirmed, it has been shown that candidates scoring high on different criteria of intercultural competence were appraised by their peers as being more adaptable to a foreign environment and more effective when posted abroad. Based on the results of the IAC, identified skill deficits enabled decision makers in the HR department of DaimlerChrysler Aerospace to customize a management-development program to meet the specific needs of aspirants for key international positions. In this way the IAC served as a needs analysis for designing an effective international-development process. The findings of a longitudinal study further indicated that managers scored considerably higher on the assessment-center criteria after participating in this program than they did before, thus pointing to the utility of the IAC as a tool to evaluate the effectiveness of international training and management-development instruments.

Despite the preliminary nature of this study, the findings are encouraging. However, more research is needed to substantiate the effectiveness of assessment centers as evaluation tools to measure intercultural competencies and global leadership skills. In particular, research is needed that examines the validity of assessment-center results to predict patterns of success and failure in international assignments. This would require a systematic follow-up monitoring of the performance of expatriate managers in their countries of assignment. In addition, the validity of specific assessment-center techniques that can be used as an economical screening device to improve international selection and development decisions should be examined as well. The findings of another exploratory study indicate that international staffing decisions can be considerably improved by utilizing structured interviews that include cross-cultural role plays and case studies (Stahl, 1995b). Such "miniature assessment centers" are very cost efficient and therefore likely to be utilized by HR and line managers responsible for international staffing decisions.

Behavioral-assessment techniques are a relatively costly way to evaluate the skills that are critical to success in international business assignments. However, compared to other instruments of management development, assessment centers can serve many different purposes at the same time (Mendenhall & Stahl, in press). In addition to providing information about the intercultural skill levels of candidates, exercises such as role plays, group discussions, and negotiating simulations enable managers to test and modify their behavior in a wide range of cross-cultural business situations and help them to develop more global orientations. International assessment centers can serve as "global mind-set training," not only for those who are participants in it, but for those executives who function as observers in the assessment center as well. As more and more candidates from foreign subsidiaries participate in the corporate assessment center, a preselected pool of global managers can be established, and, as a by-product, informal networks and a truly internationally oriented corporate culture may be created. Thus, assessment centers have a number of benefits that may be worth the expenditure.

NOTE

This research was conducted with Torsten M. Kühlmann. The author gratefully acknowledges his contribution to this paper, as well as the helpful comments of Allan Bird, Mark Mendenhall, and Ed Miller on earlier versions of this chapter.

12

International Team Building: Issues in Training Multinational Work Groups

Alois Moosmüller, Erika Spieß, and Astrid Podsiadlowski

With increasing internationalization and globalization of business, it has become vital for people from different cultural backgrounds to work together (Thomas, 1996b). The significance of work groups, project groups, or teams composed of people from different cultures is growing constantly. For international corporations, the effectiveness of intercultural and interpersonal processes in multinational work groups has become a crucial question (Adler, 1991). Multinational teams, like culturally diverse teams in general, can be more effective, but also less effective, than monocultural teams, depending essentially on the successful implementation of suited team-building measures and global leadership-development measures. The aim of this chapter is to discuss some of the issues involved with these measures and to suggest how leadership behavior can be improved. We shall begin by establishing the fundamental principles for a culturally heterogeneous team, then examine the conditions for more effective team building, and finally define these conditions using a team training example.

DIVERSITY IN WORK GROUPS

Due to growing international interlinkage and intranational differentiation, diversity has become an important factor in today's business world. Groups composed of culturally diverse members are encountered at all levels of an organization, from top management down to project groups. The fact that people with different beliefs, values, attitudes, and behavior increasingly have to work together has made diversity a much discussed topic. The differing factors named in the literature are race, sex, nationality, ethnicity, culture, occupation, and geographic origin. In this chapter we focus on diversity based on the different national origin of the group members. Multinational work groups are composed of members who are socialized in various national cultures. Consequently, they perceive, think, and react differently in the same situations. Hofstede (1980a) calls the influence of national culture on individual behavior "mental programming" and asserts it has a lasting nature.

When culturally differently programmed individuals work together, culturally related differences that occur are not viewed as justified peculiarities in their own right but rather as deviations from "normality." The culture-specific limitation of the possibilities of perception, thought, and action is simultaneously a disadvantage and an advantage. On the one hand, it makes international cooperation more difficult. On the other hand, cultural differences are necessary for generating cultural synergy. Cultural differences allow the team members to develop a "global mind-set" permitting multiperspective and flexible action (Maznevski & Peterson, 1997; Rhinesmith, 1993, 1994), which is essential for intercultural leadership development. If the respective cultural-specific strengths are exploited, multinational teams can be very effective (Adler, 1991; Moran & Harris, 1981).

To understand the risks and opportunities better, it is helpful to review empirical findings on diverse work groups, because these have potential implications for studying multinational work groups. Empirical findings on group diversity indicate that there is a potential cognitive gain through diversity and therefore greater productivity and effectiveness. Heterogeneous groups are able to solve problems more quickly provided that the members of the group are able to contribute complementary skills relevant to the task (Hoffman & Maier, 1961). They can reflect a larger number of alternatives, develop better ideas, be more creative, adapt more quickly to changing environmental conditions, and render decision making more effective than homogeneous groups (for an overview of these findings, see Milliken & Martins, 1996; Smith & Noakes,

1996; Podsiadlowski, 1998). Bantel and Jackson (1989) point out that greater diversity in top-management teams is accompanied by an increase in innovation. Moreover, group think, the danger of erroneous decisions due to conformistic behavior and group pressure, is reduced (Janis, 1982). These effects can prevail if the groups have enough time to get to know each other and to overcome their initial problems, as a study by Watson, Kumar, and Michaelsen (1993) shows. Heterogeneous teams working on business case studies improved their results continuously over a long period of time and developed more alternatives to solve a problem than the homogeneous control group.

However, these advantages also constitute the disadvantages of diverse work groups. Argote and McGrath (1993) call this the "diversity/consensus dilemma": Effective group work requires different personalities and, consequently, as wide as possible a range of perspectives, skills, and experience. Simultaneously, it demands a consensus on plans and activities as well as solutions to problems, which call for common perspectives; that is, a "team mental model" (Ilgen, LePine, & Hollenbeck, 1997, 387; see also Maznevski, 1994). Other potential problems in diverse groups are the exclusion of minorities (Kirchmeyer, 1993), hindrance of communication, and an increase in turnover and absenteeism (Ancona & Caldwell, 1992).

On the basis of the reported empirical results, the potential advantages and disadvantages of diverse work groups can be summed up as follows (Podsiadlowski, 1998):

Potential advantages	*Potential disadvantages*
Productivity	Hinders communication
Effectivity	Less group stability
Innovation	Less group cohesion
Minimizing group think	Less job satisfaction
Creativity	Increased stress

With regard to these results and conclusions, it must be taken into account that most of the studies on diversity are short-term laboratory studies with groups of students, and that they concentrate on one country, the United States. There is still a shortage of studies on performance-oriented, culturally diverse teams in companies. The same applies to multinational teams: There is very little knowledge available on multinational teams and it is not backed empirically (Granrose & Oskamp, 1997; Ilgen et al., 1997). Furthermore, attention must be drawn to the special difficulty in studying multinational teams: In order to be able to make appropriate or as undistorted statements as possible, one's own "scientific ethno-centricity" (Bourdieu, 1995) has to be put aside, multiperspectivity has to be practiced, and new heuristics have to be found.

TEAM BUILDING AND THE DEVELOPMENT OF GLOBAL LEADERSHIP COMPETENCY

How does one acquire or develop these competencies required for global leadership? According to the literature, there is some con-sensus on the characteristics required for expatriates, which over-lap with global leadership competencies (e.g., relationship skills, communication skills, and personal traits such as inquisitiveness) (Black, Morrison, & Gregersen, 1999; Gregersen, Morrison, & Black, 1998; Mendenhall, 2000; Spreitzer, McCall, & Mahoney, 1997). In general, such social skills can be called intercultural competence (Kealey, 1996; Moosmüller, 1995; Podsiadlowski & Spieß, 1996). Intercultural competence refers not only to cognitive skills, such as knowledge of the culture, language, cultural standards (as well as one's own and foreign cultural characteristics), and so forth, but also to affective and behavioral skills such as empathy, human warmth, and the ability to manage anxiety and uncertainty (Gudykunst, 1988; Spieß, 1996, 1998).

International assignments are considered the best way to obtain these competencies. However, international assignments as devel-opment tools also present problems, because they often occur with-out any formal development of the needed global leadership skills required overseas. As Mendenhall (2000) warns, "The fact remains that simply sending someone overseas does not ensure that they will automatically develop global leadership competencies," so train-ing needs to take place in "real-time," while the expatriate is in the actual situation that he or she needs training for. Another inter-esting possibility would be interactive team training, where par-ticipants approach the problems that crop up in routine team work in a safe environment.

Team-building measures can be important management tools relevant for global leaders from two perspectives. On the one hand, global leaders need to have the ability to manage teams of cross-cultural members, as they are part of multinational teams either in the role of leader or as a group member with other top managers. On the other hand, a global leader's competence is developed by learning through the experience in a multinational team and par-ticipating in team-building measures. One of the main goals of team-building measures is identical with one important global leadership competency: to work effectively with people from different cultures.

PROMOTING THE GROUP AS A MULTINATIONAL TEAM

In order to make multinational work groups capable of dealing productively with diversity and to produce the necessary consensus, the team members must develop intercultural competence, which means, above all, that they must be able to change perspectives, tolerate ambiguity, and deal with varying action adequately. To this end, appropriate team-building measures must be developed. It is important to differentiate between preparatory and accompanying measures. Both are equally important.

Preparatory Measures

Preparation should create the conditions needed for a multinational work group to be able to develop its positive potential. Management needs to create clear, transparent structures as well as define goals and tasks as unequivocally as possible. Especially important is that the group recognizes the targets as a common goal (Triandis, Kurowski, & Gelfand, 1994).

There are two possible ways of creating favorable conditions for a multinational team: team composition and situational factors. It is advisable, for example, to compose the multinational groups as homogeneously as possible with regard to education, occupation, status, and age, because this provides the best conditions for utilizing the potential of national cultural diversity (Milliken & Martins, 1996).

The danger that cultural diversity will have a negative effect is substantially larger in "weak situations" than in "strong situations." Weak situations are situations that offer no suitable incentives, are ambiguous about which behavior is successful, give the impression that there is more than one path leading to the goal, and do not motivate the team participants to strive for consensus. Strong situations are distinguished by clear behavioral guidelines and defined tasks and demands, whereas in weak situations the occurrences have to be interpreted first (Ilgen et al., 1997; Maznevski & Peterson, 1997; Shoda, Mischel, & Wright, 1993).

Accompanying Measures

Smith and Noakes (1996) divide team building into four phases. In phase 1 the members try to adapt to each other, with national stereotypes and national status playing an important role. Varying value orientations are discovered, building trust is experienced as a problem, and culture clash is encountered. In phase 2 the actual influence of cultural diversity on routine team actions is in the foreground (e.g., how time is dealt with or which leadership style predominates, how problems are solved and decisions are reached, etc.). In phase 3 dyadic or subgroup alliances are built, with cultural similarity playing an important role. There is a great danger of polarization into national subgroups and of intensifying ethnocentric attitudes. If the team is able to cope with these difficulties, phase 4 can set in, in which diversity is no longer a handicap but rather is viewed as an opportunity, setting the fundamental conditions for positive team building.

We believe that there are two critical phases in which team-building measures are especially important: the beginning of team cooperation (phase 1), and when the team has already gathered much experience in dealing with cultural diversity and wants to coordinate and harmonize actions (transition from phase 3 to phase 4). Davison (1994) discovered that it is necessary to implement "team basics" at the beginning. In particular, the team has to bring to the surface and respect hidden cultural diversity, and the working method and performance goals must be agreed upon. Often, for fear of losing time, work is started immediately, without first clarifying the basics. In all probability this will lead to loss of efficiency in the course of teamwork.

A TYPOLOGY OF MULTINATIONAL TEAMS

The complexity and diversity of the composition and organizational context of multinational teams is infinite. Preparatory and accompanying team-developing measures must reflect this diversity and complexity. A prerequisite, however, is differentiating between the teams. We have therefore drawn up categories that permit classifying the teams. However, they are of a hypothetical nature and are still open to additional research (see Figure 12.1).

There are two significant questions: First, is the organization in which the team works economically and politically dominated by a certain nation, or is there a power basis (the power to decide, execute, and control the organization's operations) independent of any national dominance? In the first instance, it must be anticipated that the culture of the nation with the greater power will exercise greater influence in the team. In the latter case, a "supranational" power basis predominates and no single culture will have precedence. Second, are teams composed of individual members from different nations, or of groups of members from different nations (e.g., Germans, Americans, and Japanese)? The former has to deal primarily with questions concerning the coordination and integra-

Figure 12.1
Ideal Typical Characteristics of Multinational Teams

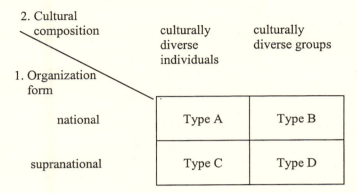

tion of such diverse backgrounds; the latter, on the other hand, has to deal with the problems of polarization, hardening of boundaries between the different groups, and stereotyping and generalization.

A type A team is composed of individuals from different national cultural backgrounds. Therefore, hardly any member is able to relate to someone with the same cultural background. As a consequence, the "cultural programming" of members is weakened for a relatively long period of time. The influence of the home-company culture is very strong, as the common cultural denominator is of special significance in team building. Such teams, for example, can be found in the offices of multinational companies in Singapore (Podsiadlowski, 1999).

A type B team is composed of two or more national cultural subgroups with at least three members each. Most of the members identify with one of these subgroups (i.e., they communicate more often and more intensely with members of the same culture). If a subgroup belongs to the same national culture as the home company, there is the danger that cultural differences will intermingle with the problem of uneven distribution of power. The result may be that cultural differences are overemphasized and mutual adaptive behavior is blocked. Team situations of this type frequently occur in foreign subsidiaries of multinational companies or in joint ventures in which one firm has the majority (Moosmüller, 1997a).

A type C team is similar to type A, but the umbrella organization of the team does not represent a national culture. Rather it is a supranational structure: perhaps an international organization (e.g., Greenpeace or Unesco), a 50/50 joint venture, or an international research project (e.g., CERN in Geneva). For such teams to be able to function effectively it is vital that important common goals are pursued and that a supportive umbrella organization exists (Bantz, 1993).

Type D will be dealt with in more detail using a case study.

A CASE STUDY:
INTERCULTURAL TRAINING IN THE TRIAD PROJECT

Description of the Team Training Approach

In 1994 and 1995 two several-day-long intercultural team-building sessions were conducted as part of an American–Japanese–German joint venture project, the "Triad Project." Started in 1993 by three companies from the United States, Japan, and Germany, this U.S.-based high-tech research and development project lasted about four years. Each of the three companies contributed about one-third of the more than 100 project staff members. All functions were organized triculturally: Americans, Japanese, and Germans shared the top management positions equally; the staff was assigned to tricultural subteams; tricultural staff distribution also reigned in the offices and rooms. The intention was to ensure that intercultural cooperation also worked on the informal level, thereby generating cultural synergy.

Some months after the project had started, it turned out that the formal exchange of information (meetings, presentations, discussions) had become ineffective and that informal information exchange did not come about to the extent expected. The initial willingness of the project staff to help each other with mutual cultural understanding had waned markedly after a few months. The three national groups began to stick to themselves and team members increasingly complained about the lack of mutual trust. Many staff members were disappointed, because the excitement of the first months ("we will show what international teams can do!") had subsided and management's proclaimed "open, innovative and synergy generating climate" did not set in. At that time, reports on the intercultural problems of the project appeared in journals ("Computer Chip Project," 1994; "Cultures Clash," 1994). In order to improve this situation, project management decided to implement intercultural training.

An intercultural team of trainers conducted the two multiday training sessions with fifteen participants in each session, five from each of the three countries (Moosmüller, 1997b). The teams were fairly homogeneous with respect to age, education, occupation, and status: The participants were generally between twenty-eight and thirty-eight, had an academic background, and worked on projects in the engineering field. The methodological basis of the three-culture training was Clackworthy's (1992) "cultural interaction training." Simulated business situations were the heart of the training. Participants' interaction was video recorded, analyzed, and discussed, thereby enabling participants to consciously experience daily cultural differences that normally remain unnoticed in the teams in handling information, meetings, decision making, problem solving, delegating, supervision, evaluation, and building trust. Thus, the participants were able to reconstruct the influence of cultural differences on the team. Different cultural backgrounds became understandable, other viewpoints could be taken, and new opportunities for cooperation could be worked out.

COPING WITH CULTURAL DIFFERENCES IN THE TEAM TRAINING APPROACHES

The most common problems in teams are the result of ignorance of culturally related different courses of action. When, for instance, Americans, Japanese, and Germans exchange information, make presentations, and discuss in order to reach a common decision, they are unaware that the courses of action and the respective expectations of these actions vary considerably. In the training simulations these differences became apparent and learnable. The participants discussed these differences and inquired about their cultural backgrounds. For example, it was discovered that the Japanese participants explain facts in detail at the beginning and do not come to the results until the end of the presentation. American participants, on the other hand, begin with the results, which they subsequently justify with arguments and facts in the course of the presentation. German participants first briefly outline the problem or even provide a historical survey of it and then continue like the Americans.

In real teamwork activities, such different "culturally programmed" courses of action remain hidden to the participants. One's own ethnocentric expectations and practice remain the unquestioned gauge according to which others' action is considered "not normal": thus, the Japanese are "not logical," Americans "not credible," and Germans "meticulous." This type of erroneous assessment of each other hinders the desired quick, uncomplicated, and trustworthy exchange of information and favors turning to one's own cultural groups. In training, erroneous assessment can be corrected, respect for different courses of action can be instilled, and effective ways for dealing with differences can be learned. The participants are encouraged to exchange their intuitive assessment of critical situations, and thus to express their tacit intercultural knowledge explicitly.

Table 12.1 shows further American–Japanese–German differences that influence participants' actions. Expressing these differences in words is the result of team training and represents an example for transforming tacit intercultural knowledge of a team into explicit intercultural knowledge.

With the aid of some cultural dimensions, cultural differences in working and learning behavior that need to be noted in the planning and conducting of team training can be reified in order to offer optimum development opportunities to all the participants and thus the team. Depending on which national cultures are involved in the training, different demands are made. In particular, it is important to know which learning style the training participants practice based on their cultural disposition. In American–Japanese–German team training, the following differences, for instance, need to be taken into account.

Japanese come from a "harmony culture"; Americans and Germans, on the other hand, come from "conflict cultures" (i.e., the former cultivate an indirect style of communication, avoid any open exchange of opinions, do not approach problems directly, and take care to save the other's "face," whereas the latter discuss controversial opinions openly and directly, approach problems directly and take care to save only one's own "face") (Condon, 1984; Gudykunst & Nishida, 1993; Lebra, 1976). In the training, the direct exchange of opinions cannot be practiced, especially not if different attitudes and behavior are being worked on. Consequently, discussions are not spontaneous but rather preplanned and more written than oral statements are worked with. Although this is frustrating, it keeps the group able to work and to learn. However, if Western habits and expectations are the basis of proceeding, chances that the training will fail are great.

Japanese and Germans have strong and Americans weak "uncertainty avoidance."[1] Americans desire a flexible schedule and are accustomed to change tasks and exercises spontaneously according to needs and the situation. For Germans and for Japanese, this would be very irritating. They, on the other hand, expect that what is announced actually occurs, that routines are established and adhered to. Compromises must be made here and learning behavior has to be reviewed repeatedly on the metalevel.

The Japanese approach is collectivistic–particularistic, whereas the German approach and much more so the American approach is individualistic–universalistic (Gudykunst, 1997; Hofstede, 1980a; Triandis, 1995). The result is that the Japanese experience a stronger ingroup–outgroup contrast, which among other things means that they are loyal, trusting, open, and informal in their ingroup,

Table 12.1
Daily Culturally Diverse Action in the Team

	Japanese Participants	German Participants	American Participants
Values and expectations	Responsibility to the group Trust, loyalty Respect for cultural differences, high commitment	Give clear definitions Explain actions, give background Be able to clearly assess the relationship between the ideal (want) and real (must) boundaries	Be clear and decisive Go own way Be innovative Good ideas and exceptional performance must be rewarded
Basis of work	Agreement on common goals	Agreement on a common premise	Individuality
Thinking process	Subtlety, compromise Distanced, objective, non-evaluating thinking	Define problem Clear, consistent thinking	Offer options Creative, open, playful thinking
Communication attitude	Non-confrontational "We" feeling	Direct Controlled	Seek quick solution Flexible
Exchange of information (Presentation)	Set scope: discuss goals and strategies Facts first Detailed presentation of facts Arguments may be associative Results	Set scope: discuss background, context, problem definition Results first Results backed by facts Conclusive argumentation	Results first Results backed by facts Clear arguments
Demands on partner who caused a problem	No explicit demands on the source "The source must know my demands"	Strong, explicit demands on the source "The source must solve the problem"	Moderate, explicit demands on the source "I offer the source my cooperation in solving the problem"

but suspicious, withdrawn, and formal within the outgroup. In contrast to this, Germans and Americans expect consistent behavior. Controversy within a Japanese group is kept inside the group and not allowed to surface, decisions are made on the basis of personality and not on objectivity, giving the impression of block building or cronyism. However, Germans and Americans expect independent, ego-driven behavior based on "true" reality. These differences contribute considerably to fostering and intensifying mutual prejudice and must be addressed continuously in training.

The Japanese and American action orientation is pragmatic and based on experience, whereas German action orientation is abstract—analytical in nature (Friday, 1989; Moosmüller, 1997a; Moritz, 1996). Germans, for example, have the need to find logical or historical reasons for cultural differences; this, however, is a waste of time in the eyes of Americans and Japanese. For them, the effects and how to behave are far more important. Japanese and Americans prefer role play and simulation; cultural differences have to be comprehensible. Germans tend to consider exercises as games and not as a way to learn, because for them learning always has an intellectual abstract dimension. Design, conducting, and processing of simulation and practical exercises have to meet these different needs.

INTERNATIONAL TEAM BUILDING AND LEADERSHIP COMPETENCE

Intercultural team training like that just described can fulfill two purposes: It can make the collaboration in a team more effective and it can improve the intercultural competence of team members. Interactive intercultural team training can also be conducted with the sole aim of promoting global leadership competence. The Triad Project training indicated the following dynamics of learning. Each section ends with suggestions for conducting intercultural training, and specifies the leadership competence (see Mendenhall, 2000) that a global leader should develop.

Ethnocentric Stances and Attitudes

- The members of the team are largely unaware of culturally related differences in perception, thinking, and action.
- The more intense the collaboration in the team and the greater the pressure for success, the more clearly visible the cultural differences become; moreover, the greater the tendency to play down or ignore the differences and to deny one's own ethnocentric stances or attitudes.
- The attitude toward cultural differences is ambivalent: Differences are realized and simultaneously negated, accepted and simultaneously denied.

Intercultural training has to work with this ambivalence: Cultural differences and ethnocentric stances and attitudes have to be discussed carefully.

Intercultural Competence

- In the course of collaborating, the members of a multinational team develop intercultural competence (knowledge of their own and foreign cultures and ability to empathize, change perspectives, and learn interculturally).
- Depending on the personality, previous experience, and sociocultural conditions, intercultural competence develops heterogeneously. The uneven distribution of intercultural competence in the team may be the source of additional communication problems.

Intercultural training has to sharpen the team members' awareness of the presence of intercultural competence, increase trust in this competence, support mutual learning, and promote the intercultural competence of each individual, thereby increasing the intercultural communication skills of the team.

Intercultural Knowledge

- Culturally heterogeneous teams produce intercultural knowledge (i.e., a collective pool of knowledge) (Assman, 1992; Goodenough, 1981). This pool results from experiences gathered in dealing with critical intercultural situations and simultaneously supplies models for action and problem-solving strategies for such critical situations. Each individual team member will draw upon the pool of knowledge for handling intercultural situations.
- The access of the individual to the pool of intercultural knowledge potentially containing a suited solution for every critical situation is limited, because intercultural knowledge is only present as "tacit knowledge" (Nonaka & Takeuchi, 1995). This means that it cannot be planned, learned, or controlled.

Intercultural training must permit transforming tacit intercultural knowledge into explicit intercultural knowledge. Only explicit intercultural knowledge is accessible to all team members, can be utilized flexibly according to the situation, can be adapted to changing conditions, and can be used as a basis for the further gaining of knowledge.

Intercultural Learning

- The participants become more aware of culturally different perceptions and ways of thinking, of their own limitations, and of their own ability to think and perceive (i.e., they become more aware of their own cultural programming).
- They gain the ability to understand how stereotyping comes about if the actions of someone from a different culture are interpreted according to one's own reference framework, and the ability to understand how reciprocal erroneous attributions hinder developing mutual trust.
- Culturally specific knowledge must be incorporated in planning and conducting the training of multinational teams from the very beginning. It is not necessary, on the other hand, to have precise knowledge of the cultural diversity present in the team. The participants will work that out themselves. However, it is important to establish suited learning conditions conducive to this process.

The greatest challenge for training and leading of multicultural teams is to do justice to the participants' different learning behaviors and learning expectations due to their different cultural backgrounds and to avoid any discrimination or disrespect.

GENERAL CONCLUSIONS

Intercultural cooperation should be considered an opportunity to utilize different approaches and strategies in order to be able to cope better with global challenges. Successful handling of cultural diversity increases creativity and the quality of decisions, and the ability to adapt decisively improves a company's competitiveness.

The abilities required by global leaders overlap extensively with the skills enhanced by team-building measures. As foreign assignments help develop a permanent learning process, so do the experiences working in a team and participating in team-building measures. International team building may not be a substitute for foreign assignments as a leadership development tool, but it can improve and support similar learning processes.

The aim of staff building and, in particular, intercultural team building is to promote creativity and innovation, to develop multiple perspectives, and to remove communication barriers, misunderstanding, and distrust. To do this it is necessary that the organization provide the appropriate conditions, that the team members are interculturally competent, and that intercultural measures are taken to make group processes more effective.

Finally, of vital significance is the implementation of suited measures during the team work process: After a certain period of working together, the team develops its own culture, of which its members are largely unaware. This culture is a pool of tacit intercultural knowledge, and thus the key to making a team effective. In order to utilize this potential it is necessary that tacit knowledge be transformed into explicit intercultural knowledge (i.e., it is made generally accessible, controllable, impartable, and selectively applicable). When this succeeds, it will be possible to profit from the diversity of multinational work groups and generate cultural synergy.

NOTE

1. "Uncertainty avoidance can therefore be defined as the extent to which the members of a culture feel threatened by uncertain or unknown situations. This feeling is, among other things, expressed through nervous stress and in a need for predictability: a need for written and unwritten rules" (Hofstede, 1991, 113).

13

Effective Global Leadership: The Role of Linguistic Analysis of Intercultural Communication Situations

Bernd Müller-Jacquier and Ellen M. Whitener

Globalization involves more than isolated transactions with a limited number of partners in foreign countries during a restricted period of time. More and more international leaders engage in long-term projects where the majority of their professional time is spent in face-to-face situations with foreign coparticipants who practice different communication styles. Many leaders realize that this situation demands a new class of communication skills. Therefore, the nature and the effects of culture-bound communication problems have to be reconsidered in detail.

In theory and in practice, intercultural communication problems are primarily explained psychologically rather than linguistically, focusing on differences in cultural values or cultural orientations (Hofstede, 1991; Kluckhohn & Strodtbeck, 1961; Maznevski, DiStefano, Gomez, Nooderhaven, & Wu, 1997). Therefore, we call this approach "culture oriented" or simply "cultural." However, such a focus on culture-oriented explanations of interaction bears a danger as participants rashly jump to conclusions about another participant's cultural value orientations without taking into consideration the impact of his or her conventions of communication.

In this chapter we have two primary goals: to challenge global leaders to develop their roles as cultural mediators and to provide direction for future research in intercultural communication and leadership. We build a foundation for these goals by reviewing the literature on linguistics and cultural orientations. We rely on these literatures to construct a framework to direct the linguistic awareness and competence of global leaders. We conclude with tentative advice for global leaders and human resource professionals, and suggestions and cautions for future research in this area. Through much of this chapter we admittedly assume a prescriptive stance and tone—rationally and reasonably, we think—relying on the literature in intercultural communication; however, we urge organizational researchers to investigate the validity and generalizability of our assertions in the global business-management arena.

INTERCULTURAL COMMUNICATION: A COMMUNICATION PROBLEM?

Knapp (1995) poses the provocative question as to whether participants in intercultural communication view misunderstandings as problems of linguistics and communication as opposed to problems of differing cultural values or orientations. As shown in Figure 13.1, both cultural orientations and linguistics impact intercultural miscommunication. As Maznevski and Zander (in press) note, cultural orientations are rooted in individuals' culture—the collection of shared, deep-level norms and values about the way things should be (Adler, 1997c; Hofstede, 1991; Lane, DeStefano, & Maznevski, 1997; Trompenaars, 1993). When individuals interact, they speak and behave on the basis of those norms and values; when individuals from different cultures interact, they speak and behave on the basis of norms and values that often differ. "These differences can damage . . . relationships, as one person interprets another's words or behavior in a way in which it was not intended, and neither person recognizes that the misinterpretation has occurred" (Maznevski & Zander, 2000).

In these moments of misinterpretation with or among foreigners (Agar, 1994), participants tend to blame culture-specific (foreign) value systems or individual preferences and characteristics, rather than different conventions of communication (Thomas, 1996a; Winter, 1994). Because of this unquestioned trust in the functioning of interpersonal communication, most individuals require great effort or individual training before they learn to systematically search for different linguistic conventions for equivalent intentions in two cultures (e.g., C_1 and C_2 in Figure 13.1).

Figure 13.1
Points and Processes in Intercultural Communication

SETTING:

Co–participant (C_1)		*Co–participant* (C_2)	
Mental lexicon, culture-specific speech acts, nonverbal and paraverbal conventions, discourse styles, scripts, etc.	Values, stereotypes, expectations, legal and economic systems, history, etc.	Mental lexicon, culture specific speech acts, nonverbal and paraverbal conventions, discourse styles, scripts, etc.	Values, stereotypes, expectations, legal and economic systems, history, etc.

         ↘   ↓   ↗

Intercultural Communication Situation

Process:

↓

Application of behavior schemes

(interpretations bound to C_1 or C_2 for analyzing foreign-culture actions)

↓

Ambiguity

↓

Attribution

(Linguistic ability is attributed to foreign value systems)

↓

Miscommunication

↓

Frustration/Stress

↓

Results:

Lack of Objectivity

(e.g., stereotypes when perceiving future intercultural situations)

↓

Avoidance of Contact

(avoiding future contact with co-participants of other cultures)

One of Knapp's (1995) findings illustrates this. British individuals who described their German colleagues as "very unfriendly and direct" and "aggressive" were presented with empirical findings indicating that their negative impressions might possibly result from the fact that their German counterparts did not make use of linguistic politeness markers such as "please" after requests and commands as frequently as they do themselves. That is to say, German speakers will habitually mark such speech acts with other politeness markers (e.g., the subjunctive or intonation; see also House, 1989), and so, in keeping with German conventions, will use the specific illocutionary marker "please" (for indicating their requests) less frequently.

The British individuals reacted to this linguistic explanation of their cultural attributions they had already made as follows: Rather than accepting the suggestion that their impression of impoliteness stems from different communicative conventions in Germany, they assumed that Germans make use of more direct speech act realizations than the British "because they *are* more impolite" (Knapp, personal communication, 1989).

Even though this impression might be true for some individuals, the example illustrates how rarely those affected by such intercultural misunderstandings are willing to accept linguistically oriented explanations of critical communicative situations. The cited culturally oriented conclusions, which they had reached from the perceived communicative behavior based upon their own behavioral conventions, seemed far more plausible. Thus, they avoided having to analyze whether different frequencies or distributions of "please" or its assumed correspondent, "bitte," exist, and whether they are themselves systematically (and wrongly) interpreting different linguistic rules as an expression of culturally explained characteristics of their partner(s).

In contrast to most research conducted to date, we call for a communication-theoretic analysis of the concrete situational interaction that should as a rule precede a cultural analysis based upon value attributions. Where this is ignored, culture-oriented analyses of intercultural situations, even though they contain correct empirical analyses, are based on incorrect analyses of actions and therefore false attributions of intentions (Müller, 1995a, 1995b). This runs the risk of systematically imposing a biased consciousness on intercultural situations; participants think they understand the reasons for a communication breakdown, but their explanation is often inadequate, based only on their culture-oriented analysis of assumed values and not also on a linguistic analysis of the communicative expressions of intended actions.

To avoid misattributions of the reasons for culturally generated problems of interaction, reduce the stress, and enhance understanding, we propose that global leaders must perform a linguistic analysis of their communications and interactions. In the following section we present a framework to guide this analysis that combines linguistic awareness with situational analytic skill. The basic idea is that linguistic analysis—combined with a situational analysis to determine what an individual from another culture is expressing, how he or she proceeds, and what at the end he or she intends— should come before the culture-oriented analysis of values and orientations in attributing causes and explanations for behavior.

A LINGUISTIC FRAMEWORK FOR ANALYSIS OF INTERCULTURAL COMMUNICATION

Our linguistic framework for analyzing intercultural communication builds on ethnography of communication (Hymes, 1974) and discourse analysis (in the sense of Gumperz, 1992, 1993). These approaches raise the issue of explicit and implicit norms of communicating, including social, verbal, and nonverbal parameters of interaction: "Conversational interpretation is cued by empirically detectable signs, contextualization cues, and that the recognition of what these signs are, how they relate to grammatical signs, how they draw on socio-cultural knowledge and how they affect understanding, is essential for creating and sustaining conversational involvement and therefore to communication as such" (Gumperz, 1992, 42). In more specific terms, communication builds on the culture-specific interpretation of speech acts, social meanings, conventions of discourse, choices of topic, directness, register, and paraverbal and nonverbal factors (Bonvillain, 1997).

Leaders can use this framework to explain unexpected foreign behavior by exploring the cultural gaps created by different underlying communication conventions. To be more precise, they can look for communication differences in how coparticipants express their speech acts and social meanings by estimating adequate conventions of discourse, choices of convenient topics, situationally shaped registers or degrees of directness, and paraverbal and nonverbal factors. This analysis has to be conducted prior to any attribution of the perceived behavior to the participant's foreign cultural value system.

Speech Acts

Speaking is an activity we perform and by which we manifest certain behavioral intentions. Frequently, we cannot unambiguously distinguish between a behavioral intention and its realization through verbal and nonverbal expressions, even in our mother tongue. In a monocultural American situation, for example, the addressee can only identify the utterance, "Why didn't you come back after *Seinfeld* last night?" as a question or a reproach when all paraverbal and nonverbal signals have been carefully considered. Only after the correct assignment has been made can the addressee react appropriately to the utterance, answering or apologizing and defending himself or herself.

In intercultural situations correct assignment is a very complex problem (e.g., as illustrated in training videos like Gumperz, 1993). The reason for this lies in the different use of the contextualizers marking specific intentions. Promises made in intercultural situations are particularly difficult because the conditions for realizing them differ from culture to culture. If a person reacts to a summarizing question such as "Also, Sie könnten morgen vorbeikommen und bei der Vorbereitung helfen?" [So, you could come round tomorrow and give me a hand with the preparations?] with a straightforward "Ja" or "Ja, gern" [Yes or Yes, I'll be glad to], that kind of response (in German) is considered to be a promise or a commitment, rather than a vague expression of intentions (such as, "At this moment in time I can imagine that I might come around").[1]

In intercultural situations we must further observe that besides their forms of realization, the frequency and distribution of speech acts and their embedding into preferred sequences are also culture specific.

Speech acts such as offering or accepting personal invitations are also sequences full of misunderstandings. Frequently, "invitations" arise spontaneously and the form in which they are uttered does not provide sufficient information about whether they are seriously meant, how serious they are, and which reactions or responses are conventionally expected (e.g., "I'd be really pleased, if you visited me/us soon."). It is also not clearly discernible for the speakers how Germans interpret such an invitation and whether the following possible reaction means that they will really plan to visit: "Ja, danke, gute Idee, wir werden es sicher einrichten können" [Thanks. That's a good idea, I'm sure we'll be able to arrange it].

Social Meaning

From a cognitive-psychological point of view, "social meaning" refers to the indication that coparticipants use words to express social representations and to evoke these in others. Such patterns of mental imagery, here also termed "concepts," are distinctly culture specific (Aitchison, 1987; Kleiber, 1990; Müller, 1980; Wierzbicka, 1991). This is why interlocuters in intercultural situations—especially when using a lingua franca—have to pay very close attention to potentially different cognitive–emotional representations of word meanings, and they should try to deduce these from the (contextualized) utterances of their conversation partner.

Take the case of an envisaged joint venture between German and French partners, where both sides agree to have developed a Konzept (written conception) for possible areas of cooperation by the first meeting. Frequently, the German side will arrive at such a meeting with a very carefully worked out written presentation of their ideas with specific mention of all relevant facts. The French, on the other hand, will present their concept as a starting point for joint brainstorming. What, to Germans, usually means a thoroughly structured presentation, the French interpret as a summary of very preliminary ideas. Rather than accepting that each side follows different semantic rules for the seemingly common and international word "concept," both sides frequently attribute the differing behavior to culture-specific work attitudes, such as "thorough" and "orderly" versus "superficial" and "easy going."

Conventions of Discourse

The communicative structure of everyday situations and work interactions is language and culture specific. Discourse parameters—for example, the structural organization of a meeting or the establishment of individual phases of discussions (such as the introduction of a situation-specific conversation pattern, the indication and length of concluding remarks, and the use of argument/counterargument)—are all subject to culture-bound conventions (Clyne, 1994).

At a micro level this is clearly illustrated in the routines of turn taking. Turn-taking routines differ across cultures. Helmolt (1997), for instance, shows that Germans speak with fewer overlaps than the French, and that long phases of simultaneous speaking and listening are common in monocultural French situations. Therefore, when French people apply their rules of turn taking and start speaking as soon as they believe they have understood what their German conversation partners are trying to say, many Germans will be frustrated and stop in the middle of their turn rather than completing their contribution (fading out). This reaction can be explained by the observation that in German interruptions are mostly caused by dissent (Helmolt, 1997), whereas in French interruptions are more often of an affirmative nature. Even the ways of defending a turn follows culture-specific rules (using loudness and/ or acceleration).

The presentation of arguments also follows culturally differenti- ated rules. The French tend to notice that many Germans attempt to support their statements with detailed background information and facts. From a French point of view, Germans formulate their statements with too much complexity and detail, so that the impli- cations of their statements become clear only at the end of their contribution; all the while, the French will be waiting impatiently for the Germans to get to the heart of the problem. In contrast, German conversation partners are likely to be irritated by the French style of talking, with their references to authority figures, their tangential topics and associations, and their play on words.

A macro sequence such as working one's way through an agenda also seems to follow culture-specific rules. In dealing with Germans, Spanish managers stress that they are not used to putting points in the agenda to rest once they have been discussed, without being able to go back to them or to (heaven forbid!) question their content anew (Herbrich, personal communication, 1992).

Topics

Different cultures have specific rules for the choice of topics. These have to do with which topics are considered taboo (Schröder, 1997), and at which point others can be chosen in certain situations (Hall, 1976; Ting-Toomey, 1988). For example, Germans are amazed by the way in which some North Americans tend to integrate their own therapy experiences into an informal conversation with apparent ease. In contrast, U.S. professionals find that Germans will frequently in- troduce political topics into situations that are rather private and informal and discuss them fervently with a considerable amount of disagreement. Such behavior seems strange to outsiders, given the perceived relations among the conversation partners.

Directness

Comparative studies (e.g., between Germans and Swedes) may reveal that German speakers are direct and Swedish speakers are indirect in expressing their communicative intentions. However, most comparative approaches fail to mention that such statements must be seen in relative terms, because, for example, a number of Asian speakers would describe the Swedes as being very direct. To be more precise, the statement should be as follows: Compared to many Germans, many Swedish speakers are less direct in express- ing their communicative intentions. This does not mean that their intentions are not expressed clearly enough, but simply that they make use of certain conventionalized contextualizers (Gumperz, 1992), which speakers from the same culture can as a rule easily interpret as indicators of these intentions. Communication is severely impeded if, as a German, one is used to receiving more explicit contextual clues, or if, as a nonnative speaker of Swedish, one is not able to fully and correctly interpret these contextualizers.

For example, many foreign businesspeople find the German way of expressing disagreement explicitly disquieting. French businessmen might criticize Germans for not making enough of an effort to phrase disagreements in a form more acceptable to the French; for example, by making use of modals or subjunctive phrases and particles instead of using "opposition formats" (Kotthoff, 1989). In German these formats, where the previous speaker's words are quoted in a negation construction (e.g., "By no means can we allow three monthly payments!"), represent a preferred way of showing disagreement. Participants from cultures preferring more indirect means of expressing their intention normally react to such provokingly expressed viewpoints by temporarily or even completely retreating from the situation.

Directness and indirectness are also related to quantity: Minutely detailed agreements have a form of explicitness that some cultures consider excessive and sometimes even insulting. The French notice, for example, how very precise work instructions are within German companies. To them this form of instruction implicitly questions their professional competence. An important and culturally difficult way to express meaning in an indirect way is the use of allusions, a technique currently under investigation (Schegloff, 1996).

Register

Register is probably the most complicated category of interaction in intercultural situations. Register denotes functional varieties of speech; that is, alternative formulations that interactors use depending on the situation (from very ritualized to informal), the status of the person being addressed, the age of those present, their rank, their gender, and the degree of formality or informality chosen by the coparticipants.

In general, all participants will attempt to take these six features of register into account and formulate their utterances appropriately. The choice of register constitutes the situation (How informal or formal do I conceive the situation to be?) and defines or confirms the relationships (How status or person related do I construct the situation? What relationships between persons and roles do I assume or plan?).

The understanding and use of register is particularly important in first encounters. They either take into account existing relations of status and power or are used to lay a claim to these. For example, Germans are often surprised when an employee of a French firm is introduced, "Et ça c'est Moinier, il travaille déjà depuis 5 ans chez nous" [And this is Moinier, he has already been working with us for five years]. Such forms of address without Mr., Ms., or Mrs. in German express a demeaning colloquial register not suitable to the professional context. In French companies, however, such forms are commonly used for reference and sometimes as a form of address.

Germans particularly struggle to decide which form of "you" they should use in professional intercultural situations: the familiar "Du" or the formal "Sie." While some have no problem adapting to the practice used abroad of addressing colleagues with the familiar "you" plus first name, problems arise as soon as German colleagues or superiors arrive who at home are addressed with the distance-keeping "Sie" (an issue they cannot hide from their U.S. colleagues unless they resort to English, which does not distinguish forms of "you").[2] There are many questions arising in this context: Which rules of register and therefore which relation definition should be applied in the German–U.S. context? What consequences might the choice of "you" and first name have for further work relations back home?

Individuals interacting with people from other cultures not only struggle to recognize differences in register, but also try hard to figure out its role and responsibility in their interactions: How are small-talk sequences marked linguistically? When and how can deformalization take place (i.e., moving from a socially defined and ritualized situational frame to one that is primarily constituted by the individuals)? How can or should one move on to business matters and which register is suitable for that?

Paraverbal and Nonverbal Factors

Cultures are clearly distinctive in their paraverbal and nonverbal conventions. They vary in paraverbal factors such as the speakers' rhythm, volume, word and sentence stress, speech rate, and intonation or division (number and length of pauses). German and French speakers prefer different rules for the regulation of turn taking in group meetings (team discussions): Germans will continue speaking with a loud volume to keep and defend their "turn" (Helmolt, 1997), while the French increase their speech rates to signal they want to continue. Such paraverbal factors of interaction have rightfully moved into the range of interest of linguistic investigations of conversation (Selting, 1992) in recent years. Their influence on the course of interaction is manifold and certainly remains underestimated to date.

Possibly even more important than messages conveyed by words are nonverbal messages imparted by facial expressions, gestures, degree of proximity, or eye contact. A general rule of communication seems to be that nonverbal forms of expression are taken more seriously than verbal ones. However, since the actual form of expression of nonverbal messages differs from one culture to another, we should point out the danger of misinterpretations.

Misinterpretations of nonverbal messages come from two sources (Bonvillain, 1997). First, a nonverbal gesture used by individuals from one culture is absent from the repertoire of individuals from another culture, who either do not notice the sign or recognize they do not know what it means. Second, a nonverbal gesture carries different meanings in different cultures. Participants recognize the gesture but do not realize that they are misinterpreting its intended meaning.

For example, pointing frequently leads to misunderstandings in intercultural situations because pointing rules are very different but at the same time have a guiding role within an interaction (Poyatos, 1983). In Germany it is customary to point to objects or persons with your arm or index finger, while people in other cultures will move their chin forward, roll their eyes, or move their heads to indicate the equivalent (see also Apeltauer, 1997).

In addition, cultures differ in their customary degree of proximity (i.e., the physical distance considered "normal" between two human beings and the spatial arrangement of objects in general) (Hall, 1976). How sensitively we react to an invasion of our imagined personal space and how differently it is defined from culture to culture can even be seen in experiments, where, for example, someone takes a seat "too close" to an uninitiated individual or moves closer to someone while speaking than that coparticipant is used to.

Differences in speaking proximity can create little "dances" as conversationalists adjust to the distance set by their partners and by the discomfort they feel as a result. At receptions in Italy some Germans feel that they are constantly "in reverse" (i.e., backing away from their Italian conversation partners). Naturally, the Italians frequently react by moving closer again to reach the proximity normal for them.

Summary

This linguistic framework represents the places where misinterpretation, misunderstanding, and miscommunication begin. It also represents a starting point for analyzing those critical incidents and reaching out to close the miscommunication gap. When they encounter moments where they do not know which intentions their coparticipants are expressing, global leaders can explore whether speech acts, social meaning, conventions of discourse, choices of topics, directness, register, and paraverbal and nonverbal factors provide a plausible explanation for their confusion and misinterpretation of their partners' intentions.

IMPLICATIONS OF LINGUISTIC ANALYSIS FOR GLOBAL LEADERS

Morrison (in press) reviews the literature on global leadership and summarizes the results of an extensive investigation into the characteristics of global leaders (Black, Morrison, & Gregersen, 1999). Based on his analysis, he suggests that global leaders need to develop three competencies:

1. Exhibiting character by developing close relationships and demonstrating integrity with individuals outside the organization and coworkers inside the organization.
2. Demonstrating savvy in building and negotiating successful global business ventures.
3. Embracing duality by managing uncertainty and balancing global and local pressures.

Finally, he asserts that across all three competencies global leaders need to exhibit a key ability: inquisitiveness.

Most global leaders recognize the need to build awareness of language (including grammar and vocabulary) and culture in order to effectively lead global corporate enterprises. But we propose that truly effective global leaders will demonstrate extraordinary awareness of communication and cultural issues as they lead their enterprises. In particular, we propose that they will try to determine how, in different cultures, the specific expressions for effectively exhibiting character, for demonstrating savvy, for embracing duality, and for practicing inquisitiveness vary. The following case illustrates our points:

Dr. Greiner has just been appointed department head in a German company's branch office in Seoul, Korea. After he arrives, he calls his first team meeting. He prepared questions in advance to help him get oriented to the work at that branch, to gather important information, and, at the same time, to begin to "socialize" with his future colleagues. However, not very long into the meeting, he realizes that his Korean colleagues' answers are very vague. Indeed, they seem to become increasingly vague and even evasive the more precisely he phrases his questions. To ensure that they understand his English, he repeats his questions whenever the answers are provided reluctantly. He smiles and attempts to make eye contact. Finally, he states that if his colleagues have any questions, he would be very happy to answer them. But there are none. After the meeting he does not know much more than he did before and is quite irritated. He assumes they have hidden agendas and want something from him. He resolves to gather some of the needed information in formal and informal face-to-face conversations (in his office and also at the lunch table) and to phrase his questions even more precisely at the next meeting.

Many leaders would, like Dr. Greiner, attempt to find culturally oriented explanations and solutions to their experience; however, the results would be limited. We propose that a truly effective leader will also generate hypotheses about the different linguistic conventions that might explain the situation. A linguistic analysis would yield a number of additional hypotheses. For example, relying on a linguistically based explanation of directness and indirectness, leaders might consider that the Korean colleagues are giving contextualized answers to the questions. However, they would note that Dr. Greiner seems to be misinterpreting these context-sensitive statements as vague even though, according to Korean conventions, they are quite clear. Therefore, he cannot understand why he was not provided with concrete information.

Linguistically sensitive leaders might also propose that speech acts explain the situation. They might hypothesize that Dr. Greiner posed questions in a way that seemed to be calling for a decision or yes/no response without realizing that in a high-context culture (Hall, 1976) like Korea, such questions may be seen as requiring a face-threatening commitment that the Koreans want to avoid.

Third, they could propose that Dr. Greiner was not introduced according to Korean discourse conventions. Because proper introductions may be an important prerequisite for communication in first-contact situations, the Koreans may have been hesitant to respond to his questions.

Relying on the linguistic perspective of nonverbal communication, leaders might contemplate that Dr. Greiner wrongly interpreted his colleagues' lowered eyes as a sign of embarrassment or ignorance. He may not have recognized it as a gesture of politeness towards their superior.

Global leaders would also benefit from analyzing Dr. Geiner's reactions to the Korean's responses using a linguistic–interactionist point of view. Considering the effects of foreign behavior on the situation and relying on the linguistic notion of speech acts, they might propose that Dr. Greiner's reaction to his interpretation of the Korean answers of asking even more concrete decision questions was unsuitable for the situation. Thereby, he provoked his colleagues to give even vaguer answers and avoid eye contact more strongly, interactively causing even more misunderstanding.

In addition, they may analyze the nonverbal communication, noting that Dr. Greiner reacted to the Koreans' convention of avoidance of eye contact by trying even harder to obtain it. Thereby, he might have provoked an even more intense avoidance of eye contact.

Finally, linguistically savvy leaders would analyze the conventions of discourse and observe that Dr. Greiner caused further insecurity in the response behavior of his coparticipants by repeating questions that had been understood and even answered already.

This analysis illustrates how important it is to come up with multiple explanations for reconstructed critical incidents (regardless of whether they are personal experiences or documented in the literature). All the explanatory hypotheses have the potential of being accurate, for the given case study as well as for other German–Korean or U.S.–Korean interactions.

Exhibiting Character

Morrison (in press) says that exhibiting character includes connecting emotionally with people, and "in connecting emotionally, global leaders overcome the very real barriers to communication that separate people within and across cultures and vast geographic distances." Certainly, the case presented demonstrates that the way people connect personally and how they demonstrate "connecting emotionally with others" underlies different linguistic and culturally determined conventions. Dr. Greiner exhibits character in his behavior; that is, calling for and conducting his first meeting as the actual leader of the company, gathering relevant information, and smiling to his colleagues, combined with the democratic attempt to be ready to answer any questions. But because of other communication conventions, he fails, looking almost like a fool in the eyes of his Korean colleagues because he was too direct in a face-threatening way, trying to destroy the equilibrium of the group in questioning its individual members, and at the same time he demonstrated weak leadership in asking questions instead of giving answers.

As they develop their own personal linguistic awareness, global leaders will need to determine, by using the framework of linguistic analysis as outlined in the previous section, how exactly the emotional-connection process is performed cross-culturally and how the ways of exhibiting character in one's own culture are received and interpreted in others.

Demonstrating Savvy

Morrison (in press) also asserts that global leaders require organization savvy to effectively capture global business opportunities. Leaders with savvy can identify organizational resources (including their human resources) and can tap and mobilize their managers and staff to work for the success of the organization. Obviously, Dr. Greiner attempted to show the savvy that had made him so successful in Germany. But because the interpersonal interactions that stimulate these processes are highly culture bound, as a global leader he needed instead to direct those interactions consciously, taking into consideration the cultural and linguistic preferences of his staff and subordinates.

In addition, leaders need to develop others' linguistic awareness both personally and strategically. Periodically and on a meta-communicative level, global leaders need to model and coach linguistic and culture awareness for their managers and staff: As they practice their linguistic awareness of cultures, they occasionally need to make their framework and processes explicit (e.g., in cooperation with experienced intercultural trainers) (Landis & Bhagat, 1996). They may need to act as a communication facilitator or counselor to help others analyze their own culture-sensitive conventions. Strategically, they need to use the tools of human resource professionals to build skills in linguistic awareness throughout the organization. For example, they could utilize selection instruments (e.g., interview questions or personality tests) that measure inquisitiveness, and develop intercultural training programs that teach the linguistic framework and facilitate the development of linguistic-analysis skills.

Embracing Duality

Finally, global leaders need to embrace duality, recognizing the ongoing tensions and complexities of uncertainty, fast-paced change, and conflicting global and local requirements (Morrison, in press). In the case presented, much of the ambiguity stems from different linguistic conventions: The Western Dr. Greiner has to accept that his subordinates normally would demonstrate a cooperative behavior (at least there was no reason for not cooperating), but actually did not in avoiding his questions and nonverbal contacts. And he has to realize that his Korean subordinates' responses to him were reactions to his nonstandard behavior as a leader and to the way he had shown the commonly accepted key competence of global leaders, inquisiveness.

Rather than accepting or tolerating the culturally created tensions and complexities in international cooperations, effective global leaders actively manage the conflicts (Black, Morrison et al., 1999). In managerial terms, they have to develop, manage, and reinforce an organizational culture that all members of the organization share. In linguistic terms, they should mediate and mold the creation of a multicultural speech community that supercedes the natural speech communities of all the members of their organization.

As participant observers, global leaders should self-consciously watch the interactions (Agar, 1994) and try to understand what exactly had been done by what is said. As they analyze the observations and responses, they should look for similarities and differences and identify situationally relevant patterns in the communication. From these patterns they can build new expectations of how to communicate in this context with this person, thereby enhancing their communicative competence (Hymes, 1974).

But still, to date much of the empirical research has relied on interviews or surveys of managers and executives. Managers who are linguistically ignorant and cannot differentiate between different cultural communication conventions regularly run into intercultural and communication difficulties themselves and systematically report situations that are heavily biased by their inability to correctly interpret the communication and intentions of culturally different speakers resulting in episodes like the case presented. Their data may be highly reliable, consistently reflecting the specific cultural orientations of German, U.S., or Korean expatriates, but contain so much systematic error variance that the validity of their data and conclusions is suspect. Researchers who wish to continue to query executives and managers, therefore, need to become linguistically aware themselves, designing research that investigates intercultural communication and linguistic issues and probing for ways to identify and remove the systematic bias of linguistic ignorance.

Our main implication for research comes in the form of a caution. If linguistic awareness of cultures is as important to intercultural communication as we have argued and if global leaders to date have been as linguistically unaware as we have feared, then we are in considerable danger of basing research conclusions on systematically biased data (for reported episodes without mentioning the relativity of cultural-specific human actions and reactions, see Müller, 1995a).

NOTES

1. Their acceptance presupposes culture-specific conditions, such as "I, as a person, am willing and physically able to do X at the specified time" (where my conversation partner considers X to be a positive event), and adds culture-bound implications such as "If I can't make it, I will let my 'partner' know and provide an acceptable explanation as to why I can't come."

2. A similar situation is described and analyzed in Speicher (1985).

14

Strategic Repatriation Policies to Enhance Global Leadership Development

Paula M. Caligiuri and Mila Lazarova

This chapter will examine the strategic global HR practices for repatriating employees after their global assignments. In particular, it will examine best practices against the contrasting benefits and concerns of repatriation, for both organizations and employees. Most multinational companies would state that having an increase in global competence is the greatest benefit of successful repatriation. In stark contrast, most MNCs would also state that the low retention rate of global assignees upon repatriation is their greatest concern. This contrast creates the elusive and yet very common repatriation problem for MNCs. In this chapter we will discuss the four reasons for the repatriation problem and offer a series of strategic best practices to address each. The four reasons addressed are (1) MNCs often do not integrate selection, performance management, and repatriation systems into one strategic process when it is necessary; (2) some turnover upon repatriation is functional, and possibly even strategic; (3) MNCs tend to treat all global assignments as if they had the same strategic objective, when they do not; and (4) MNCs believe that all global assignees intend to have long-term careers with the MNC, when they do not. We also provide proactive repatriation practices for developing a comprehensive strategic-repatriation system.

BENEFITS AND CONCERNS
OF REPATRIATION TO THE MNC

Benefits to the MNC

The recent past has seen an accelerated interest in the strategic role of HR on firm performance (Becker & Huselid, 1998; Burack, Burack, Miller, & Morgan, 1994; Huselid, 1995; Lengnick-Hall & Lengnick-Hall, 1998). Strategic human resources is "the pattern of planned human resource deployments and activities intended to enable an organization to achieve its goals" (Wright & McMahan, 1992, 298). Strategic human resources is concerned with the integration of the human resource function in the strategic planning of the organization and, more specifically, with aligning HR practices horizontally (by coordination and congruence among the various HRM practices) and vertically (by linking the HRM practices with the strategic management process; Wright & McMahan, 1992).

Researchers in the area of global HR have also followed this trend, investigating the impact of global HR practices on the MNC's bottom line. A recent large-scale study by Stroh and Caligiuri (1998) examined the effectiveness of certain guiding global HR principles on the organization's bottom line. Their study revealed that "developing leadership through developmental cross-cultural assignments" was among the top five organizationwide practices affecting the effectiveness of the MNC. In short, the results of the study suggest that a positive relationship exists between the MNCs' bottom-line financial success and the MNCs' ability to successfully repatriate and utilize the global leadership competencies of their global assignees.

Concerns for the MNC

The Stroh and Caligiuri (1998) study suggests a strong strategic motivation for MNCs to develop successful repatriation programs. The benefit of repatriation, however, needs to be interpreted in light of the repatriation reality in many MNCs: Many MNCs have difficulty retaining their employees upon repatriation. Past research suggests that between 20 and 25 percent of repatriated employees leave their firms within a year after returning to the United States (Black, Gregersen, & Mendenhall, 1992a, 1992b; O'Boyle, 1989). Some companies have reported losing between 40 and 55 percent of their repatriates through voluntary turnover within three years after repatriation. Other studies suggest that 74 percent of repatriates did not expect to be working for the same company within one year after returning to their home country, 42 percent had seriously considered leaving their companies after repatriation, and 26 percent had been actively searching for alternative employment (Black et al., 1992a). The reasons for this high turnover rate among repatriates will be discussed later.

To better understand the reasons for this repatriation problem, it is important to understand why this problem is a concern for MNCs. The repatriation problem presents two key concerns for MNCs: They either lose a human-capital investment that was needed internally or they lose a human-capital investment to a competitor, making their competition stronger. Consistent with Stroh and Caligiuri's (1998) findings, the first concern suggests that the newly developed global skills are needed within the MNC as a source of competitive advantage. The second suggests that the newly developed global skills may or may not be needed within the MNC, but losing repatriates to the competition produces an external competitive risk. While past discussions have focused on only the former concern, a truly strategic repatriation policy will need to consider the latter as well.

BENEFITS AND CONCERNS
OF REPATRIATION FOR THE INDIVIDUAL

Benefits to the Individual

While strategically beneficial for the MNC, repatriation is also beneficial for individuals who have been on a global assignment, both personally and professionally. Personally, repatriates report that they are more open minded and flexible after they come back. They have acquired and expanded an ability to adapt to foreign environments and tolerate ambiguity. Global assignees report that they develop an appreciation for new things, become culturally sensitive, and learn to respect values and customs different from their own (Adler, 1997c; Osland, 1995).

Repatriation also has professional benefits. Although professional repatriation concerns still exist, repatriates today describe their global assignments as having a more positive influence on their careers as a whole (Tung, 1998). From a professional standpoint, the majority of today's global assignees report that they have developed valuable skills through their international experiences (Tung, 1998), and that these newly developed skills greatly enhance their expertise in both the domestic and the international context (Adler, 1981, 1997c; Baughn, 1995; Black et al., 1992a; Napier & Peterson, 1991).

Concerns for the Individual

While the experience of a global assignment is viewed positively by most repatriates, the experience does come with some costs. From the perspective of the individual global assignee, repatriation is associated with several concerns, both personal and professional. From a personal perspective, the majority of repatriates experience "reverse culture shock." Some suggest that coming home is more emotionally stressful than going abroad (Adler, 1981, 1997c; Baughn, 1995). For instance, global assignees may be expecting everything they encounter in their host country to be different from their home country. When going home, however, most repatriates expect that nothing would have changed. The latter expectation is generally wrong: The political, economic, social, and cultural climate has changed. Moreover, the expatriates themselves have changed, which, in turn, produces an even wider gap between repatriates' expectations and their reality upon return (Adler, 1981, 1997c; Black et al., 1992a; Shilling, 1993). In addition to the personal adjustment problems the expatriate is experiencing, he or she may also have family members going through the same difficult readjustment period. Research has suggested that expatriates' and spouses' repatriation adjustments are significantly correlated (Black & Gregersen, 1991b). These family adjustment difficulties usually magnify the problems repatriates face upon return (Harvey, 1982, 1989).

Several other factors related to the repatriates' sudden change in lifestyles create personal concerns upon repatriation. For example, repatriates may experience cash-flow or disposable-income problems, housing problems, and other problems associated with loss of social status and lifestyle changes (Harvey, 1982; Kendall, 1981). While on assignment many expatriates usually receive generous financial allowances to accommodate the "hardships" of living away from home, allowing them live in excellent housing conditions and to enjoy a relatively more affluent way of life while they are abroad (Black et al., 1992b; Harvey, 1982, 1989; Kendall, 1981; Stroh, Gregersen, & Black, 1998). While on global assignment expatriates are usually occupying high-level positions in a host national subsidiary and have a unique social status that gives them prominence in both the local community and at work (Black & Gregersen, 1991b; Engen, 1995; Gomez-Mejia & Balkin, 1987; Kendall, 1981). It is difficult for global assignees when these are taken away upon repatriation. In addition to the loss of financial and social status, repatriates soon learn that others' interest in their international experience fades fairly quickly, and that they no longer hold any special social position (Black et al., 1992a; Gregersen & Black, 1995; Kendall, 1981; Shilling, 1993).

Repatriates describe their global assignments as career enhancing (Tung, 1998); however, the career enhancement may often be realized only by finding a position with another company. In short, repatriates' newly developed global skills may not be needed in the organizations sending them on global assignment. A recent study indicated that less than 40 percent of repatriates had the opportunity to utilize their international experience upon returning home (Black et al., 1992a). Often, due to poor career planning, repatriates are placed in a "holding pattern," and are assigned jobs that are available without regard to the individuals' abilities, qualifications, and needs (Baughn, 1995; Harvey, 1982, 1989). Many repatriates perceive their new jobs at home as lacking in autonomy, authority, and significance compared to their global assignments (Black et al., 1992a; Gomez-Mejia & Balkin, 1987; Harvey, 1982; Kendall, 1981). Not surprisingly, many repatriates report dissatisfaction with the repatriation process (Adler, 1997c; Baughn, 1995; Black et al., 1992a, 1992b; Gomez-Mejia & Balkin, 1987; Harvey, 1989; O'Boyle, 1989; Stroh et al., 1998).

THE DISCONNECT BETWEEN THE BENEFITS AND CONCERNS OF REPATRIATION

While the benefits of global assignments for both MNCs and individuals are great, the concerns associated with repatriation pose a formidable challenge for global HR. Clearly, the greatest concern is the disconnect between the desired state and the reality of repatriation in most MNCs: In the desired state, the competencies the global assignees have developed (Adler, 1997c; Tung, 1998) are the competencies the MNCs need their leaders to possess to be more competitive in the global market (Stroh & Caligiuri, 1998). In reality (at least for now), the competencies the global assignees have developed are indeed valuable—but not immediately relevant in the MNC. This reality, compounded with the personal and professional problems associated with repatriation, has caused the high rate of turnover among repatriates.

The overarching concern is that MNCs tend to be reactive, rather than strategic, in their approach to solving this repatriate turnover problem. As observed in the previous section, we believe that the repatriation problem is a strategic one. The solution, likewise, must be strategic. The following section will identify the four reasons for the repatriation problem, and offer a series of strategic best practices to address each. The section will also provide a comprehensive list of proactive practices to be included in a strategic global assignment program.

Integration Needed among Selection, Performance Management, and Repatriation Systems

The low retention rates of repatriates are not surprising given that global assignments generally have not been viewed by companies as a component in employees' career development. A study of HR managers from fifty-six U.S.–based MNCs found that 65 percent of the HR managers said that their employees' global assignments were not integrated into their overall career planning, and 56 percent said that a global assignment was either detrimental or immaterial to one's career (O'Boyle, 1989). The 1994 Global Survey Relocation Report found that repatriation support programs offered by companies typically do not include long-term career-development plans. While 97 percent of the U.S.–based MNCs in the survey offer to pay for the return shipment of household goods, only 31 percent offer any expatriate career-development assistance (Windham International & National Foreign Trade Council, 1994). This lack of strategic integration seems to be a concern not limited to U.S.–based MNCs. A 1996 repatriation report found that only 13 percent of U.S.–based companies, 22 percent U.K.-based companies, and 46 percent of continental European-based MNCs plan for their global assignees' return (Conference Board, 1996).

Recommendations for Practice

While these surveys and many others bemoan the need to integrate the skills acquired by the global assignee upon repatriation, little has been done to examine the entire strategic global assignment process, including selection, performance management, and repatriation. The career-development concern cannot be addressed by a repatriation system in isolation. Rather, it needs to be integrated into all three processes. To be truly strategic, an MNC's purpose for selecting an individual for a global assignments should be a part of a greater developmental career path. MNCs should assess expatriates' performance on the basis of desired developmental competencies. It follows that MNCs could then repatriate employees with their greater career development in mind.

Some Turnover upon Repatriation Is Functional

In a survey of personnel managers, almost half of the respondents state that their repatriates are not guaranteed jobs within the company upon return (O'Boyle, 1989), and 45 percent viewed returning expatriates as a problem because they considered them "hard to fit back into the company" (p. B1). Another study found that 77 percent of U.S. repatriates were demoted to a lower-level position than they had held during their global assignment (Black et al., 1992a). As discussed in the previous section, one explanation for this is the lack of strategic integration of the global assignment process. Another, more straightforward explanation is that not all global assignments have a strategic purpose. It is the reality that some MNCs do not want or need all of their global assignees back. The global competencies gained on assignment, in some cases, are needed only for the global assignment and are not needed upon repatriation. While the subsequent section will discuss different types of global assignments and how repatriation will differ accordingly, this section was simply intended to address the issue that some repatriate turnover is, in fact, strategic.

Recommendations for Practice

Clearly the best recommendation for building a strategic repatriation system is honesty. If an individual will truly not be needed upon repatriation, then they must be given a realistic preview of the global assignment process, stating the "no guarantee" reality of the position.

Different Global Assignments Will Have Different Repatriation Strategies

As addressed in the previous section, not all global assignees are created or intended to be equal in terms of their strategic significance to the organization. While researchers have outlined the different categories of global assignments (Caligiuri, 1998; Hays, 1974; Oddou, 1991), recommendations for repatriation simply lump all global assignees into a single category. This is simply unrealistic in a typically complex MNC with many global assignees serving many different purposes. This section will disentangle the categories of global assignments and then describe how strategic repatriation strategies differ within each category.

A global assignment is a job context, not a job description. Thus, the requirements needed for the successful completion of the assignment, the goals of the assignment (both functional and developmental), and the strategic need for the global assignee's competencies upon repatriation (either present or acquired) will differ depending on the type of assignment. Caligiuri (1998) has suggested the classification of global assignments into four categories: (1) technical, (2) developmental/high potential, (3) strategic/executive, and (4) functional/tactical. The classification was proposed within the framework of expatriate performance evaluation, and is a useful foundation for a discussion of repatriation policies and practices of MNCs. Each category of global assignment will be described briefly in the following section, with suggestions for repatriation. In addition to the recommendations for each individual category, this chapter will also offer a comprehensive list of proactive repatriation practices that apply to all categories of global assignees.

Technical Assignments

This type of assignment is becoming increasingly more common as organizations are expanding their technical expertise worldwide. When technical skills do not exist in one geographic region, a global assignment may be necessary to fill a technical need. The typical technical assignment is similar in content to the assignee's domestic position. Specifically, these technical assignees are in an organizational setting fairly typical to the setting of the home country. Many of the global assignees on technical assignments will describe their work experience as "quite similar" to what they were doing back home. It is not expected that these global assignees will have significant interactions with the host nationals working at the subsidiary location, and those interactions that inevitably occur will not greatly affect the outcome of the assignment. In other words, the person is being sent for his or her technical skills. It is those technical skills that will determine the outcome of the assignment. These assignments include technicians at an oil refinery, systems engineers on continuation client site, systems analysts interfacing with a computer system, and the like.

In order for repatriation strategies to be effective, organizations have to consider their needs for these individuals' technical skills after the assignment is completed. In most MNCs these technical experts are needed throughout the organization and are in relatively high demand. However, it may not always be the case that these expatriates' technical skills are needed back in the home country. Sometimes technical experts may rotate from host country to host country, going where their technical skills are needed. In either case, a repatriation system for these assignees would assess technical skills and determine where the skills are needed most in the organization. In some MNCs technical experts are needed only for a fixed period of time in the host country to complete a given project. These expatriates are "contract assignees." MNCs hire these assignees solely to do the job. Once the job is completed, the employment contract with the MNC is over.

Developmental/High Potential Assignments

For some MNCs, sending expatriates abroad for two or more years to develop global competencies is consistent with their overall strategic human resource plan. Most organizations that utilize this type of global assignments do this within the context of their managerial-development program. These programs are often rotational, with one of the rotations being in another country. While on this type or assignment, the goal is individual development.

These developmental rotational assignments often have a very structured series of experiences. Given the structured nature of these assignments for the repatriates, their next assignment is often very clear and known well in advance of the completion of the global assignment. Repatriation, in this case, is rather straightforward and predetermined by the rotations within the leadership-development program.

Strategic/Executive Assignments

Many MNCs, when asked to analyze their ideal staffing strategy for global assignments, will identify the strategic/executive assignment as the ideal. These strategic assignments are usually filled by individuals who are being developed for high-level management positions in the future. The purpose of these assignments tend to be high profile (e.g., general managers, vice presidents) and the experience is viewed as both developmental and strategic. Thus, these individuals are not sent solely for developmental assignments; rather, they are there to fill a specific need in the organization. These global assignees are the core "critical" group of assignees. They may have the task of entering a new market, developing a country base in a new area, being the general manager of a joint venture, or the like. An inpatriate assignment, where high-profile managers from other countries take a global assignment in the headquarters country, is an example of a strategic assignment (Black et al., 1992a; Kobrin, 1988).

For these individuals, repatriation is often well thought out and a part of the overall succession-planning initiative of the organization. In many cases these expatriates are very well aware that they are being groomed for a given position. An important aspect of the repatriation process will be to ensure that the position for which these individuals are being groomed will actually utilize their developed global skills. Often considered the highest human-capital investment for MNCs, companies must ensure that these individuals have the appropriate levels of autonomy and job discretion upon repatriation. Turnover upon repatriation among this category of assignee is seriously detrimental to the strategic management of a MNC's human capital.

Functional/Tactical Assignments

The functional/tactical assignment is similar to the technical assignment with one distinct difference: Significant interactions with host nationals are necessary in order for the assignment to be deemed successful. As with the technical assignment, a person will be sent to fill a technical or managerial gap in a given host country. While they are there they will need to interact with host nationals in order for the assignment to be deemed successful. This type of global assignment is the most common global assignment (Windham International & National Foreign Trade Council, 1994).

These assignees are sent to fill a technical need. However, once they are there they realize that cross-cultural skills are needed in order to be successful. If the global skills are an afterthought to the assignment, global assignees are possibly being sent without the skills necessary to be successful on the job (Black et al., 1992a, 1992b). This tends to be an oversight in selection.

In addition to selection, this category of assignees poses the greatest challenge for MNCs in terms of retention upon repatriation. Given that intercultural communication and effectiveness is needed to successfully complete one's global assignment, these functional/tactical assignments have an unintended developmental component. The global assignees within this category are the ones most likely to turn over upon repatriation, because they are the ones who have developed new international skills and competencies that were not needed (or intended in the first place). As such, the global assignees within this category are the ones most likely to feel unfulfilled upon repatriation.

As a part of their repatriation strategy, MNCs need to first consider whether the skills and competencies are truly needed within the organization upon repatriation. If the skills and competencies are needed, MNCs should assess (via a performance-management system) the additional developmental skills gained during the global assignment. These should be acknowledged and rewarded, and considered as a part of the MNC's human-capital investment. Where possible, these skills should be utilized in the domestic position.

If the skills and competencies of repatriates are not needed, then the repatriates should be given the realistic expectation prior to accepting the global assignment. In some cases, MNCs will hire more contract assignees to fill these functional positions. As the following section suggests, some individuals are very attracted to these contract assignments, because they are consistent with their overall career goals.

Individuals' Career Motivations Differ

While the repatriation "problem" may be a very strategic concern for MNCs, organizations should expect some natural attrition, as they would from any other "high-demand" professional. In some cases, even with the best possible repatriation program, MNCs will not be able to retain certain repatriates. Harvey (1982) found that many returnees may have better career opportunities in multinational companies other than the company that sent them on the global assignment. He suggested that in such cases many repatriates would be likely to leave for "both motivational and monetary reasons" (p. 54). As with other individual career decisions, rather than staying, some repatriates may choose to leave for a better job offer elsewhere and do not perceive the organizational exit (initiated by them) as a negative job move.

Clearly, international experience is a competitive asset that may enhance the opportunities for future career advancement, even though this may take place in another company. Given that international experience is an asset in today's job market, MNCs are often making their repatriates more valuable for the external labor market. A 1998 study of 409 expatriates on assignment to fifty-one countries found that most expatriates overwhelmingly agree that the global assignment had "a positive impact upon subsequent career advancement either in the current organization or elsewhere" (Tung, 1998, 129). In addition, most of the expatriates in the sample reported that an international assignment presented them with an opportunity to acquire skills and expertise usually not available at home.

Tung's (1998) study suggests that "boundaryless" careers are becoming the pattern for international assignees—as with other high-demand professionals (such as information-technology [IT] engineers). A boundaryless career assumes that individuals will move from one company to another to pursue the best opportunities for their own professional development. Recently, authors have suggested that professionals may accept global assignments to gain the additional skills and experience they perceive to be valuable for their advancement in their career, not in their company (Inkson, Pringle, Arthur, & Barry, 1997; Tung, 1998).

This trend is even more problematic in countries with a tight job market. In the United States there is increased "job-hopping" and shorter average tenure (in some cases of highly valued professionals only amounting to several months). Data from the United States suggest that in the early 1970s a manager worked for one or two companies in his or her entire career. The U.S. managers of today are more likely to hold seven to ten jobs in their lifetimes (Cascio, 1993; Kransdorrf, 1997). The average tenure for the managers has also been dropping continuously. In some professions (e.g., accounting and auditing), typical tenure ranges from three to six months (Grossman, 1998). Among information-technology managers, the turnover rate is 15.5 percent for twelve months (Cone, 1996). Given these trends among managers and technical professionals, it is not surprising that some repatriates are interested in changing companies after their global assignment is completed.

Recommendations for Practice

It is a challenge for MNCs to retain their global leaders who are in high demand and have a high internal career motivation. Some recommendations may be borrowed from other industries, such as the information-technology industry, where the labor market has enabled IT professionals to job hop with relative ease. Studies of IT professionals suggest many ways to retain high-quality employees. These studies suggest the importance of recognition, encouragement, praise, and opportunities for professional growth (Grossman, 1998). Additional incentives, besides higher pay and competitive benefits, are suggested for high-potential professionals. These incentives include career development, training programs, promotions, better corporate communications, flexible staffing, and stock options (Comeau-Kirchner, 1999; Fryer, 1998).

PROACTIVE RECOMMENDATIONS
FOR STRATEGIC REPATRIATION

In addition to the practices already addressed, there are some proactive repatriation practices that have been found to be highly effective for successful repatriation. These practices are important from a strategic standpoint because they address the common concerns that most repatriating employees will face (e.g., financial, professional, and emotional concerns). Unlike the previous recommendations, these proactive strategies will apply to almost all repatriates and should be used in the context of a strategic repatriation system. There are eleven such practices:

1. Organizations should make an effort to manage expectations upon repatriation. This will be helpful in reducing the expatriate's ambiguity

while on assignment (Black, 1992; Conference Board, 1996; Hammer, Hart, & Rogan, 1998). Organizations should give detailed predeparture briefings before the expatriate leaves for his or her global assignment, detailing for the expatriate what to expect while on the assignment and what to expect upon return (Conference Board, 1996). For example, organizations can create accurate expectations prior to the assignment by using former repatriates to help train and brief future expatriates on what to expect (Conference Board, 1996).

2. Career planning is another critical function for retaining expatriates upon repatriation. Between six and twelve months before the end of the global assignment, MNCs should offer multiple reentry sessions or career-planning sessions to discuss the expatriate's concerns regarding repatriations; for example, career objectives and performance (Adler, 1981, 1997c; Black, 1992; Black et al., 1992a; Conference Board, 1996). The intention of these career-planning reentry sessions is to give the expatriate a sense of security regarding his or her future with the company. This planning may utilize the skills of a team, including HR, the sending manager, and the business-unit leader (Black et al., 1992a).

3. To reduce ambiguity about the expatriates' future, offer a written guarantee or repatriation agreement. This repatriation agreement outlines the type of position the expatriate will be placed in upon return from global assignment (Gomez-Mejia & Balkin, 1987).

4. One popular practice used in proactive repatriation systems is mentoring. Mentors keep the expatriate abreast of important occurrences while he or she is on global assignment and help the expatriate stay connected with the organization (Black et al., 1992b; Conference Board, 1996; Gomez-Mejia & Balkin, 1987; Napier & Peterson, 1991). A mentor also guides the expatriate's future career with the organization by being the expatriate's internal champion.

5. Organizations should offer a reorientation program to brief returning expatriates on the changes in the company, such as in policies, personnel, and strategy (Gomez-Mejia & Balkin, 1987; Harvey, 1982). This should be provided immediately upon return from the assignment, when the repatriate returns to work.

6. Repatriation training seminars should be offered to employees and their families. These repatriation training seminars will address expatriates' emotional concerns upon returning home (Black, 1992, 1994; Black et al., 1992a, 1992b; Conference Board, 1996; Hammer et al., 1998). This repatriation training should improve reentry adjustment. Examples of their concerns may include leaving their expatriate social lifestyle, their private schools, and so forth. Repatriation training may be provided through the company's preexisting international employee assistance program (Gomez-Mejia & Balkin, 1987).

7. Another recommendation is financial counseling and financial or tax assistance. This counseling helps repatriates adjust back to their lifestyles without the additional allowances of the expatriate position

(Gomez-Mejia & Balkin, 1987; Harvey, 1982; Kendall, 1981). For example, some organizations offer bridge loans, low-interest loans for the purchase of a house, or assistance with mortgages. Other organizations are willing to pay for private school back home to have educational continuity for the children of global assignees (Kendall, 1981; Napier & Peterson, 1991).

8. In addition to financial counseling, lifestyle counseling is also beneficial to employees and their families, as their lifestyles are likely to change dramatically when they return to their home countries (Black, 1994; Harvey, 1989; Kendall, 1981). For example, to try to encourage a continuity of lifestyle after the global assignment, the organization can pay for their repatriated families to join expatriate clubs, enter private schools, and so on upon return.

9. MNCs can also offer a repatriation adjustment period for the employees to reintegrate without added pressure from the organization (Harvey, 1989; Kendall, 1981). Given the pressures of repatriation both at home and at work, some organizations will reduce the repatriates' travel time, give more vacation time, and so forth.

10. While the expatriate is still on assignment, MNCs should offer opportunities for communication with their home office. For example, the expatriate could be offered extended home visits during which he or she is expected to be visible at the office (Black, 1994; Gomez-Mejia & Balkin, 1987; Gregersen & Stroh, 1997). Another possibility is to include the expatriate on e-mail memos, send them newsletters, encourage communication with colleagues and mentors back home to maintain his or her network, and so on (Adler, 1997c).

11. Organizations should show visible signs that they value the international experience (e.g., promoting the repatriate upon return, maintain position prestige and status, or additional compensation for completing the assignment). This will create the perception within the organization that global experience is beneficial for one's career (Adler, 1981, 1997c; Black et al., 1992a; Black, 1994; Gomez-Mejia & Balkin, 1987; Gregersen & Black, 1995). This will also help produce a culture in which global experience should not be disregarded as "different, and not relevant here" (Adler 1981, 1997c; Hammer et al., 1998).

Repatriation remains a high priority for global HR managers. This chapter suggests several reasons for the existence of the "repatriation problem" in MNCs. MNCs today will need to take a more strategic approach to the entire global assignment process. As such, MNCs will need to do a thorough needs assessment of the competencies and skills needed from their current and future workforce. When (and if) global assignees' developed or existing competencies and skills are needed, MNCs will need to develop repatriation systems that align the MNC's and the repatriate's interests, expectations, and competencies.

15

Conclusion: Future Issues in Global Leadership Development

Nancy J. Adler, Edwin L. Miller,
and Mary Ann Von Glinow

To conclude this volume, we asked three well-known and highly respected scholars and consultants from the field of international human resource management to briefly share their views on global leadership-development issues. They were asked to comment briefly regarding their thoughts, observations, and intuitive sense about the challenge of developing global leaders.

NANCY J. ADLER, McGILL UNIVERSITY

Historically, global leadership "that goes beyond the nation-state and seeks to address all human beings [has been] . . . the most important but rarest and most elusive, variety of leadership" (Gardner, 1995, 20). Today, however, the "rare" is becoming a necessity.

Although all too infrequently recognized as such, global leadership is not the same as domestic leadership (see Adler, 1997b; Boyacigiller & Adler, 1996; Bartlett & Ghoshal, 1989; Dorfman, 1996). As we move into the twenty-first century, the domain of influence of leadership has shifted rapidly from the circumscribed geographies of the past to the globally encompassing geographies of the present and future; that is, leadership has shifted from focusing on a part of the world—most commonly a nation or domestic economy—to focusing on the whole world. Competition has and will continue to force companies that formerly succeeded by using either domestic or multidomestic strategies to completely replace such approaches with integrated cross-culturally interactive global strategies.

Do we know how to lead globally? No, not yet. First, there is still significant confusion between leading and managing. Especially in this era of empowered managers and the "leader-ful" organization, there is a tendency to equate everything that every manager does with leadership. Yet as Kotter (1996) first pointed out years ago, management is not leadership, and the work of the entry-level manager is not the same as the leadership demanded of the CEO. As organizations flatten into networks, leadership is becoming a more dispersed function—although the dispersion appears to be happening more rapidly within management theories than within actual organizations. The bottom line is that everything that managers do is not leadership. Leaders focus the vision of an organization, give direction, and inspire people to embrace the vision and follow in the collectively agreed-upon direction. Global leaders focus the worldwide vision of an organization, give direction, and inspire people from multiple cultures to work simultaneously and interactively toward reaching the collectively agreed-upon vision.

Second, even when attempting to focus specifically on leadership rather than management, there is still no agreement as to what leadership is. As Bennis and Nanus (1985) pointed out over a decade ago, following exhaustive reviews of the leadership research and literature, "Decades of academic analysis have given us more than 350 definitions of leadership. Literally thousands of empirical investigations of leaders have been conducted in the last 75 years alone, but no clear and unequivocal understanding exists as to what distinguishes leaders from non-leaders and, perhaps more important, what distinguishes effective leaders from ineffective leaders" (p. 4).

Third, among the hundreds of definitions of leadership and leadership theories, there are few, if any, theories that are truly global. Most leadership theories, although failing to state so explicitly, are still domestic theories masquerading as universal theories (Boyacigiller & Adler, 1991, 1996). Most commonly, they describe the behavior of leaders in one particular country. Historically, male American leaders working in the United States have been used most frequently as the source on which leadership generalizations, theoretical and otherwise, have been based. This is particularly unfortunate for understanding global leadership, because the focus of study has been domestic organizations, not global companies, and because, culturally, "Americans' extreme individualism combined with their highly participative managerial climate, renders U.S. management practices [including leadership] unique; that is, differentiated from the approaches [used by leaders] in most areas of the world" (Dorfman, 1996, 292; also see Dorfman & Howell, 1988; Dorfman & Ronen, 1991; Hofstede, 1991).

Fourth, in the last decade numerous studies have focused on leadership in countries other than the United States. However, the vast majority of leadership research has yet to focus on that which makes global leadership different from its domestic and multidomestic predecessors; that is, global strategic scope and cross-cultural interaction. Global leaders, unlike their domestic counterparts, address people worldwide. Global leadership involves the ability to inspire and influence the thinking, attitudes, and behavior of people from around the world who are in direct or indirect contact with each other. Global leadership theory, unlike its domestic counterpart, is concerned with the interaction of people and ideas among cultures, rather than with either the efficacy of particular leadership styles within the leader's home country or with the comparison of leadership approaches among leaders from various countries. Global leadership, therefore, is not an isolated phenomenon of any one country or a set of countries.

Fifth, given their global influence, which, by definition, transcends national borders, global leaders have a responsibility for the well-being of society that far exceeds that of their domestic counterparts of yesteryear. Since no government body can regulate companies that span the globe, the social-responsibility function must be internalized by the company and its leaders in ways that have never been needed or seen before. To succeed is to create a healthy bottom line for the company and for society.

Sixth, global leadership theory and practice needs to recognize the increasing numbers of senior women leaders and their influence on the organizations and societies they lead (see, among others, Adler 1999, 1998, 1997a). Heretofore, senior levels of leadership and most leadership theories focused primarily on men, while claiming, sometimes implicitly and sometimes explicitly, to be generic. Today the face of leadership is changing (see Adler, Brody, & Osland, 2000). For example, more than 80 percent of the women who have ever led their countries as president or prime minister have held office in just the last decade (Adler, 1997a, 1997b). To ignore women leaders and their contribution would be to render any theory of global leadership incomplete (Adler, 1997d).

EDWIN L. MILLER, UNIVERSITY OF MICHIGAN
BUSINESS SCHOOL

In the professional literature and in everyday conversations, the term "global competence" is used indiscriminately without much thought being devoted to what the author, scholar, or business practitioner had in mind. For example, global leadership has been applied to a firm judged to be successful in the global marketplace, a functional unit that is deeply involved in the development and implementation of the firm's global strategy, and to an individual or individuals who turn the competitive challenges and opportunities of global competition into extraordinary organizational successes. For purposes of this discussion, I will focus on the individual, and the skills and behavioral competencies they are to be measured against.

What are some of the agreed-upon indicators of global competence of managerial, executive, professional, and technical personnel regardless of their functional orientation? Global competency is multidimensional, and it is composed of at least three basic skill categories:

1. Demonstrated professional knowledge and functional competence.
2. Exhibited intellectual, social, and interpersonal skills.
3. Demonstrated cross-cultural competence.

Demonstrated professional knowledge and functional competence are the necessary qualities and the starting point for the global competency equation. Knowing the business and its strategic intent helps the employee to respond to organizational demands in the ever-changing circumstances of the world. Grounding in one's functional area and successful performance within that function and ascending positions of functional and managerial responsibilities are essential building blocks in the global leadership equation.

Regardless of functional specialization, employees who seek to be labelled as global leaders must be competent in knowing and delivering state-of-the art recommendations, and knowledgable about the global business conditions facing the enterprise. In the final analysis this set of competencies requires the employee to deliver when called upon.

Exhibited intellectual, social, and interpersonal skills represent another category of skills considered to be essential for inclusion in the measurement of global competence. Although there are many skills associated with this skill set, intellectual capability is one of the most important. As an example of this bundle of qualities, one of the criteria is the requirement that employees be prepared and committed to the task of continuing to learn throughout their careers. This characteristic is essential for the growth and development of professional and managerial personnel. Employees must grow with their jobs and learn from the changing circumstances in which they find themselves, because they represent the future leadership of the enterprise. Keeping up with the ever-changing and ever-quickening pace of change within the global marketplace requires employees who are adaptive, flexible, and willing to try new approaches for doing business in the world market.

Social skills must be included among the criteria for global competence, and one of the critical skills is the ability to communicate effectively across functional boundaries, as well as cross-culturally. Global leaders will have to communicate their visions of the firm's future, its strategy, and the importance of their employees dedicating their efforts to the accomplishment of the global vision and strategy.

Interpersonal skills represent another set of skills associated with global competence. Communication, leadership, and change management will become scarce resources as firms restructure themselves, because there will be increased stimulation of interaction across functional boundaries, organizational levels, and cross-cultural frontiers. Understanding the dynamics of working in diverse work-groups or cross-national work teams increases the importance and urgency of acquiring and utilizing these skills. Being able to work well with others becomes pivotal in the competence equation. Employees, regardless of organizational level or functional expertise, will be required to interact with confidence and consideration among individuals from different cultural backgrounds and functional orientation.

Cross-cultural competence has come to be regarded as the critical new human resource requirement for corporations engaged in global competition. Cross-cultural competence is an elusive set of skills and behaviors, and they may not be distributed uniformly across all employees. I'm tempted to say that some individuals may never acquire cross-cultural competence regardless of the time and effort they devote to it.

Cross-cultural competence is multivariate and is composed of the following variables: (1) an internationalized understanding of the worldwide business environment, and especially where the firm is doing business; (2) an international perspective integrated with one's professional knowledge and its application; and (3) an incorporation of an internationalized perspective into one's interpersonal skill set.

I have examined little more than the tip of the global competency iceberg, and there is much more that can be said. I'm sure that others will probably have a different set of dimensions and variables comprising them. However, this is an excellent place to begin the discussion and establishment of an agenda for future research and practice.

Challenges Facing the Scholar and Practitioner

To begin the discussion, I would list seven research challenges that need to be explored:

1. Are people born with the latent attitudes and behaviors to become global leaders, or can people become global (can one acquire the necessary skills and attitudes in other ways)? This question harkens back to earlier discussions of leadership and the question, "Are leaders born or are they developed?"

2. Are there specific work- and academic-related experiences that have a positive impact on enhancing one's cross-cultural competence? Are there situations and experiences that will prevent one from acquiring the necessary skills and experiences necessary to become a global leader?

3. What is known about the transference of knowledge and behaviors acquired in formal management programs?

4. Is the global competence equation considered to be similar regardless of the firm and its circumstances?

5. Is foreign-language acquisition a precursor to cross-cultural competence?

6. Can one become globally competent and ultimately a global leader without having served abroad?

7. Can one be labelled a global leader without demonstrating competency on each of the global competence categories? Stated in a slightly different way, what is the source of the global competencies I have listed?

I believe these questions will provide scholars and practitioners with a menu for expanding the knowledge base and organizational practices that will help to develop global competency, and help to determine who will ultimately become a global leader.

Can Managers and Executives Be Developed into Global Leaders?

It is not clear to me that each and every individual can acquire the degree of knowledge, skills, and attitudes that will guarantee they will be labelled a global leader. Development activities and experiences can help to improve one's global competency, but that does not mean that the individual will become a global leader. I sometimes wonder if one becomes known as a global leader after he or she has proven to be highly successful in leading a firm or a functional unit to new heights in the world of global competition. The enterprise's culture, strategy, and human resource systems are necessary elements in the development of its employees' global competencies. Systematic efforts by the corporation and its management must be clear and positive about the importance of international and global types of activities. It is not likely that an individual will seek out opportunities to acquire global knowledge, skills, and cross-cultural competence without consistent reinforcement of employees' commitment to acquiring such knowledge and behaviors.

If development activities are to be successful, the firm will need to make human resource decisions that are in harmony with its global strategy, and those decisions should reflect the organization's culture and its strategy. The organization can provide the opportunities. However, it will be the individual who makes the decision whether to exert the time and effort to acquire international-oriented skills and use them. To the firm's employees, management's behavior will signal what is important and what will be rewarded.

The human resource management function and its specialists have an important role in the development of global leaders. For example, it will have responsibility for recruiting candidates who have had some international work experience, developing performance-appraisal systems that stress the desirability of international exposure, design compensation systems that reward those who acquire it, and the planning and administration of management-succession programs.

It is time for the HR function to look closely at itself and evaluate its level of global leadership and global competence. If it is to add value to the development and implementation of the organization's global strategy, it is time for HR professionals to acquire global skills and experiences. Development of these skills and experiences will contribute to the transformation of the function into an important partner in adapting HR practices to the changing global needs of the firm. No longer can the HR function and its specialists be exempted from inclusion in the globalization process.

What Aspects of Human Nature and Corporate Life Hinder Enhancement of Global Leaders?

I believe that the fear of dealing with the unknown, the hesitancy of interacting with employees from diverse backgrounds, and the fear of trying to integrate an international or global perspective with one's functional competence are examples of how human nature can hinder one's progress toward global competence. Some people, because of their personalities or perceived commitments to family and friends, are reluctant to venture into the complex world of international or global business. They are satisfied where they are and with what they are doing, and there isn't much that can be done to develop them into global leaders. That is, there is resistance to change. The challenge for the manager of such employees is to demonstrate that acquiring such skills and knowledge will enable the employees to perceive that their needs and goals can be best served by the acquisition of such competencies.

Acquiring cross-cultural competence in terms of attitude changes, developing different ways of looking at a firm's strategy development, and integrating a global perspective into one's functional area is much easier said than done. The individual employee may not be interested in developing global competencies, and this may be the Achilles heel for the development of global competence. It will be disastrous if those who have an interest in developing the skills and attitudes associated with cross-cultural competence are ridiculed by their colleagues or superiors who have little or no interest in global orientation or activities.

From the corporation's perspective, it is essential that its policies, practices, and procedures be aligned with the overall corporate strategy. If the firm and its management fail to reward what they would like to see occur then there will be little employee effort and interest in becoming globally competent. Without a systematic and conscientious plan to review the linkage between promotion decisions, job assignments, the compensation plan and development opportunities, the corporation may be hindering the acquisition of global competencies. The firm may express an interest in its employees developing global competencies, but simultaneously it must be prepared to reward employees taking advantage of opportunities to gain global skills and knowledge. As I have noted, it is the individual who will ultimately decide whether to become globally competent.

MARY ANN VON GLINOW, CIBER DIRECTOR, FLORIDA INTERNATIONAL UNIVERSITY

Fidel Castro is a global leader. So was Mother Teresa (although she probably wouldn't have called herself that). So too were Hitler, Ghandi, Mao, Thatcher, and Clinton, as well as Bill Gates, Donald Trump, Yasser Arafat, Anita Roddick, and Nelson Mandela. All are or have been in strong positions of power, spanning national and cultural boundaries, and have been highly influential in their domain. But what do these global leaders have in common, if anything? Hitler was short, Clinton is tall. Mandela is a black male, Roddick a white female. Clearly, the obvious descriptors of height, weight, gender, or ethnicity do not seem to apply; similarly, doing right or good doesn't apply to some of their behaviors. And would we still think of them as global leaders if they had not been as successful at doing what they do? Indeed, who ever remembers failures, unless they were spectacular ones?

Now, perched on the edge of the millennium, what *do* we know about the competencies of global leaders, and are these competencies transferable or capable of being developed across an array of domestic to transnational enterprises, NGOs, or public-sector organizations? Are there such things as universal competencies that a global leader needs to have, quite apart from his or her cultural and national milieu? This question begs our attention to the convergence/divergence debate (Webber, 1969), global versus local practices (Bartlett & Ghoshal, 1989), and the emic/etic debate (Berry, 1990) that has long befuddled IHRM researchers and seems to prequel any discussion of global leadership competencies. For two decades these pairs of concepts have been at the nexus of the controversy about theory development and method in cross-cultural research, with the focus on how to generalize from one situation or perspective to another (Drost & Von Glinow, 1999).

Toward a Competency Model of Global Leadership

Now, perhaps more than any time in our commercial history, there are profound demands for managerial and leadership competence across multiple boundaries that are both national and cultural. The notion of aligning the MNE's core competencies with more specific decisions about performance appraisal, training and development, selection, compensation, and the like is not controversial. Indeed, a competency-based firm fits extremely well with the needs of today's global companies, whose needs for coordination and aligning offices across national and cultural boundaries have escalated daily. Yet despite the need for competency models, identifying the right set of competencies for a MNE has proved illusive, not because of disagreement about them, but because they often reflect generic management skills rather than a particular MNE's strengths and unique culture (Kroeck, Von Glinow, & Wellinghoff, 1999). In general, most global firms seem to hone in on three or four basic categories of competence; for example, communication, leadership, and administration. However, other MNEs expand this to thirty or more. With too few or too many competencies identified comes the automatic problem of measuring them and linking them to desired outcomes, naturally including performance. Then, once competencies have been defined, some have interpreted them as an exhaustive list of what is expected, thus influencing the employees' future expectations of promotability and compensation.

This is not to dispute competency models, because the HR community has uniformly rallied around them when properly crafted. The roll out of these models (whether in the United States or elsewhere) has been met with much less enthusiasm however, due to several factors: definitional imprecision, levels effects, and cultural contaminants.

Definitional imprecision relates to the fact that some managers equate competencies with skills and abilities, while others view them as capabilities of doing something by employing a range of skills and abilities. Then, too, there are strong and relatively weak competency models, all of which use the same terms. This definitional clouding of the term makes its measurement all the more problematic.

Levels effects pertains to different levels of the MNE requiring different competencies. Dalton and Sandholtz (1990) note that the skills of the first-line supervisor are not relevant at the middle level, and those skills at the middle are not sufficient for the executive level. Parry (1993) notes that managers at all levels must be learning, building upon, and reinforcing those competencies. Most probably all of us have known good global leaders who are not at the top of the MNE, but are instead the seconds, thirds, and elsewhere in the chain of command. Logically, if a competency is fundamentally anchored in the culture and strategy of the MNE, it should be independent of hierarchical level, or, alternatively, not anchored only at one level.

Cultural contaminants are those cultural and nation-specific factors that necessarily muddy the competency equation. For example, the global manager should have some core competency in managing human resources, which from a managerial perspective means selecting, hiring, appraising, and rewarding employees. Reasonable outcomes of this HR competency would be the attraction, motivation, and retention of competent employees worldwide, with systems and structures in place to support performance using good and fair employment practices. The hitch is that some practices vary so fundamentally across different countries and cultures to the point where they would be contraindicated (Von Glinow, 1993, in press; Teagarden, 1995). Thus, the competency models cannot be all things to all people if they are acutely specific, nor can they be terribly useful if they are too generic in focus. This suggests that global leadership competencies need to be anchored in sufficiently specific cultural and national settings. To accurately capture which global leadership competencies are critical in which settings requires some insight from those who know the challenges of the position and are capable of generating dimensions and behaviors that will be used for performance management as well as management development. Therefore, some type of balancing act is required to pinpoint which global leadership competencies are necessary and sufficient to ensure relevance of the competency model and avoid the definitional levels and cultural contaminants traps.

The Balancing Act for Researchers

IHRM researchers interested in identifying global leadership competencies must simultaneously step back as well as delve into the emic/etic debate. This is not meant to sound cryptic, but I believe we need to think seriously about conducting a "sequence" of research whereby parallel indigenous studies within several countries may lead to a validly generalized universal, or a "derived etic," which lies in direct contrast to the more popular (perhaps for ease of publication) dependence upon the imposed-etic measures inferred from primarily North American samples (Berry, 1990; Drost & Von Glinow, 1999). The derived-etic construct (of global leadership competencies) needs to be identified through such repeated studies so that we can arrive at similarities in competencies at a more generic and even a country level. We have long had access to single case studies at the country level, revealing strictly emic practices. However necessary, these studies rarely allow sufficiency in generalizability, nor do they permit commonalities within and between cultures (Drost & Von Glinow, 1999). Parallel indigenous studies allow researchers to embed MNE context into imposed-etic constructs (e.g., global leadership competencies), so that we may finally come to learn why our findings differ or cohere with our theories in use (Drost & Von Glinow, 1999).

The Balancing Act for MNE Global Leaders

Managers of the MNE need to focus on a reasonable set of core competencies necessary for global leadership; however, these core competencies don't exist in a vacuum. In perhaps one of only a few studies of its kind delving into global leadership competencies by Kroeck, Von Glinow, and Wellinghoff (1999), one particular MNE's leadership competencies were found to be centered around ten general dimensions, with several subcategories of competencies (see Table 15.1). As discussed, these ten competencies will most likely vary across different cultural contexts, and since this study is specific to one large MNE, care needs to be taken in any generalization. However, as a first start in identifying global leadership competencies (derived etic), we culled information from MNE managers who know the challenges and demands of global leadership, and facilitated a process whereby the MNE managers generated their own competencies and specific behavioral outcomes associated with each competency.

Although the derived global leadership competencies were initially diverse and plentiful (there were 240 in all), we initially clustered groups of competencies that were directly relevant to the industry as well as the different countries in which the MNE operated. Broadly speaking (and running the risk of sounding too generic), ten groups of competencies were seen to be vital for this MNE's continued success: broad knowledge, thinking and planning strategically, managing remotely and globally, managing the operation, managing the work environment, managing learning, managing human resources, problem solving, decision making, and customer focus. For a specific focus of each of these broad competencies, please refer to Table 15.1.

Although there were 160 subcompetencies identified, the ten aggregate categories are presented, as are their outcomes to which the MNE managers would be held accountable. Space limitations here preclude any extensive discussion of these global leadership competencies; however, this MNE developed a plan to nurture the leadership competencies (which matched their organizational strategy to the industry context) among its various levels of managers as it pursued its globalization strategy. The trick is in the carry through, which is why this is somewhat of a balancing act. The vision of this senior group of MNE managers must be communicated to all involved throughout the MNE, there needs to be system and structural infrastructure in place to continuously reinforce this new model in order to make this change last, and, ultimately, the focus then shifts from effort to outcomes.

Global Leadership Development

It would be folly to have gone on this long about developing global competencies, such as managing learning, if managers couldn't learn or be developed into global leaders. As was implicit in the earlier discussion, some managers are thrust into the spotlight of global leadership without any mentoring or training. And while

Table 15.1
Overview of Ten Core Competencies

Core Competency	Management Focus	Competency Outcomes
Broad Knowledge	Deep understanding of business law, marketing, finance, management, and own functional area. Wisdom regarding people, corporate, and regional cultures; credibility.	Consistent knowing what, when, where, how, why and who.
Planning Strategically	Thinking ahead. Recognizing need for change; identifying optimal direction and objectives.	Able to set the stage for action.
Managing Globally and Remotely	Connecting distant units and staff. Attending to issues and concerns of different regions.	Synchrony of efforts; local effectiveness.
Managing the Operation	Getting the work done every day. Overcoming obstacles; maximizing efficiency and effectiveness.	Regularly accomplished objectives.
Managing the Work Environment	Creating the appropriate mind-set in the workplace; motivating staff; managing commitments.	Sense of urgency, respect, trust, teamwork, and integrity.
Managing Learning	Learning from both wins and losses; establishing ongoing processes for learning and improving; recognizing needed self and staff development.	Long-term development of the unit and the careers of all those working in it.
Managing Human Resources	Hiring, appraising, and compensating; interpreting personnel policies and procedures; providing the needed direction, coaching, and support for accomplishing the work.	Assembly and retention of competent staff; work structured and supported; fair employment practices.
Problem Solving	Putting problems into perspective; analyzing and identifying solutions; managing creatively.	Regularly able to generate feasible alternative solutions.
Decision Making	Choosing among feasible alternatives; sound reasoning; seizing opportunities and taking immediate action.	Good judgement; can make quick or tough decisions.
Customer Focus	Creating strong service and quality rapport; developing mutual understanding.	First and best.

this "drop-kick" strategy usually fails at achieving its intended purpose, there are nevertheless whole volumes devoted to management development and the role that mentoring plays. Scholars like Bob House claim charismatic leadership can be created and developed sufficiently to show results. One could quibble with how important that is when it comes to managing the operation, which is a competency with which few will argue. However, as a substitute for one competency (i.e., managing the operation), a strong secondary or tertiary one such as charismatic leadership could deflect criticism away from a "failure" and turn it into a success story. In other words, while the global leader may have failed to meet the criterion of managing the operation successfully, the strength of his or her personality and charisma may obviate that to some extent. This suggests some type of prioritization scheme needs to be crafted. Those global leadership competencies necessary and sufficient within a country or culture context need to be identified first, then prioritized.

Do Human Nature and Corporate Life Get in the Way?

What prevents us from actualizing the type of core competencies identified by the one MNE reported on in this section? Having broad knowledge, or managing learning, or managing the operation with its respective competency outcomes seem reasonable enough; however, most senior managers have "templates" on how to manage that they have crystallized over time, where "a" leads to "b" regularly. These templates both enable and disable new learning. They probably influence how most of us believe the operation needs to be managed. This is part of what makes us capable of stepping outside of the box, as well as being imprisoned inside, a somewhat paradoxical equation. Global leaders that seem to be successful in the eyes of their followers seem capable of achieving the required competency outcomes despite the paradoxical forces that both enable and disable them. It almost seems trite to say that global leaders have a capacity to listen, to ferret out the good stuff from the bad stuff, and to fully communicate and trust. This is a reflective capacity, not mentioned in the ten core competencies identified by the MNE, but significant in this writer's mind. Global leadership implies criss-crossing time zones routinely, and quite apart from the armchair travelers or suitcase expats (Taylor & Napier, 1995) identified as the new global leader communication or traveling modality, this requires the ability to take the time to step back and reflect. Most of the global leaders I know don't have the luxury of such reflection due to institutional factors, Wall Street, and other stakeholder expectations influencing their reputational cachet. Such constraints ultimately hinder our capacity to grow, as do most organizational reward systems, which inhibit long-term insights due to short-term demands.

However, there are factors that enhance the development of global leadership competencies, and these include (in addition to the ones identified earlier) one's ability to maneuver across multiple boundaries, generating good ideas with high impact (Yeung, Ulrich, Nason, & Von Glinow, 1999), and successfully utilizing the full capacities of the management team.

Ultimately, global leadership competencies must be anchored within the company and country context, and while there is some element of intrigue about their discovery, the outcomes of those competencies are routinely embraced in most MNEs. Such is the nature of global leadership competencies.

References

Abe, H., & Wiseman, R. L. 1983. A cross-cultural confirmation of the dimensions of intercultural effectiveness. *International Journal of Intercultural Relations, 7*, 53–68.

Abramson, N. R., Lane, H. W., Nagai, H., & Takagi, H. 1993. A comparison of Canadian and Japanese cognitive styles: Implications for management interaction. *Journal of International Business Studies, 24*, 575–587.

Aburdene, P., & Naisbitt, J. 1992. *Megatrends for women.* New York: Villard Books.

Adler, N. J. 1981. Re-entry: Managing cross-cultural transitions. *Group and Organizational Studies, 6*, 341–356.

Adler, N. J. 1986. *International dimensions of organizational behavior.* Boston: Kent.

Adler, N. J. 1991. *International dimensions of organizational behavior* (2d ed.). Boston: Kent.

Adler, N. J. 1994. Competitive frontiers: Women managing across borders. In N. J. Adler & D. N. Izraeli (Eds.), *Competitive frontiers: Women managers in a global economy* (pp. 22–40). Cambridge, MA: Blackwell.

Adler, N. J. 1996. Global women political leaders: An invisible history, an increasingly important future. *Leadership Quarterly, 7*, 133–161.

Adler, N. J. 1997a. Global leaders: A dialogue with future history. *International Management, 1* (2), 21–33.

Adler, N. J. 1997b. Global leadership: Women leaders. *Management International Review, 37* (special issue 1), 171–196.

Adler, N. J. 1997c. *International dimensions of organizational behavior* (3d ed.). Cincinnati: South-Western College Publishing.

Adler, N. J. 1997d. Societal leadership: The wisdom of peace. In S. Srivastva (Ed.), *Executive wisdom and organizational change* (pp. 205–221). San Francisco: Jossey-Bass.

Adler, N. J. 1998. Did you hear? Global leadership in charity's world. *Journal of Management Inquiry, 7* (2), 135.

Adler, N. J. 1999. Global entrepreneurs: Women, myths, and history. *Business and the Contemporary World, 11* (4).

Adler, N. J., & Bartholomew, S. 1992. Managing globally competent people. *Academy of Management Executive, 6* (3), 52–65.

Adler, N. J., Brody, L. W., & Osland, J. S. 2000. The women's global leadership forum: Enhancing one company's leadership capability. *Human Resource Management.*

Adler, N. J., & Ghadar, F. 1989. Globalization and human resource management. In A. M. Rugman (Ed.), *Research in global strategic management: A Canadian perspective.* Greenwich, CT: JAI Press.

Adler, N. J., & Ghadar, F. 1990. Strategic human resource management: A global perspective. In R. Pieper (Ed.), *Human resource management: An international comparison* (pp. 235–260). Berlin: DeGruyter.

Adler, P. A., & Adler, P. 1994. Observational techniques. In N. Denzin & Y. Lincoln (Eds.), *Handbook of qualitative research.* Thousand Oaks, CA: Sage.

Adler, P. S. 1975. The transitional experience: An alternative view of culture shock. *Journal of Humanistic Psychology, 15,* 13–23.

Agar, M. 1994. *Language shock: Understanding the culture of conversation.* New York: William Morrow.

Ah Chong, L. M., & Thomas, D. C. 1997. Leadership perceptions in cross-cultural context: Pakeha and Pacific Islanders in New Zealand. *Leadership Quarterly, 8,* 275–293.

Aitchison, J. 1987. *Words in the mind: An introduction to the mental lexicon.* Oxford: Basil Blackwell.

Albert, R. 1983. The intercultural sensitizer or culture assimilator: A cognitive approach. In D. Landis & R. Brislin (Eds.), *Handbook of intercultural training:* Vol. 2. *Issues in training methodology* (pp. 186–217). Elmsford, NY: Pergamon.

Al-Jafary, A., & Hollingsworth, A. T. 1983. An exploratory study of managerial practices in the Arabian Gulf region. *Journal of International Business Studies, 14,* 143–152.

Allaire, Y., & Firsirotu, M. E. 1984. Theories of organizational culture. *Organization Studies, 5,* 193–226.

Ancona, D. G., & Caldwell, D. F. 1992. Bridging the boundary: External activity and performance for organizational teams. *Administrative Science Quarterly, 37,* 634–666.

Anderson, L. R. 1983. Managing of the mixed-cultural work group. *Organization Behavior and Human Performance, 31,* 303–330.

Anderson, N. F. 1993. Benazir Bhutto and dynastic politics: Her father's daughter, her people's sister. In M. A. Genovese, (Ed.), *Women as national leaders* (pp. 41–69). Newbury Park, CA: Sage.

Antoni, C. H. 1998. Kooperationsförderliche Arbeitsstrukturen. In E. Spieß (Ed.), *Formen der Kooperation—Bedingungen und Perspektiven* (pp. 157–168). Göttingen: Hogrefe.

Apeltauer, E. 1997. Zur Bedeutung der Körpersprache für die interkulturelle Kommunikation. In A. Knapp-Potthoff & M. Liedke (Eds.), *Aspekte interkultureller Kommunikationsfähigkeit* (pp. 17–39). München: Iudicium.

Argote, L., & McGrath, J. E. 1993. Group process in organizations: Continuity and change. In C. L. Cooper & I. T. Robertson (Eds.), *International review of industrial and organizational psychology* (pp. 333–389). New York: Wiley.

Argyle, M. 1991. *Cooperation, the basis of sociability*. London: Routledge.

Arnold, D. J., & Qualch, J. A. 1998. New strategies in emerging markets. *Sloan Management Review, 40* (1), 7–20.

Arthur, M. B., Hall, D. T., & Lawrence, B. S. 1989. *Handbook of career theory*. New York: Cambridge University Press.

Arthur, W., & Bennett, W. 1995. The international assignee: The relative importance of factors perceived to contribute to success. *Personnel Psychology, 48*, 99–114.

Assman, J. 1992. *Das kulturelle Gedächtnis: Schrift, Erinnerung und politische Identität in früheren Hochkulturen*. München: Beck.

Astin, H. S., & Leland, C. 1991. *Women of influence, women of vision*. San Francisco: Jossey-Bass.

Aycan, Z. 1997. Acculturation of expatriate managers: A process model of adjustment and performance. In Z. Aycan (Ed.), *Expatriate management: Theory and research* (Vol. 4, pp. 1–41). Greenwich, CT: JAI Press.

Aycan, Z., & Berry, J. W. 1996. Impact of employment-related experiences on immigrants' psychological well-being and adaptation to Canada. *Canadian Journal of Behavioral Science, 28* (3), 240–251.

Aycan, Z., Kanungo, R. N., Mendonca, M., Yu, K., Deller, J., Stahl, G., & Khursid, A. in press. Impact of culture on human resource management practices: A ten-country comparison. *Applied Psychology: An International Review.*

Ayman, R., Kreiker, N. A., & Masztal, J. J. 1994. Defining global leaderships in business environments. *Consulting Psychology Jounal, 46*, 1061–1087.

Badawy, M. K. 1980. Styles of Mid-Eastern managers. *California Management Review, 22* (1), 51–58.

Baker, J. C. & Ivancevich, J. M. 1971. The assignment of American executives abroad: Systematic, haphazard or chaotic? *California Management Review, 13*, 39–44.

Bamberger, I., Eßling, R., Evers, M., & Wrona, T. 1995. *Internationalisierung und strategisches Verhalten von Klein–und Mittelunternehmen*. Essen: University of Essen.

Bantel, K. H., & Jackson, S. E. 1989. Top management and innovations in banking: Does the composition of the top team make a difference? *Strategic Management Journal, 10*, 107–124.

Bantz, C. R. 1993. Cultural diversity and group: Cross-cultural team research. *Journal of Applied Communication Research*, February, 1–20.

Barham, K. 1990. *An international human resource strategy study.* Hertfordshire, UK: Ashridge Management Center.

Barham, K., & Antal, B. 1994. Competences for the Pan European manager. In P. S. Kirkbride (Ed.), *Human resource management in Europe: Perspectives for the 1990s.* London: Routledge.

Barham, K., & Oates, D. 1991. *The international manager.* London: Economist Books.

Barna, L. M. 1983. The stress factor in intercultural relations. In L. A. Samovar & R. E. Porter (Eds.), *Intercultural communication: A reader* (5th ed., pp. 322–330). Belmont, CA: Wadsworth.

Barney, J. 1991. Firms resource and sustained competitive advantage. *Journal of Management, 17*, 99–120.

Bartlett, C. A., Doz, Y., & Hedlund, G. (Eds.). 1990. *Managing the global firm.* London: Routledge.

Bartlett, C. A., & Ghoshal, S. 1987a. Managing across borders: New organizational responses. *Sloan Management Review*, Autumn, 43–53.

Bartlett, C. A., & Ghoshal, S. 1987b. Managing across borders: New strategic requirements. *Sloan Management Review*, Summer, 7–17.

Bartlett, C. A., & Ghoshal, S. 1989. *Managing across borders: The transnational solution.* Boston: Harvard Business School Press.

Bartlett, C. A., & Ghoshal, S. 1992, September–October. What is a global manager? *Harvard Business Review*, 124–132.

Bass, B. M. 1990. *Bass & Stogdill's handbook of leadership: Theory, research, and managerial applications* (3d ed.). New York: Free Press.

Bass, B. M., Burger, P. C., Doktor, R., & Barrett, G. V. 1979. *Assessment of managers: An international comparison.* New York: Free Press.

Baughn, C. 1995. Personal and organizational factors associated with effective repatriation. In J. Selmer (Ed.), *Expatriate management: New ideas for international business* (pp. 215–230). Westport, CT: Quorum Books.

Baumgarten, K. 1995. Training and development of international staff. In A.-W. Harzing & J. van Ruysseveldt (Eds.), *International human resource management: An integrated approach* (pp. 205–228). London: Sage.

Becker, B. E., & Huselid, M. A. 1998. High performance work systems and work performance: A synthesis of research and managerial implications. *Research in Personnel and Human Resources Management, 16*, 53–101.

Belenky, M. F., Clinchy, B. M., Goldberger, N. R., & Tarule, J. M. 1986. *Women's ways of knowing: The development of self, voice, and mind.* New York: Basic Books.

Benn, M. 1995. Women who rule the world. *Cosmopolitan*, February issue.

Bennett, A. 1989, February 27. The chief executives in year 2000 will be experienced abroad. *The Wall Street Journal*, p. A1.

Bennett, M. J. 1993. Towards ethnorelativism: A developemental model of intercultural sensitivity. In M. R. Paige (Ed.), *Education for the intercultural experience* (pp. 21–71). Yarmouth, ME: Intercultural Press.

Bennis, W. 1989a. *On becoming a leader*. Reading, MA: Addison-Wesley.

Bennis, W. 1989b. *Why leaders can't lead: The unconscious conspiracy continues*. San Francisco: Jossey-Bass.

Bennis, W., & Nanus, B. 1985. *Leaders: The strategies for taking charge*. New York: Harper and Row.

Berger, P. L., & Luckmann, T. 1966. *The social construction of reality*. Garden City, NY: Doubleday.

Bernard, J. 1981. *The female world*. New York: Free Press.

Berry, J. W. 1980. Social and cultural change. In H. C. Triandis & R. Brislin (Eds.), *Handbook of cross-cultural psychology* (Vol. 5, pp. 211–279). Boston: Allyn & Bacon.

Berry, J. W. 1983. Acculturation: A comparative analysis of alternative forms. In R. J. Samuda & S. L. Woods (Eds.), *Perspectives in immigrant and minority education*. Lanhan, MD: University Press of America.

Berry, J. W. 1990. Imposed etics, emics, and derived emics: Their conceptual and operational status in cross-cultural psychology. In T. Heartlund, K. L. Pike, & M. Harris (Eds.), *Emics and etics: Insider / outsider debate*. Newbury Park, CA: Sage.

Berry, J. W. 1992. Acculturation and adaptation in a new society. *International Migration Quarterly Review, 30*, 69–87.

Berry, J. W., & Sam, D. L. 1997. Acculturation and adaptation. In J. W. Berry, M. H. Segall & C. Kagitcibasi (Eds.), *Handbook of cross-cultural psychology* (3d ed., pp. 291–325). Boston: Allyn & Bacon.

Bettenhausen, K. L., & Murnighan, J. K. 1985. The emergence of norms in competitive decision-making groups. *Administrative Science Quarterly, 30*, 350–372.

Bettenhausen, K. L., & Murnighan, J. K. 1991. The development and stability of norms in groups facing interpersonal and structural challenge. *Administrative Science Quarterly, 36*, 20–35.

Bhagat, R. S., & Prien, K. O. 1996. Cross-cultural training in organizational contexts. In D. Landis & R. S. Bhagat (Eds.), *Handbook of intercultural training* (2d ed., pp. 216–230). Thousand Oaks, CA: Sage.

Bittner, A., & Reisch, B. 1991. *Internationale Personalentwicklung in deutschen Großunternehmen: Eine Bestandsaufnahme*. Bad Honnef: Institut für interkulturelles Management.

Black, J. S. 1990. The relationship of personal characteristics with the adjustment of Japanese expatriate managers. *Management International Review, 30*, 119–134.

Black, J. S. 1992. Coming home: The relationship of expatriate expectations with repatriation adjustment and job performance. *Human Relations, 45*, 177–192.

Black, J. S. 1994. O Kaerinasai: Factors related to Japanese repatriation adjustment. *Human Relations, 47*, 1489–1508.

Black, J. S., & Gregersen, H. B. 1991a. The other half of the picture: Antecedents of spouse cross-cultural adjustment. *Journal of International Business Studies, 22*, 461–477.

Black, J. S., & Gregersen, H. B. 1991b. When Yankee comes home: Factors related to expatriate and spouse repatriation adjustment. *Journal of International Business Studies, 22,* 671–694.

Black, J. S., Gregersen, H. B., & Mendenhall, M. E. 1992a. *Global assignments: Successfully expatriating and repatriating international managers.* San Francisco: Jossey-Bass.

Black, J. S., Gregersen, H. B., & Mendenhall, M. E. 1992b. Toward a theoretical framework of repatriation adjustment. *Journal of International Business Studies, 24,* 737–760.

Black, J. S., Gregersen, H. B., Mendenhall, M. E., & Stroh, L. K. 1999. *Globalizing people through international assignments.* New York: Addison-Wesley Longman.

Black, J. S., & Mendenhall, M. E. 1989. A practical but theory-based framework for selecting cross-cultural training programs. *Human Resource Management, 28* (4), 511–539.

Black, J. S., & Mendenhall, M. E. 1990. Cross-cultural training effectiveness: A review and a theoretical framework for future research. *Academy of Management Review, 15,* 113–136.

Black, J. S., & Mendenhall, M. E. 1991. The U-curve adjustment hypothesis revisited: A review and theoretical framework. *Journal of International Business Studies, 22,* 225–247.

Black, J. S., & Mendenhall, M. E., & Oddou, G. 1991. Toward a comprehensive model of international adjustment: An integration of multiple theoretical perspectives. *Academy of Management Review, 16* (2), 291–317.

Black, J. S., Morrison, A., & Gregersen, H. B. 1999. *Global explorers: The next generation of leaders.* New York: Routledge.

Black, J. S., & Stephens, G. K. 1989. The influence of the spouse on American expatriate adjustment and intent to stay in Pacific Rim overseas assignments. *Journal of Management, 15,* 529–544.

Bolman, L., & Deal, T. 1995. *Leading with soul.* San Francisco: Jossey-Bass.

Bonvillain, N. 1997. *Language, culture, and communication: The meaning of messages* (2d ed.). Upper Saddle River, NJ: Prentice Hall.

Bottger, P. C., Hallein, I. H., & Yetton, P. W. 1985. A cross-national study of leadership: Participation as a function of problem structure and leader power. *Journal of Management Studies, 22,* 358–368.

Bourdieu, P. 1995: Narzißtische Reflexivität und wissenschaftliche Reflexivität. In E. Berg & M. Fuchs (Eds.), *Kultur, soziale Praxis, Text. Die Krise der ethnographischen Repräsentation* (pp. 365–374). Frankfurt: Suhrkamp.

Boyacigillar, N. 1990. The role of expatriates in the management of interdependence, complexity and risk in multinational corporations. *Journal of International Business Studies, 21,* 357–381.

Boyacigiller, N., & Adler, N. J. 1991. The parochial dinosaur: The organizational sciences in a global context. *Academy of Management Review, 16,* 262–290.

Boyacigiller, N., & Adler, N. J. 1996. Insiders and outsiders: Bridging the worlds of organizational behavior and international management. In B. Toyne & D. Nigh (Eds.), *International business inquiry: An emerging vision* (pp. 22–102). Columbia: University of South Carolina Press.

Brake, T. 1997. *The global leader: Critical factors for creating the world class organization.* Chicago: Irwin Professional.

Brewster, C., & Scullion, H. 1997. Expatriate HRM: A review and an agenda. *Human Resource Management Journal, 7,* 32–41.

Brocker, M., & Nau, H. H. (Eds.). 1997. *Ethnozentrismus. Möglichkeiten und Grenzen des interkulturellen Dialogs.* Darmstadt: Primus Verlag.

Brod, H., & Kaufman, M. (Eds.). 1994. *Theorizing masculinities.* Thousand Oaks, CA: Sage.

Buckley, P. J., & Casson, M. 1998. Models of the multinational enterprise. *Journal of International Business Studies, 29,* 21–44.

Bunch, C. 1991. Foreword. In H. S. Astin & C. Leland, *Women of influence, women of vision* (pp. xi–xiv). San Francisco: Jossey-Bass.

Bungard, W., & Antoni, C. H. 1993. Gruppenorientierte Interventionstechniken. In H. Schuler (Ed.), *Lehrbuch Organisationspsychologie* (pp. 377–404). Göttingen: Huber.

Burack, E. H., Burack, M. D., Miller, D. M., & Morgan, K. 1994. New paradigm approaches in strategic human resource management. *Group and Organization Management, 19,* 141–159.

Calas, M. B., & Smircich, L. 1993. Dangerous liaisons: The "feminine-in-management" meets "globalization." *Business Horizons, 36,* 71–81.

Caligiuri, P. M. 1997. Assessing expatriate success: Beyond just "being there." In Z. Aycan (Ed.), *Expatriate management: Theory and research* (pp. 117–141). Greenwich, CT: JAI Press.

Caligiuri, P. M. 1998. *Evaluating the success of global assignments: Performance measurement in a cross-national context.* Paper presented at the 1998 Academy of Management Meeting, San Diego, CA, August.

Campbell, J. 1968. *Hero with a thousand faces.* Princeton, NJ: Princeton University Press.

Cantor, D., & Bearnay, T. 1992. *Women in power.* New York: Houghton Mifflin.

Carroll, S. J. 1984. Feminist scholarship on political leadership. In B. Kellerman (Ed.), *Leadership: Multidisciplinary perspectives.* Englewood Cliffs, NJ: Prentice Hall.

Cascio, W. F. 1993. Downsizing: What do we know? What have we learned? *Academy of Management Executive, 7,* 95–104.

Casmir, F. L. 1999. Foundations for the study of intercultural communication based on a third-culture building model. *International Journal of Intercultural Relations, 23,* 91–116.

Cattell, R. 1948. Concepts and methods in the measurement of group syntality. *Psychological Review, 55,* 48–63.

Cherrington, D. J., & Middleton, L. 1995, July. An introduction to global business issues. *Human Resource Magazine, 40,* 124.

Chodorow, N. 1978. *The reproduction of mothering.* Berkeley and Los Angeles: University of California Press.

Church, A. T. 1982. Sojourner adjustment. *Psychological Bulletin, 91,* 540–572.

Clackworthy, D. 1992. *Cultural interaction training: Creating understanding and handling conflict in German/American teams.* Paper presented at Management Centre Europe 11th International Training Conference, Brussels.

Clarke, C., & Hammer, M. R. 1995. Predictors of Japanese and American managers job success, personal adjustment, and intercultural interaction effectiveness. *Management International Review, 35,* 153–170.

Clyne, M. 1994. *Inter-cultural communication at work: Cultural values in discourse.* Cambridge: Cambridge University Press.

Cohn, S. 1985. *The process of occupational sex-typing: The feminization of clerical labor in great britain.* Philadelphia: Temple University Press.

Col, J.-M. 1993. Managing softly in turbulent times: Corazon C. Aquino, president of the Philippines. In M. A. Genovese (Ed.), *Women as national leaders* (pp. 13–40). Newbury Park, CA: Sage.

Collins, B. E., & Guetzkow, H. 1964. *A social psychology of group processes for decision-making.* New York: John Wiley & Sons.

Comeau-Kirchner, C. 1999. Reducing turnover is a tough job. *Management Review, 88,* 9.

Computer chip project brings rivals together, but the cultures clash. Foreign work habits get in the way of creative leaps, hobbling joint research. 1994, May 3. *Wall Street Journal.*

Condon, J. C. 1984. *With respect to the Japanese. A guide for Americans.* Yarmouth, ME: Intercultural Press.

Cone, E. 1996. Nice money, if you can get it. *Information Week, 592,* 64.

Conference Board. 1996. *Managing expatriates return: A research report* (Report Number 1148-96-RR). New York: Author.

Conger, J. A. 1989. *The charismatic leader: Behind the mystique of exceptional leadership.* San Francisco: Jossey-Bass.

Conger, J. A., & Kanungo, R. 1988. *Charismatic leadership.* San Francisco: Jossey-Bass.

Council for International Exchange. 1988. *Educating for global competence: The report of the Advisory Council for International Exchange.* Washington, DC: Author.

Coyle, W. 1988. *On the move: Minimizing the stress and maximizing the benefit of relocation.* Sydney: Hampden.

Cullen, J. B. 1999. *Multinational management: A strategic approach.* Cincinnati: South-Western College Publishing.

Cultures clash in three-country project: Putting Japanese, Germans and Americans together has proved harder than first thought. 1994, July. *Electronic Business Asia.*

Daft, R., & Weick, K. 1984. Toward a model of organization as interpretation systems. *Academy of Management Review, 9,* 284–296.

Dalton, G., & Sandholtz, K. 1990. How am I doing? *Executive Excellence, 7,* 6–7.

Dalton, M. A. 1998. Developing leaders for global roles. In C. D. McCauley, R. S. Moxley, & E. Van Velsor (Eds.), *The Center for Creative Leadership handbook of leadership development* (pp. 379–402). San Francisco: Jossey-Bass.

Dalton, M., & Wilson, M. 1998. *Antecedents of effectiveness in a group of Arab expatriates: The role of personality and learning.* Paper presented at the 24th International Congress of Applied Psychology, San Francisco, California, August 9–14.

Davenport, T. H., & Prusak, L. 1998. *Working knowledge: How organizations manage what they know.* Boston: Harvard Business School Press.

Davis, R. V., & Lofquist, L. H. 1984. *A psychological theory of adjustment.* Minneapolis: University of Minneapolis Press.

Davison, S. C. 1994. Creating high performance international teams. *Journal of Management Development, 13,* 81–90.

Deller, J. 1997. Expatriate selection: Possibilities and limitations of using personality scales. In Z. Aycan (Ed.), *Expatriate management: Theory and research* (Vol. 4, pp. 93–116). Greenwich, CT: JAI Press.

Demorgon, J., & Molz, M. 1996. Bedingungen und Auswirkungen der Analyse von Kultur(en) und interkulturellen Interaktionen. In A. Thomas (Ed.), *Psychologie interkulturellen Handelns* (pp. 43–86). Göttingen: Hogrefe.

Denzin, N., & Lincoln, Y. 1994. *Handbook of qualitative research.* Thousand Oaks, CA: Sage.

Derr, C. B., & Oddou, G. 1991. Are U.S. multinationals adequately preparing future American leaders for global competition? *International Journal of Human Resource Management, 2,* 227–244.

Deshpande, S. P., & Viswesvaran, C. 1992. Is cross-cultural training of expatriate managers effective? A meta analysis. *International Journal of Intercultural Relations, 16,* 295–310.

Deutsch, M. 1958. Trust and suspicion. *Journal of Conflict Resolution, 2,* 265–279.

Deutsche Bundesbank. 1999. *Monatsbericht Februar 1999.* Frankfurt: Author.

Diaz-Guerrero, R. 1979. The development of coping style. *Human Development, 22,* 320–331.

Die Zeit. 1999. *Wettkampf der Giganten, 19,* 38.

Dinges, N. G., & Baldwin, K. D. 1996. Intercultural competence. In D. Landis & R. S. Bhagat (Eds.), *Handbook of intercultural training* (2d ed., pp. 106–123). Thousand Oaks, CA: Sage.

Dinnerstein, D. 1976. *The mermaid and the minotaur.* New York: Harper and Row.

Dobrzynski, J. H. 1996, November 6. Somber news for women on corporate ladder. *New York Times,* p. D1.

Dorfman, P. W. 1996. International and cross-cultural leadership. In B. J. Punnett & Oded Shenkar (Eds.), *Handbook for international management research* (pp. 267–349). Cambridge: Blackwell.

Dorfman, P. W., & Howell, J. P. 1988. Dimensions of national culture and effective leadership patterns: Hofstede revisited. In R. N. Farmer (Ed.), *Advances in international comparative management* (Vol. 3, pp. 127–150). Greenwich: JAI Press.

Dorfman, P. W., & Ronen, S. 1991. *The universality of leadership theories: Challenges and paradoxes.* Paper presented at the Academy of Management Annual Meeting, Miami, Florida, August.

Douglas, A. 1977. *The feminization of american culture.* New York: Avon Books.

Dowling, P. J. in press. Completing the puzzle: Issues in the Development of the Field of International Human Resource Management. *Management International Review, 39* (4), 27–43 [Special Issue].

Dowling, P. J., Welch, D. E., & Schuler, R. S. 1999. *International human resource management: Managing people in a multinational context* (3d ed.). Cincinnati: South-Western College Publishing.

Doz, Y. L. 1979. *Government control and multinational strategic management: Power systems and telecommunications equipment.* New York: Praeger Special Studies.

Doz, Y. L., & Prahalad C. K. 1986. Controlled variety: A challenge for human resource management in the MNC. *Human Resource Management, 25,* 55–71.

Doz, Y. L., & Prahalad, C. K. 1991. Managing DMNCs: A search for a new paradigm. *Strategic Management Journal, 12,* 145–164.

Driskell, J. E., Hogan, R., & Salas, E. 1987. Personality and group performance. In C. Hendrick (Ed.), *Group processes and intergroup relations* (pp. 91–112). Newbury Park, CA: Sage.

Drosdowski, G., Grebe, P., Köster, R., Müller, W., & Scholze-Stubenrecht, W. (Eds.). 1963. *Duden Band 7—das Herkunftswörterbuch.* Mannheim: Bibliographisches Institut, Dudenverlag.

Drosdowski, G., Grebe, P., Köster, R., Müller, W., & Scholze-Stubenrecht, W. (Eds.). 1982. *Duden Band 5—das Fremdwörterbuch* (4th ed.). Mannheim: Bibliographisches Institut, Dudenverlag.

Drost, E., & Von Glinow, M. A. 1999. Leadership behavior in Mexico: Etic philosophies and emic practices. In T. Scandura & M. Serapio (Eds.), *Research in international business and international relations* (Vol. 7, pp. 3–28). Greenwich, CT: JAI Press.

Dugan, A. 1991. State sell-offs stall. *International Management,* November, 44–47.

Dunbar, E. 1992. Adjustment and satisfaction of expatriate U.S. personnel. *International Journal of Intercultural Relations, 16,* 1–16.

Dutton, J., & Jackson, S. 1987. Categorizing strategic issues: Links to organizational action. *Academy of Management Review, 12,* 76–90.

Earley, P. C. 1987. Intercultural training for managers: A comparison of documentary and interpersonal methods. *Academy of Management Journal, 30,* 685–698.

Earley, P. C. 1993. East meets West meets Mideast: Further explorations of collectivistic and individualistic work groups. *Academy of Management Journal, 36,* 319–348.

Earley, P. C. 1994. Self or group? Cultural effects of training on self-efficacy and performance. *Administrative Science Quarterly, 39,* 89–117.

Editor's viewpoint. 1990, May 2. *Business International Council.*

Edström, A., & Galbraith, J. 1977. Transfer of managers as a coordination and control strategy in multinational organizations. *Administrative Science Quarterly, 22,* 248–263.

Edström, A., & Lorange, P. 1984. Matching strategy and human resources in multinational corporations. *Journal of International Business Studies, 15,* 125–137.

Eisler, R. 1987. *The chalice and the blade.* San Francisco: Harper.

Elmuti, D., & Kathalawa, Y. 1991. An investigation of the human resource management practices of Japanese subsidiaries in the Arabian Gulf region. *Journal of Applied Business Research, 7,* 82–88.

Engen, J. R. 1995. Coming home. *Training, 32*, 37–40.

Erez, M., & Earley, P. C. 1993. *Culture, self-identity, and work.* Oxford: Oxford University Press.

Euromanagers. 1990, June 14. *International Herald Tribune,* p. 10.

Evans, P.A.L. 1992. Management development as glue technology. *Human Resource Planning, 15*, 85–106.

Evans, P.A.L., Lank, E., & Farquhar, A. 1990. Managing human resources in the international firm: Lessons from practice. In P. Evans, J. Doz, & A. Laurent (Eds.), *Human resource management in international firms* (pp. 113–143). London: Macmillan.

Feldman, D. C., & Thomas, D. C. 1991. Career management issues facing expatriates. *Journal of International Business Studies, 23*, 271–293.

Ferguson, K. E. 1984. *The feminist case against bureaucracy.* Philadelphia: Temple University Press.

Festing, M. 1996. *Strategisches Internationales Personalmanagement. Eine transaktionskostenthoeretisch fundierte Analyse.* München/Mering: Rainer Hampp Verlag.

Festing, M. 1997. International human resource management strategies in multinational corporations: Theoretical assumptions and empirical evidence from German firms. In J. Wolf (Guest Ed.), International Human Resource and Cross Cultural Management [Special Issue No. 1]. *Management International Review, 37*, 43–65.

Festing, M. 1999a. *Tacit knowledge linking strategic management and international human resource management.* Paper submitted for consideration to the Australia and New Zealand Academy of Management, Hobart.

Festing, M. 1999b. Wissenstransfer durch internationale Personalentwicklung—strategische Bedeutung bei Globalisierung der Geschäftstätigkeit. In A. Martin, W. Mayrhofer, & W. Nienhüser (Eds.), *Die Bildungsgesellschaft im Unternehmen? Festschrift für Wolfgang Weber* (pp. 243–268). München/Mering: Rainer Hampp Verlag.

Festing, M. 1999c. *Tacit knowledge linking strategic management and international human resource management.* Paper presented to the Australia and New Zealand Academy of Management, Hobart.

Fiedler, F. E. 1966. The effect of leadership and cultural heterogeneity on group performance: A test of the contingency model. *Journal of Experimental Social Psychology, 2*, 237–264.

Finlay, F. 1990. *Mary Robinson: A president with a purpose.* Dublin: O'Brien Press.

Fiske, S., & Taylor, S. 1984. *Social cognition.* Reading, MA: Addison-Wesley.

Flanagan, J. C. 1954. The critical incident technique. *Psychological Bulletin, 51*, 327–358.

Fondas, N. 1997. The origins of feminization. *Academy of Management Review, 22*, 257–282.

Forster, N. 1997. The persistent myth of high expatriate failure rates: A reappraisal. *International Journal of Human Resource Management, 8*, 414–433.

Franke, R., Hofstede, G., & Bond, M. 1991. Cultural roots of economic performance: A research note. *Strategic Management Journal, 12*, 165–173.

Frese, M., & Zapf, D. 1994. Action as the core of work psychology: A German approach. In H. C. Triandis, M. D. Dunette, & L. M. Hough (Eds.), *Handbook of industrial and social psychology* (2d ed., Vol. 4, pp. 271–340). Palo Alto, CA: Consulting Psychologists Press.

Friday, R. A. 1989. Contrasts in discussion: Behaviors of German and American Managers. *International Journal of Intercultural Relations, 13*, 429–446.

Fryer, B. 1998. IT departments face high staff turnover. *Information Week, 675*, 104.

Furnham, A. 1997. *The psychology of behaviour at work*. Hove East Sussex: Psychology Press.

Furnham, A., & Bochner, S. 1986. *Culture shock: Psychological reactions to unfamiliar environments*. New York: Methuen.

Gardner, H. 1995. *Leading minds: An anatomy of leadership*. New York: Basic Books.

George, J. M., & Bettenhausen, K. 1990. Understanding prosocial behavior, sales performance, and turnover: A group-level analysis in a service context. *Journal of Applied Psychology, 75*, 698–709.

Gerlach, K., & Lorenz, W. 1992. Arbeitsmarkttheorie/-ökonomie. In E. Gaugler & W. Weber (Eds.), *Handwörterbuch des Personalwesens* (pp. 169–179). Stuttgart: Schäffer Poeschel Verlag.

Gertsen, M. C. 1990. Intercultural competence and expatriates. *International Journal of Human Resource Management, 3*, 341–362.

Ghadar, F., & Adler, N. 1989. Management culture and the accelerated product life cycle. *Human Resource Planning, 12*, 37–42.

Gilligan, C. 1982. *In a different voice: Psychological theory and women's development*. Cambridge: Harvard University Press.

Glennon, L. M. 1979. *Women and dualism*. New York: Longman.

Godfrey, J. 1996. Mind of the manager. *Inc., 18* (3), 21.

Goinrich, J. A. 1999. Young markets ripe for picking. *Asian Business, 35* (7), 34–39.

Gomez-Mejia, L., & Balkin, D. B. 1987. The determinants of managerial satisfaction with the expatriation and repatriation processes. *Journal of Management Development, 6*, 7–17.

Goodenough, W. H. 1981. *Culture, language, and society* (2d ed.). Menlo Park, CA: Benjamin Cummings.

Goodwin, D. K. 1995. *No ordinary time: Franklin & Eleanor Roosevelt. The home front in World War II*. New York: Simon & Schuster.

Goold, M., & Campbell, A. 1998. Desperately seeking synergy. *Harvard Business Review, 76*, 131–143.

Grace, N. M. 1995. *The feminized male character in twentieth-century literature*. Lewiston, NY: Edwin Mellen Press.

Granrose, C. S., & Oskamp, S. (Eds.). 1997. *Cross-cultural work groups*. Thousand Oaks, CA: Sage.

Grant, J. 1988. Women as managers: What can they offer organizations? *Organizational Dynamics, 16* (1), 56–63.

Grant, R. M. 1991. The resource-based theory of competitive advantage: Implications for strategy formulation. *California Management Review, 33* (3), 114–135.

Grant, R. M. 1996. Toward a knowledge-based theory of the firm. *Strategic Management Journal, 17,* 109–122.

Graubmann, G. 1997. *Aufgabenbereiche der internationalen Personalarbeit: Eine empirische Untersuchung bei deutschen Großunternehmen.* Unpublished master's thesis. University of Bayreuth.

Green, R., & Larsen, T. 1991, November–December. Changing patterns of U.S. trade: 1985–1989. *Business Horizons,* pp. 7–13.

Gregersen, H. B., & Black, J. S. 1992. Antecedents to commitment to a parent company and a foreign operation. *Academy of Management Journal, 35,* 65–90.

Gregersen, H. B., & Black, J. S. 1995. Global executive development: Keeping high performers after international assignments. *Journal of International Management, 1,* 3–31.

Gregersen, H. B., Morrison, A. J., & Black, J. S. 1998. Developing leaders for the global frontier. *Sloan Management Review, 40,* 21–32.

Gregersen, H. B., & Stroh, L. K. 1997. Coming home to the Arctic cold: Antecedents to Finnish expatriate and spouse repatriation adjustment. *Personnel Psychology, 50,* 635–654.

Grossman, R. J. 1998. How recruiters woo high-demand candidates. *HR Magazine, 43,* 122–130.

Gudykunst, W. B. 1988. Uncertainty and anxiety. In Y. Y. Kim & W. B. Gudykunst (Eds.), *Theories in intercultural communication.* Newbury Park, CA: Sage.

Gudykunst, W. B. 1997. *Communicating with strangers.* New York: McGraw-Hill.

Gudykunst, W. B. 1998. Applying anxiety/uncertainty management (AUM) theory to intercultural adjustment training. *International Journal of Intercultural Relations, 22,* 227–250.

Gudykunst, W. B., Guzley, R. M., & Hammer, M. R. 1996. Designing intercultural training. In D. Landis & R. S. Bhagat (Eds.), *Handbook of intercultural training* (2d ed., pp. 61–80). Thousands Oaks, CA: Sage.

Gudykunst, W. B., & Nishida, T. 1993. Interpersonal and intergroup communication in Japan and the United States. In W. B. Gudykunst (Ed.), *Communication in Japan and the United States* (pp. 149–214). Albany: State University of New York Press.

Gullahorn, J. T., & Gullahorn, J. E. 1963. Extension of the U-curve hypothesis. *Journal of Social Issues, 19,* 45–46.

Gumperz, J. J. 1992. Contextualization revisited. In P. Auer & A. Di Luzio (Eds.), *The contextualization of language* (pp. 39–53). Amsterdam/ Philadelphia: John Benjamins.

Gumperz, J. J. 1993. *Crosstalk II. Entreprises training video: Counselling and advice across cultures.* London: Mosaic, BBC Education.

Gutteridge, T., Leibowitz, Z., & Shore, J. 1993. *Organizational career development.* San Francisco: Jossey-Bass.

Guzzo, R. A., & Dickson, M .W. 1996. Teams in organizations: Recent research on performance and effectiveness. In J. T. Spence, J. M. Darley, & D. J. Foss (Eds.), *Annual review of psychology* (Vol. 47, pp. 307–338). Palo Alto: Annual Reviews.

Hackman, J. R. 1998. Why teams don't work. In R. S. Tindale, L. Heath, J. Edwards, E. J. Posavac, F. B. Bryant, Y. Suarez-Balcazar, E. Henderson-King, & J. Myers (Eds.), *Social psychological applications to social issues*: Vol. 4. *Theory and research on small groups* (pp. 245–267). New York: Plenum Press.

Hackman J. R., & Morris, C. G. 1975. Group tasks, group interaction process, and group performance effectiveness: A review and proposed integration. In L. Berkowitz (Ed.), *Advances in experimental social psychology* (Vol. 8, pp. 45–99). New York: Academic Press.

Haire, M., Ghiselli, E. E., & Porter, L. W. 1966. *Managerial thinking: An international study*. New York: Wiley.

Hall, E. T. 1976/1989. *Beyond culture*. New York: Anchor Books.

Hall, E. T. 1983. *The dance of life: The other dimension of time*. Garden City, NY: Anchor Books.

Hall, J., & Watson, W. H. 1970. The effects of a normative intervention on group decision-making performance. *Human Relations, 23*, 299–315.

Hall, J., & Williams, M. S. 1970. Group dynamics training and improved decision making. *Journal of Applied Behavioral Science, 6*, 39–68.

Hamel, G., & Prahalad, C. K. 1989. Strategic intent. *Harvard Business Review, 67* (3), 63–76.

Hamel, G., & Prahalad, C. K. 1994. *Competing for the future*. Boston: Harvard Business School Press.

Hammer, M. R., Hart, W., & Rogan, R. 1998. Can you go home again? An analysis of the repatriation of corporate managers and spouses. *Management International Review, 38*, 67–86.

Hampden-Turner, C. 1993, December 9–10. *The structure of entrapment: Dilemmas standing in the way of women managers and strategies to resolve these*. Paper presented at the Global Business Network Meeting, New York.

Handy, A., & Barham, C. 1989, October 28. *The European*, p. 14.

Harrison, R., & Hopkins, R. L. 1967. The design of cross-cultural training: An alternative to the university model. *Journal of Applied Behavioral Science, 3* (4), 431–460.

Hartsock, N. C. 1983. *Money, sex, and power: Toward a feminist historical materialism*. New York: Longman.

Harvard Business School Press (Ed.). 1992. *Leaders on leadership*. Boston: Author.

Harvey, M. G. 1982. The other side of foreign assignments: Dealing with the repatriation dilemma. *Columbia Journal of World Business, 17*, 53–59.

Harvey, M. G. 1989. Repatriation of corporate executives: An empirical study. *Journal of International Business Studies, 20*, 131–144.

Harvey, M. G., & Buckley, M. R. 1997. Managing inpatriates: Building a global core competency. *Journal of World Business, 32*, 35–52.

Harzing, A.-W.K. 1999. *Managing the multinationals. An international study of control mechanisms*. Cheltenham, UK: Elgar.

Hasbach, C. P. 1996. *Die Erfahrungen von Mitarbeitern bei der Wiedereingliederung nach einem Auslandseinsatz*. Unpublished master's thesis. University of Bayreuth.

Havel, V. 1994, July 8. The new measure of man. *New York Times*, p. A27.

Hawes, F., & Kealey, D. J. 1981. An empirical study of Canadian technical assistants. *International Journal of Intercultural Relations, 5,* 239–258.

Hays, R. D. 1974. Expatriate selection: Insuring success and avoiding failure. *Journal of International Business Studies, 4,* 25–37.

Hedlund, G. 1986. The hypermodern MNC—a heterarchy. *Human Resource Management, 25,* 9–25.

Hedlund, G., & Rolander, D. 1990. Action in heterarchies: New approaches to managing the MNC. In C. A. Bartlett, Y. Doz, & G. Hedlund (Eds.), *Managing the Global Firm* (pp. 15–46). London: Routledge.

Helgesen, S. 1990. *The female advantage: Women's ways of leadership.* New York: Doubleday.

Heller, F. A., & Wilpert, B. 1981. *Competence and power in managerial decision-making.* Chichester, UK: Wiley.

Helmolt, K. 1997. *Kommunikation in internationalen Arbeitsgruppen. Eine Fallstudie über divergierende Konventionen der Modalitätskonstituierung.* München: Iudicium.

Hendry, C. 1994. *Human resource strategies for international growth.* New York: Routledge.

Himelstein, L. 1996, October 28. Shatterproof glass ceiling. *Business Week,* p. 55.

Hirai, T. 1989 *Tokyo Business Today,* pp. 20–24.

Hirschbrunn, H.-W., & Schlossberger, C. 1996. Internationale Führungskräfte-Entwicklung bei der Daimler Benz AG. In K. Macharzina & J. Wolf (Eds.), *Handbuch Internationales Führungskräfte-Management* (pp. 30–65). Stuttgart: Raabe Verlag.

Hitt, M. A., Ireland, R. D., & Hoskisson, R. E. 1995. *Strategic management: Competitiveness and globalization* (Annotated Instructor's Ed.). Minneapolis/St. Paul: West.

Hoffman, L. R., Harburg, E., & Maier, N.R.F. 1962. Differences and disagreement as factors in creative group problem solving. *Journal of Abnormal Social Psychology, 64,* 206–214.

Hoffman, L. R., & Maier, N.R.F. 1961. Quality and acceptance of problem solutions by members of homogeneous and heterogeneous groups. *Journal of Abnormal and Social Psychology, 62,* 401–407.

Hofstede, G. 1980a. *Culture's consequences: International differences in work-related values.* London: Sage.

Hofstede, G. 1980b. Motivation, leadership, and organization: Do American theories apply abroad? *Organizational Dynamics, 9,* 42–63.

Hofstede, G. 1991. *Cultures and organizations: Software of the mind.* London: McGraw-Hill.

Hofstede, G. 1996. An American in Paris: The influence of nationality on organization theories. *Organization Science, 17,* 525–537.

Hofstede, G. 1999. Cultural constraints in personnel management. In W. Weber, M. Festing, P. J. Dowling (Guest Eds.), Cross-Cultural and Comparative International Human Resource Management [Special Issue No. 2]. *Management International Review, 38,* 7–26.

Hollander, E. P. 1985. Leadership and power. In G. Lindzey & E. Aronson (Eds.), *Handbook of social psychology*. New York: Random House.

Holmes, T. H., & Rahe, R. H. 1967. The social readjustment rating scale. *Journal of Psychosomatic Research, 11*, 213–218.

Homans, G. C. 1958. Social behavior and exchange. *American Journal of Sociology, 63*, 597–606.

Horsch, J. 1995. *Auslandseinsatz von Stammhaus-Mitarbeitern*. Frankfurt am Main: Peter Lang.

House, J. 1989. Politeness in English and German. In S. Blum-Kulka, J. House, & G. Kasper (Eds.), *Cross-cultural pragmatics: Requests and apologies* (pp. 98–119). Norwood, NJ: Ablex.

Howell, J. P., Dorfman, P. W., Hibino, S., Lee, J. K., & Tate, U. 1994. *Leadership in Western and Asian countries: Commonalities and differences in effective leadership processes and substitutes across cultures*. Las Cruces: New Mexico State University.

Huselid, M. A. 1995. The impact of human resource management practices on turnover, productivity, and corporate financial performance. *Academy of Management Journal, 38*, 635–670.

Hymes, D. 1974. *Foundations of sociolinguistics*. Philadelphia: University of Pennsylvania Press.

Iannello, K. P. 1992. *Decisions without hierarchy: Feminist interventions in organization theory and practice*. New York: Routledge.

Ilgen, D. R., LePine, J. A., & Hollenbeck, J. R. 1997. Effective decision making in multinational teams. In P. C. Earley & M. Erez (Eds.), *New perspectives on international industrial/organizational psychology* (pp. 377–409). San Francisco: New Lexington Press.

Industrial Democracy in Europe (IDE). 1976. International research group: An international comparative study. *Social Science Inform, 15*, 177–203.

Industrial Democracy in Europe (IDE). 1979. International research group: Participation, formal rules, influence and involvement. *Industrial Relations, 18*, 273–394.

Industrial Democracy in Europe (IDE) Revisited. 1993. *International research group*. Oxford: Oxford University Press.

Inkson, K., Pringle, J., Arthur, M. B., & Barry, S. 1997. Expatriate assignment versus overseas experience: Contrasting models of international human resource development. *Journal of World Business, 32*, 351–368.

Iqtidar, H., & Webster, L. J. 1996. *Frene Ginwalda: Speaker of the South African National Assembly*. Unpublished paper, McGill University, Faculty of Management.

Ireland, R. D., & Hitt, M. A. 1999. Achieving and maintaining strategic competitiveness in the 21st century: The role of strategic leadership. *Academy of Management Executive, 13*, 43–57.

Jackson, S. E. 1996. The consequences of diversity in multidisciplinary work teams. In M. A. West (Ed.), *Handbook of work group psychology* (pp. 53–75). Baffins Lane, Chichester: John Wiley & Sons.

Jackson, S. E., & Ruderman, M. N. 1996. Introduction: Perspectives for understanding diverse work teams. In S. E. Jackson & M. N. Ruderman (Eds.), *Diversity in work teams: Research paradigms for a changing workplace* (pp. 1–13). Washington, DC: American Psychological Association.

Janis, I. L. 1982. *Group think: Psychological studies of policy decisions and fiascos* (2d ed.). Boston: Houghton Mifflin.

Jennings, E. 1960. *The anatomy of leadership.* New York: Harper and Row.

Kakar, S. 1971. Authority patterns and subordinate behavior in Indian organizations. *Administrative Science Quarterly, 16,* 298–308.

Kamoche, K. 1996. Strategic human resource management within a resource-capability view of the firm. *Journal of Management Studies, 33,* 213–233.

Kannheiser, W., Hormel, R., & Aichner, R. 1993. *Planung im Projektteam* (Vol. 1). München: Hampp.

Kanter, R. M. 1977. *Men and women of the corporation.* New York: Basic Books.

Kanungo, R. N., & Menon, S. 1995. *Managerial resourcefulness: Measuring a critical component in leadership role.* Paper presented at the Academy of Management Meeting, Vancouver, Canada, August.

Kanungo, R. N., & Misra, S. 1992. Managerial resourcefulness: A reconceptualization of management skills. *Human Relations, 45,* 1311–1332.

Kealey, D. J. 1989. A study of cross-cultural effectiveness: Theoretical issues, practical applications. *International Journal of Intercultural Relations, 13,* 387–428.

Kealey, D. J. 1990. *Cross-cultural effectiveness: A study of Canadian technical advisors overseas.* Hull: CIDA.

Kealey, D. J. 1996. The challenge of international personnel selection criteria, issues and methods. In D. Landis & R. Bhagat (Eds.), *Handbook of Intercultural Training* (2d ed., pp. 81–105). Thousand Oaks, CA: Sage.

Kealey, D. J., & Protheroe, D. R. 1996. The effectiveness of cross-cultural training for expatriates: An assessment of the literature on the issue. *International Journal of Intercultural Relations, 20,* 141–165.

Kealey, D. J., & Ruben, B. D. 1983. Cross-cultural personnel selection: Criteria, issues and methods. In D. Landis & R. W. Brislin (Eds.), *Handbook of intercultural training* (Vol. 2, pp. 155–175). New York: Pergamon Press.

Kelly, C. 1996. 50 world-class executives. *Worldbusiness, 2* (2), 20–31.

Kendall, D. 1981. Repatriation: An ending and a beginning. *Business Horizons, 24,* 21–25.

Kets de Vries, M. F., & Mead, C. 1992. The development of the global leader within the multinational corporation. In V. Pucik, N. M. Tichy, & C. K. Barnett (Eds.), *Globalizing management: Creating and leading the competitive organization* (pp. 187–205). New York: John Wiley & Sons.

Kim, P. S. 1999. Globalization of human resource management: A cross-cultural perspective for the public sector. *Public Personal Management, 28*, 227–244.

Kirchmeyer, C. 1993. Multicultural task groups. An account of the low contribution level of minorities. *Small Group Research, 24*, 127–148.

Kirchmeyer, C., & Cohen, A. 1992. Multicultural groups: Their performance and reactions with constructive conflict. *Group and Organization Management, 17*, 153–170.

Kleiber, G. 1990. *La sémantique du prototype. Catégories et sens lexical.* Paris: PUF.

Klein, V. 1972. *The feminine character: History of an ideology.* Urbana: University of Illinois Press.

Klenke, K. 1996. *Women and leadership: A contextual perspective.* New York: Springer.

Kluckhohn, F., & Strodtbeck, F. 1961. *Variations in value orientations.* Evanston, IL: Row, Peterson.

Knapp, K. 1995. Interkulturelle Kommunikationsfähigkeit als Qualifikationsmerkmal für die Wirtschaft. In J. Bolten (Ed.), *Cross culture—Interkulturelles Handeln in der Wirtschaft* (pp. 8–23). Berlin: Wissenschaft/Praxis.

Kobrin, S. J. 1988. Expatriate reduction and strategic control in American multinational corporations. *Human Resource Management Journal, 27*, 63–75.

Kobrin, S. J. 1994. Is there a relationship between a geocentric mind-set and multinational strategy? *Journal of International Business Studies, 25*, 493–511.

Kogut, B., & Zander, U. 1992. Knowledge of the firm, combinative capabilities and the replication of technology. *Organization Science, 3*, 383–397.

Köhler, R. 1997. Internationale Kooperationsstrategien kleinerer Unternehmen. In M. Bruhn & H. Steffenhagen (Eds.), *Marktorientierte Unternehmensführung* (pp. 183–203). Wiesbaden: Gabler.

Kopp, R. 1994. International human resource policies and practices in Japanese, European, and United States multinationals. *Human Resource Management, 33*, 581–599.

Kotter, J. 1988. *The leadership factor.* New York: Free Press.

Kotter, J. 1991. What leaders really do. In J. Gabarro (Ed.), *Managing people and organization.* Boston: Harvard Business School Press.

Kotter, J. P. 1996. *Leading change.* Boston: Harvard Business School Press.

Kotthoff, H. 1989. *Pro und Kontra in der Fremdsprache. Pragmatische Defizite in interkulturellen Argumentationen.* Frankfurt a.M.: Lang.

Kozan, M. K. 1989. Cultural influences on styles of handling interpersonal conflicts: Comparisons among Jordanian, Turkish, and United States managers. *Human Relations, 42*, 787–799.

Kramer, R., & Tylor, T. R. 1995. *Trust in organizations.* Thousand Oaks, CA: Sage.

Kransdorrf, A. 1997. Fight organizational memory lapse. *Workforce, 76*, 34–39.

Kroeck, G., Von Glinow, M. A., & Wellinghoff, A. 1999. *Revealing competencies for global managers: Using decision room technology to identify and align management competence with corporate strategy* (Working Paper), Florida International University.

Kühlmann, T. M. 1995a. Die Auslandsentsendung von Fach- und Führungskräften: Eine Einführung in die Schwerpunkte und Ergebnisse der Forschung. In T. M. Kühlmann (Ed.), *Mitarbeiterentsendung ins Ausland* (pp. 1–25). Göttingen: Verlag für Angewandte Psychologie.

Kühlmann, T. M. 1995b. *Mitarbeiterentsendung ins Ausland: Auswahl, Vorbereitung, Betreuung und Wiedereingliederung.* Göttingen: Verlag für Angewandte Psychologie.

Kühlmann, T. M., & Stahl, G. K. 1995. Die Wiedereingliederung von Mitarbeitern nach einem Auslandseinsatz: Wissenschaftliche Grundlagen. In T. M. Kühlmann (Ed.), *Mitarbeiterentsendung ins Ausland: Auswahl, Vorbereitung, Betreuung und Wiedereingliederung* (pp. 177–215). Göttingen: Verlag für Angewandte Psychologie.

Kühlmann, T. M., & Stahl, G. K. 1996. Fachkompetenz allein genügt nicht—Interkulturelle Assessment Center unterstützen die gezielte Personalauswahl. *Personalführung Plus, 96,* 22–24.

Kühlmann, T. M., & Stahl, G. K. 1998. Diagnose interkultureller Kompetenz: Entwicklung und Evaluierung eines Assessment Centers. In C. Barmeyer & J. Bolten (Eds.), *Interkulturelle Personalorganisation* (pp. 213–223). Berlin: Verlag Wissenschaft & Praxis.

Kumar, B. N. 1992. Personalpolitische Herausforderungen für im Ausland tätige Unternehmen. In E. Dichtl & O. Issing (Eds.), *Exportnation Deutschland* (2d ed., pp. 305–337). München: Beck.

Kumar, K., Subramanian, R., & Nonis, S. A. 1991. Cultural diversity's impact on group processes and performance: Comparing culturally homogeneous and culturally diverse work groups engaged in problem solving tasks. *Southern Management Association Proceedings.*

Landis, D., & Bhagat, R. S. (Eds.). 1996. *Handbook of intercultural training* (2d ed.). Thousand Oaks, CA: Sage.

Lane, H. W., DiStefano, J. J., & Maznevski, M. L. 1997. *International management behavior* (3d ed.). Cambridge, MA: Blackwell.

Larkey, L. K. 1996. Toward a theory of communicative interactions in culturally diverse workgroups. *Academy of Management Review, 21,* 463–491.

Lau, D. C., & Murnighan, J. K. 1998. Demographic diversity and faultlines: The compositional dynamics of organizational groups. *Academy of Management Review, 23,* 325–340.

Laurent, A. 1983. The cultural diversity of Western conceptions of management. *International Studies of Management and Organization, 13,* 75–96.

Laurent, A. 1986. The cross-cultural puzzle of international human resource management. *Human Resource Management, 25,* 91–102.

Lazarus, R. S., & Folkman, S. 1984. *Stress, appraisal and coping.* New York: Springer.

Lebra, T. S. 1976. *Japanese patterns of behavior.* Honolulu: University of Hawaii Press.

Lei, D., Hitt, M. A., & Bettis, R. 1996. Dynamic core competences through meta-learning and strategic context. *Journal of Management, 22*, 549–560.

Lengnick-Hall, C. A., & Lengnick-Hall, M. L. 1998. Strategic human resource management: A review of the literature and a proposed typology. *Academy of Management Review, 13*, 454–470.

Leung, K., & Bond, M. H. 1984. The impact of cultural collectivism on reward allocation. *Journal of Personality and Social Psychology, 47*, 793–804.

Levine, J. M., & Moreland, R. L. 1990. Progress in small group research. *Annual Review of Psychology, 41*, 585–634.

Ling, S. C. 1990. *The effects of group cultural composition and cultural attitudes on performance.* Unpublished Ph.D. diss., University of Western Ontario, London, Canada.

Lipman-Blumen, J. 1983. Emerging patterns of female leadership in formal organizations. In M. Horner, C. C. Nadelson, & M. T. Notman (Eds.), *The challenge of change* (pp. 61–91). New York: Plenum Press.

Lord, R. G., & Foti, R. J. 1986. Schema theories, information processing, and organizational behavior. In H. P. Sims, Jr. & D. A. Gioia (Eds.), *The thinking organization* (pp. 20–48). San Francisco: Jossey-Bass.

Louis, M. R. 1980. Surprise and sense making: What newcomers experience in entering unfamiliar organizational settings. *Administrative Science Quarterly, 25*, 226–251.

Lubritz, S. 1998. *Internationale strategische Allianzen mittelständischer Unternehmen.* Frankfurt: Peter Lang.

Lysgaard, S. 1955. Adjustment in a foreign society: Norwegian Fulbright grantees visiting the United States. *International Science Bulletin, 7*, 45–51.

Macharzina, K. 1992. Internationalisierung und Organisation. *Zeitschrift für Organisation, 61*, 4–11.

Macharzina, K., & Wolf, J. 1996. Internationales Führungskräfte-Management und strategische Unternehmenskoordination—Kritische Reflexionen über ein ungeklärtes Beziehungssystem. In K. Macharzina & J. Wolf (Eds.), *Handbuch Internationales Führungskräfte-Management* (pp. 16–64). Stuttgart: Raabe.

Maier, N.R.F. 1967. Assets and liabilities in group problem solving: The need for an integrative function. *Psychological Review, 74*, 239–249.

Marshall, J. 1984. *Women managers: Travelers in a male world.* New York: Wiley.

Martin, J. N. 1986. Orientation for the reentry experience: Conceptual overview and implications for researchers and practitioners. In R. M Paige (Ed.), *Cross-culture orientation: New conceptualization and applications* (pp. 147–173). New York: Lanham.

Martinez, J. I., & Jarillo, J. C. 1989. The evolution of research on coordination mechanisms in multinational corporations. *Journal of International Business Studies, 19*, 489–514.

Martinez, J. I., & Jarillo, J. C. 1991. Coordination demands of international strategies. *Journal of International Business Studies, 22*, 429–443.

Marx, E. 1996. *International human resource practices in Britain and Germany.* London: Anglo-German Foundation for the Study of Industrial Society.

Mason, J. 1991. Stuck deep in the red. *International Management*, November, 38–43.

Mayrhofer, W. 1996. *Mobilität und Steuerung in international tätigen Unternehmen.* Stuttgart: Schäffer-Poeschel.

Maznevski, M. L. 1994. *Synergy and performance in multicultural teams.* Unpublished Ph.D. diss., University of Western Ontario, London, Canada.

Maznevski, M. L. 1994. Understanding our differences: Performance in decision-making groups with diverse members. *Human Relations, 47,* 531–552.

Maznevski, M. L., & DiStefano, J. J. 1996. *The mortar in the mosaic: A new look at process and performance in diverse teams.* Paper presented at the Academy of Management annual meeting, San Diego, California, August.

Maznevski, M. L., DiStefano, J. J., Gomez, C. B., Noorderhaven, N. G., & Wu, P. 1997. *The cultural orientations framework and international management research.* Paper presented at the Academy of International Business annual meeting.

Maznevski, M. L., & Peterson, M. F. 1997. Societal values, social interpretation, and multinational teams. In C. S. Granrose & S. Oskamp (Eds.), *Cross-cultural work groups* (pp. 61–89). Thousand Oaks, CA: Sage.

Maznevski, M. L., & Zander, L. 2000. Leading global teams: Overcoming the challenge of the power paradox. In M. E. Mendenhall, T. Kühlmann, & G. K. Stahl (Eds.), *Developing global leaders: Policies, processes, and innovations.* Westport, CT: Quorum Books.

McCall, M. W., Jr. 1992. *Identifying leadership potential in future international executives: Developing a concept* (Working Paper, 92-01). Massachusetts: ICEDR.

McCall, M., Lombardo, M., & Morrison, A. 1988. *The lessons of experience: How successful executives develop on the job.* Lexington, MA: Lexington Books.

McFarland, L. J., Senn, L. E., & Childress, J. R. 1993. *21st century leadership: Dialogues with 100 top leaders.* New York: Leadership Press.

McGrath, J. E., Berdahl, J. L., & Arrow, H. 1995. Traits, expectations, culture and clout: The dynamics of diversity in work groups. In S. E. Jackson & M. N. Ruderman (Eds.), *Diversity in work teams: Research paradigms for a changing workplace* (pp. 17–45). Washington, DC: American Psychological Association.

McLeod, P. L., & Lobel, S. A. 1992. The effects of ethnic diversity on idea generation in small groups. In *Best papers proceedings: Academy of Management annual meeting* (pp. 227–231). AOM.

McMillan, C. 1982. *Reason, women and nature: Some philosophical problems with nature.* Princeton, NJ: Princeton University Press.

Mendenhall, M. E. 1999. On the need for paradigmatic integration in international human resource management. *Management International Review, 39* (2), 1–23.

Mendenhall, M. E. 2000. New perspectives on expatriate adjustment and its relationship to global leadership development. In M. E. Mendenhall, T. M. Kühlmann, & G. K. Stahl (Eds.), *Developing global leaders: Policies, processes, and innovations.* Westport, CT: Quorum Books.

Mendenhall, M. E., Dunbar, E., & Oddou, G. R. 1987. Expatriate selection, training, and career-pathing: A review and critique. *Human Resource Management, 26,* 331–345.

Mendenhall, M. E., & Macomber, J. 1997. Rethinking the strategic management of expatriates from a nonlinear dynamics perspective. In Z. Aycan (Ed.), *Expatriate management: Theory and research* (Vol. 4, pp. 41–61). Greenwich, CT: JAI Press.

Mendenhall, M. E., Macomber, J., Gregersen, H., & Cutright, M. 1998. Nonlinear dynamics: A new perspective on international human resource management research and practice in the 21st century. *Human Resource Management Review, 8,* 5–22.

Mendenhall, M. E., & Oddou, G. R. 1985. The dimensions of expatriate acculturation: A review. *Academy of Management Review, 10,* 39–47.

Mendenhall, M. E., & Stahl, G. K. in press. Expatriate training and development: Where do we go from here? *Human Resource Management.*

Merriam-Webster. 1977. *Webster's new collegiate dictionary.* Springfield, MA: G. & C. Merriam Co.

Mervosh, E. M., & McClenahen, J. S. 1997, December 1. The care and feeding of exports. *Industry Week, 246,* 68–72.

Meyer, J. P., & Allen, N. J. 1991. A three-component conceptualization of organizational commitment. *Human Resource Management Review, 1,* 61–89.

Michaelsen, L. K., Watson, W. E., & Black, R. H. 1989. A realistic test of individual versus group consensus decision making. *Journal of Applied Psychology, 74,* 834–839.

Miller, E. L. 1973. The international selection decision: A study of some dimensions of managerial behavior in the selection decision process. *Academy of Management Journal, 16,* 239–252.

Miller, J. B. 1976. *Toward a new psychology of women.* Boston: Beacon Press.

Milliken, F. J., & Martins, L. L. 1996. Searching for common threads: Understanding the multiple effects of diversity in organizational groups. *Academy of Management Review, 21,* 402–433.

Millington, A., & Bayliss, B. 1990. The process of internationalization: UK companies in the EC. *Management International Review, 30,* 151–161.

Moosmüller, A. 1995. Learning objectives in intercultural competence: Decoding German everyday knowledge from a Japanese perspective. In A. Jensen, K. Jaeger, & A. Lorentsen (Eds.), *Intercultural competence* (Vol. 2, pp. 191–207). Aalborg: Aalborg University Press.

Moosmüller, A. 1997a. *Kulturen in Interaktion: Deutsche und US–amerikanische Firmenentsandte in Japan.* Münster: Waxmann.

Moosmüller, A. 1997b. Kommunikationsprobleme in amerikanisch-japanisch-deutschen Teams: Kulturelle Synergie durch interkulturelles Training? *Zeitschrift für Personalforschung, 3,* 282–297.

Moran, R. T., & Harris, P. R. 1981. *Managing cultural synergy.* Houston: Gulf.

Moran, R. T., and Riesenberger, J. 1994. *The global challenge: Building the new worldwide enterprise.* New York: McGraw-Hill.

Moreland, R. L., Levine, J. M., & Wingert, M. L. 1996. Creating the ideal group: Composition effects at work. In E. Witte & J. H. Davis (Eds.), *Understanding group behavior. Vol. 2: Small group processes and interpersonal relations* (pp. 11–35). Mahwah, NJ: Lawrence Erlbaum.

Morgan, P. V. 1986. International human resource management: Fact or fiction. *Personnel Administrator, 31* (9), 43–47.

Moritz, E. F. 1996. *Im Osten nichts Neues. Theorie und Praxis von Produktinnovation in Japan im Vergleich zu Deutschland.* Sottrum: Artefact Verlag.

Morrison, A. in press. The characteristics of global leaders. *Human Resource Management Journal.*

Müller, B. 1980. Zur Logik interkultureller Verstehensprobleme. *Jahrbuch Deutsch als Fremdsprache, 6,* 102–119.

Müller, B. 1995a. Sekundärerfahrung und Fremdverstehen. In J. Bolten (Ed.), *Cross culture—Interkulturelles Handeln in der Wirtschaft* (pp. 43–58). Berlin: Sternenfels.

Müller, B. 1995b. Steps towards an intercultural methodology for teaching foreign languages. In L. Sercu (Ed.), *Intercultural competence: A new challenge for language teachers and trainers in Europe* (Vol. 1, pp. 71–116). Aalborg: Aalborg University Press.

Müller, S. 1991. *Die Psyche des Managers als Determinante des Exporterfolges: Eine kulturvergleichende Studie zur Auslandsorientierung von Managern aus sechs Ländern.* Stuttgart: Verlag für Wissenschaft und Forschung.

Murphy, E. 1996. *Leadership IQ.* New York: John Wiley & Sons.

Murtha, T. P., Lenway, S. A., & Bagozzi, R. P. 1998. Global mindsets and cognitive shift in a complex multinational corporation. *Strategic Management Journal, 19,* 97–114.

Napier, N., & Peterson, R. 1991. Expatriate re-entry: What do expatriates have to say? *Human Resource Planning, 14,* 19–28.

Naumann, E. 1992. A conceptual model of expatriate turnover. *Journal of International Business Studies, 23,* 499–531.

Negandi, A. R., Eshghi, G. S., & Yuen, E. C. 1985. The management practices of Japanese subsidiaries overseas. *California Management Review, 27* (4), 93–105.

Nemiroff, P. M., & King, D. C. 1975. Group decision-making performance as influenced by consensus and self-orientation. *Human Relations, 28,* 1–21.

Nemiroff, P. M., Pasmore, W. A., & Ford, D. L., Jr. 1976. The effects of two normative structural interventions on established and ad hoc groups: Implications for improving decision making effectiveness. *Decision Sciences, 7,* 841–855.

Newman, K. L., & Nollen, S. D. 1996. Culture and congruence: The fit between management practices and national culture. *Journal of International Business Studies, 27,* 753–779.

Nonaka, I. 1990. *Managing innovation as a knowledge-creation process: A new model for a knowledge-creating organization.* Paper presented at New York University, Stern School of Business, International Business Colloquium.

Nonaka, I. 1991a. The knowledge-creating company. *Harvard Business Review, 69* (6), 96–104.

Nonaka, I. 1991b. Managing the firm as an information creation process. In J. R. Meindl et al. (Eds.), *Advances in Information Processing in Organizations* (Vol. 4, pp. 239–275). Greenwich, CT: JAI Press.

Nonaka, I. 1994. A dynamic theory of organizational knowledge creation. *Organization Science, 5,* 14–37.

Nonaka, I., & Takeuchi, H. 1995. *The knowledge-creating company.* New York: Oxford University Press.

O'Boyle, T. F. 1989, December 11. Grappling with the expatriate issue: Little benefit to careers seen in foreign stints. *The Wall Street Journal,* pp. B1, B4.

Oddou, G. R. 1991. Managing your expatriates: What the successful firms do. *Human Resource Planning, 14,* 301–308.

Oddou, G. R., & Derr, B. 1992. *European MNCs: Strategies to internationalize managers.* Paper presented at the Third Conference on International Personnel and Human Resources Management, Ashridge Management College, Berkhamsted, England.

Oddou, G. R., Gregersen, H., Black, J. S., & Derr, J. B. 2000. Internationalizing managers: Comparative strategies of U.S., Japanese, and European MNCs. In M. E. Mendenhall, T. M. Kühlmann, & G. K. Stahl (Eds.), *Developing global leaders: Policies, processes, and innovations.* Westport, CT: Quorum Books.

Oddou, G. R., & Mendenhall, M. E. 1988. Succession planning for the 21st century: How well are we grooming our future business leaders? *Business Horizons, 34* (1), 26–34.

Oddou, G. R., Mendenhall, M. E., & Bonner Ritchie, J. in press. Leveraging travel as a tool for global leadership development. *Human Resource Management.*

OECD. 1993. *Globalisation and small and medium enterprises (SMEs).* Vol. 3: *Country studies.* Paris: OECD.

Ones, D. S., & Viswesvaran, C. 1997. Personality determinants in the prediction of aspects of expatriate job success. In Z. Aycan (Ed.), *Expatriate management: Theory and research* (Vol. 4, pp. 63–92). Greenwich, CT: JAI Press.

Osland, J. 1995. *The adventure of living abroad: Hero tales from the global frontier.* San Francisco: Jossey-Bass.

Pagé, M. 1993. Kooperatives Lernen und sozialer Pluralismus. In G. L. Huber (Ed.), *Neue Perspektiven der Kooperation* (pp. 11–21). Baltmannsweiler: Schneider-Verlag.

Parry, S. 1993. The missing "M" in TQM. *Training, 30* (9), 29–31.

Pedersen, P. 1995. *The five stages of culture shock.* Westport, CT: Greenwood Press.

Penrose, E. 1959. *The theory of the growth of the firm.* New York: Wiley.

Perlmutter, H. V. 1969. The tortuous evolution of the multinational corporation. *Columbia Journal of World Business, 4,* 9–81.

Peters, T. 1989, April 11. Listen up, guys: Women fit profile of execs of future. *Seattle Post-Intelligencer,* p. B6.

Peterson, M. F., Smith, P. B., & 21 other authors. 1995. Role conflict, ambiguity, and overload: A 21-nation study. *Academy of Management Journal, 38*, 429–452.

Peterson, M. F., Smith, P. B., & Tayeb, M. H. 1993. Development and use of English versions of Japanese PM leadership measures in electronics plants. *Journal of Organizational Behavior, 14*, 251–267.

Petrick, J. A., Scherer, R. F., Brodzinski, J. D., Quinn, J. F., & Ainina, M. F. 1999. Global leadership skills and reputational captial: Intangible resources for sustainable competitive advantage. *Academy of Management Executive, 13*, 58–69.

Pfeffer, J. 1994. *Competitive advantage through people: Unleashing the power of the work force.* Boston: Harvard Business School Press.

Picot, A., Reichwald, R., & Wiegand, R. T. 1996. *Die grenzenlose Unternehmung* (2d ed.). Wiesbaden: Gabler Verlag.

Podsiadlowski, A. 1998. Zusammenarbeit in interkulturellen Teams. In E. Spieß (Ed.), *Formen der Kooperation—Bedingungen und Perspektiven* (pp. 193–209). Göttingen: Hogrefe.

Podsiadlowski, A. 1999. *Cooperation in cross-cultural teams: What factors are decisive for the success or failure of internationally composed work groups?* Presentation at the 6th European Congress of Psychology, Rome.

Podsiadlowski, A., & Spieß, E. 1996. Zur Evaluation eines interkulturellen Trainings in einem deutschen Großunternehmen. *Zeitschrift für Personalforschung, 1*, 48–66.

Pogrebin, R. 1996, October 18. Pearson picks an American as executive. *The New York Times*, p. D7.

Polanyi, M. 1966. *The tacit dimension.* London: Routledge & Kegan Paul.

Pond, E. 1996. Women in leadership: A letter from Stockholm. *Washington Quarterly, 19* (4), 59.

Porter, M. E. 1985. *Competitive advantage: Creating and sustaining superior performance.* New York: Free Press.

Porter, M. E. 1986. Competition in global industries: A conceptual framework. In M. E. Porter (Ed.), *Competition in Global Industries* (pp. 15–61). Boston: Harvard Business School Press.

Poyatos, F. 1983. *New perspectives in nonverbal communication: Studies in cultural anthropology, social psychology, linguistics, literature and semiotics.* New York: Pergamon.

Price Waterhouse. 1997. *International assignments: European policy and practice.* Price Waterhouse.

Pucik, V. 1992. Globalization and human resource management. In V. Pucik, N. M. Tichy, & C. K. Barnett (Eds.), *Globalizing management: Creating and leading the competitive organization.* New York: John Wiley & Sons.

Pucik, V. 1998. Creating leaders that are world-class. *Mastering Global Business* (supplement to the *Financial Post* and *Financial Times*), pp. 3–4.

Pucik, V., & Saba, T. 1998. Selecting and developing the global versus the expatriate manager: A review of the state-of-the-art. *Human Resource Planning, 21* (4), 40–54.

Quinn, R., & Cameron, K. 1988. *Paradox and transformation*. Cambridge, MA: Ballinger.

Rahim, A. 1983. A model for developing key expatriate executives. *Personnel Journal, 62*, 312–317.

Rajan, A. 1990. *A zerosum game: Business, know-how, and training challenges in an integrated Europe*. London: Industrial Society Press.

Rall, W. 1989. Organisation für den Weltmarkt. *Zeitschrift für Betriebswirtschaft, 59*, 1074–1089.

Ratiu, I. 1983. Thinking internationally: A comparison of how international executives learn. *International Studies of Management and Organization, 13*, 139–150.

Rechtschaffen, S. 1996. *Timeshifting*. New York: Bantam Doubleday Audio.

Redding, S. G., & Richardson, S. 1986. Participative management and its varying relevance in Hong Kong and Singapore. *Asia Pacific Journal of Management, 3*, 76–98.

Redfield, R., Linton, R., & Herskovits, M. 1936. Memorandum on the study of acculturation. *American Anthropologists, 38*, 149–152.

Reskin, B. F., & Roos, P. A. 1990. *Job queues, gender queues: Explaining women's inroads into male occupations*. Philadelphia: Temple University Press.

Rhinesmith, S. H. 1993. *A manager's guide to globalization*. Alexandria, VA: Irwin.

Rhinesmith, S. H. 1994. Training in the era of globalization. In Institute for International Business Communication (Ed.), *The seventh corporate communications seminar* (pp. 10–21). Tokyo.

Rhinesmith, S. H. 1995. Open the door to a global mindset. *Training and Development*, May, 35–43.

Rhinesmith, S. H. 1996. *A manager's guide to globalization: Six skills for success in a changing world*. Chicago: Irwin.

Robbins, S. 1997. *Organizational behavior*. London: Simon & Schuster.

Robinson, G., & Wick, C. 1992. Executive development that makes a business difference. *Human Resource Planning, 15*, 63–76.

Robinson, M. 1996, May. Speech to International Women's Leadership Forum. Stockholm.

Roddick, A. 1991. *Body and soul*. New York: Crown.

Ronen, S. 1986. *Comparative and multinational management*. New York: Wiley.

Ronen, S. 1989. Training the international assignee. In I. L. Goldstein (Ed.), *Training and development in organizations* (pp. 417–453). San Francisco: Jossey-Bass.

Rosen, R. H. 1996. *Leading people*. New York: Viking.

Rosenbaum, J. E. 1984. *Career mobility in a corporate hierarchy*. New York: Academic Press.

Rosenstiel, L. von. 1992. *Organisationspsychologie* (3d ed.). Stuttgart: Poeschel.

Rosner, J. 1990. Ways women lead. *Harvard Business Review, 68* (6), 119–125.

Ross, S. 1996, November 11. More multinational firms sending executives abroad. *St. Louis Post-Dispatch*, p. 18.

Rost, J. 1991. *Leadership for the 21st century.* New York: Praeger.

Ruben, B. D. 1989. The study of cross-cultural competence: Traditions and contemporary issues. *International Journal of Intercultural Relations, 13,* 229–239.

Ruben, B. D., & Kealey, D. J. 1979. Behavioral assessment of communication competency and the prediction of cross-cultural adaptation. *International Journal of Intercultural Relations, 3,* 15–47.

Sackley, N., & Ibarra, H. 1995. *Charlotte Beers at Ogilvy & Mather Worldwide* (Case No. 9-495-031). Boston: Harvard Business School Press.

Sadowski, D., & Frick, B. 1989. Unternehmerische Personalpolitik in organisations-ökonomischer Perspektive: Das Beispiel der Schwerbehindertenbeschäftigung. *Mitteilungen aus Arbeitsmarkt und Berufsforschung, 3,* 408–418.

Saint-Germain, M. A. 1993. Women in power in Nicaragua: Myth and reality. In M. A. Genovese (Ed.), *Women as national leaders* (pp. 70–102). Newbury Park, CA: Sage.

Sandel, M. J. 1982. *Liberalism and the limits of justice.* Cambridge: Cambridge University Press.

Sasseen, J. 1991. Japan takes it gently. *International Management,* November, 48–51.

Schachter, J. 1988, July 10. When hope turns to frustration. *Los Angeles Times.*

Schaupp, D. L. 1978. *Cross-cultural study of a multinational company: Attitudinal responses to participative management.* New York: Praeger.

Schegloff, E. A. 1996. Confirming allusions: Toward an empirical account of action. *American Journal of Sociology, 102,* 161–216

Schein, E. H. 1984. Coming to a new awareness of organizational culture. *Sloan Management Review, 25* (2), 3–16.

Schein, E. 1988. *Organizational culture and leadership.* San Francisco: Jossey-Bass.

Scherm, M. 1998. Synergie in Gruppen—mehr als eine Metapher? In E. Ardelt-Gattinger, H. Lechner, & W. Schlögl (Eds.), *Gruppendynamik. Anspruch und Wirklichkeit in Gruppen* (pp. 62–70). Göttingen: Verlag für Angewandte Psychologie.

Schmidt, J., & Ruiz, J. 1992, May 25–27. *Meeting the challenge of Europe '92: A comparison of cross-cultural and foreign language training for European and American business students.* Paper presented at the Academy of International Business (Western Region) Conference.

Schröder, H. 1997. Tabus, interkulturelle Kommunikation und Fremdsprachenunterricht. Überlegungen zur Relevanz der Tabuforschung für die Fremdsprachendidaktik. In A. Knapp-Potthoff & M. Liedke (Eds.), *Aspekte interkultureller Kommunikationsfähigkeit* (pp. 93–106). München: Iudicium.

Schuler, H., & Funke, U. 1993. Diagnose beruflicher Eignung und Leistung. In H. Schuler (Ed.), *Organisationspsychologie.* Bern: Verlag Hans Huber.

Schuler, R. S. 1995. Internationales Personalmanagement. In C. Scholz & J. Zentes (Eds.), *Strategisches Euromanagement* (pp. 260–274). Stuttgart: Schäffer-Poeschel.

Schultz, A. 1944. The stranger: An essay in social psychology. *American Journal of Sociology, 49*, 499–507.

Schwartz, S. H. 1994. Beyond individualism/collectivism: New cultural dimensions of values. In U. Kim, H. C. Triandis, C. Kagitcibasi, S.-C. Choi, & G. Yoon (Eds.), *Individualism and collectivism: Theory, method, and applications* (pp. 85–119). Thousand Oaks, CA: Sage.

Scott, A. F. 1992. *Natural allies: Women's associations in American history.* Urbana: University of Illinois Press.

Scullion, H. 1993. Creating international managers. In P. S. Kirkbride (Ed.), *Human resource management* (pp. 197–212). London: Routledge.

Searle, W., & Ward, C. 1990. The prediction of psychological and sociocultural adjustment during cross-cultural transitions. *International Journal of Intercultural Relations, 14*, 449–464.

Seidler, V. J. 1994. *Unreasonable men: Masculinity and social theory.* London: Routledge.

Selting, M. 1992. Intonation as a contextualization device: Case studies on the role of prosody, especially intonation, in contextualizing story telling in conversation. In P. Auer & A. Di Luzio (Eds.), *The contextualization of language* (pp. 233–258). Amsterdam: John Benjamins.

Sevillon, H. 1994. Staffing policies and strategic control in British multinationals. *International Studies of Management and Organization, 24* (3), 86.

Shetty, Y. K. 1991. Strategies for U.S. competitiveness: A survey of business leaders. *Business Horizons*, November–December, 43–48.

Shilling, M. S. 1993. How to win at repatriation. *Personnel Journal, 72*, 40–46.

Shoda, Y., Mischel, W., & Wright, J. 1993. The role of situational demands and cognitive competencies in behavior organization and personality coherence. *Journal of Personality and Social Psychology, 65*, 1023–1035.

Simon, P. 1997. *Die Entwicklung eines Beobachtungssystems zur Erfassung von Interaktionsmustern und Leistungsdeterminanten in plurinationalen Arbeitsgruppen.* Unpublished diploma thesis, Regensburg University, Institute of Psychology.

Sinclair, A. 1992. The tyranny of a team ideology. *Organization Studies, 13*, 611–626.

Smith, P. B., Misumi, J., Tayeb, M. H., Peterson, M. F., & Bond, M. H. 1989. On the generality of leadership style measures across cultures. *Journal of Occupational Psychology, 62*, 97–109.

Smith, P. B., & Noakes, J. 1996. Cultural differences in group processes. In M. A. West (Ed.), *Handbook of work group psychology* (pp. 477–501). New York: John Wiley & Sons.

Smith, P. B., & Peterson, M. F. 1988. *Leadership, organizations and culture.* London: Sage.

Smith, P. B., Peterson, M., Misumi, J., & Bond, M. H. 1992. A cross-cultural test of the Japanese PM leadership theory. *Applied Psychology: An International Review, 41*, 5–19.

Snow, C. C., Snell, S. A., Davison, S. C., & Hambrick, D. C. 1996. Use transnational teams to globalize your company. *Organizational Dynamics, 24*, 50–67.

Speicher, J. K. 1985. The (mal)functioning of address forms in inter-cultural situations. In R. J. Brunt & W. Enninger (Eds.), *Interdisciplinary perspectives at cross-cultural communication* (pp. 93–102). Aachen: Rader.

Spender, D. 1983. *Women of ideas and what men have done to them from Aprha Behn to Adrienne Rich.* Boston: Routledge & Kegan Paul.

Spieß, E. 1996. *Kooperatives Handeln in Organisationen.* München: Peter Hampp Verlag.

Spieß, E. 1998. Das Konzept der Empathie. In E. Spieß (Ed.), *Formen der Kooperation—Bedingungen und Perspektiven* (pp. 53–62). Göttingen: Hogrefe.

Spieß, E., & Winterstein, H. 1998. *Verhalten in Organisationen.* Stuttgart: Kohlhammer.

Spreitzer, G. M., McCall, M. W., Jr., & Mahoney, J. D. 1997. Early identification of international executive potential. *Journal of Applied Psychology, 82*, 6–29.

Stahl, G. K. 1995a. Die Auswahl von Mitarbeitern für den Auslandseinsatz: Wissenschaftliche Grundlagen. In T. M. Kühlmann (Ed.), *Mitarbeiterentsendung ins Ausland* (pp. 31–66). Göttingen: Verlag für Angewandte Psychologie.

Stahl, G. K. 1995b. Ein strukturiertes Auswahlinterview für den Auslandseinsatz. *Zeitschrift für Arbeits- und Organisationspsychologie, 39*, 84–90.

Stahl, G. K. 1998a. *Development and evaluation of an assessment center to select managers for international assignments.* Paper presented at the 24th International Congress of Applied Psychology, San Francisco, California, August.

Stahl, G. K. 1998b. *Internationaler Einsatz von Führungskräften.* München: Oldenbourg.

Steiner, I. D. 1972. *Group process and productivity.* New York: Academic Press.

Stening, B. W. 1979. Problems of cross-cultural contact: A literature review. *International Journal of Intercultural Relations, 3*, 269–313.

Stewart, T. 1990, January. How to manage in the global era. *Fortune*, pp. 58–72.

Stogdill, R. 1974. *Handbook of leadership.* New York: Free Press.

Streufert, S., & Swezey, R. W. 1986. *Complexity, managers, and organizations.* Orlando, FL: Academic Press.

Stroebe, W., Diehl, M., & Abakoumkin, G. 1996. Social compensation and the Köhler effect: Toward a theoretical explanation of motivation gains in group productivity. In E. Witte & J. H. Davis (Eds.), *Understanding group behavior.* Vol. 2: *Small group processes and interpersonal relations* (pp. 37–65). Mahwah, NJ: Lawrence Erlbaum.

Stroh, L. K. 1995. Predicting turnover among repatriates: Can organizations affect retention rates? *International Human Resource Management, 6*, 443–456.

Stroh, L. K., & Caligiuri, P. M. 1996. *Strategic human resources: A new source for competitive advantage in the global arena.* Alexandria, VA: International Personnel Association.

Stroh, L. K., & Caligiuri, P. M. 1997. *Increasing global competitiveness through effective people management.* San Diego, CA: Global Leadership Institute.

Stroh, L. K., & Caligiuri, P. M. 1998. Strategic human resources: A new source for competitive advantage in the global arena. *International Journal of Human Resource Management, 9,* 1–17.

Stroh, L. K., Gregersen, H. B., & Black, J. S. 1998. Closing the gap: Expectations versus reality among repatriates. *Journal of World Business, 33,* 111–124.

Sullivan, J., & Nonaka, I. 1988. Culture and strategic issue categorization theory. *Management International Review, 28* (3), 6–10.

Sundstrom, E., De Meuse, K. P., & Futrell, D. 1990. Work teams: Applications and effectiveness. *American Psychologist, 45,* 120–133.

Suutari, V. 1996. *Comparative studies on leadership beliefs and behavior of European managers.* Vasa, Finland: ACTA Wasaensia, No. 50, Business Administration 19.

Tajfel, H. (Ed.). 1978. *Differentiation between social groups: Studies in intergroup behaviour.* London: Academic Press.

Tannen, D. 1990. *You just don't understand: Women and men in conversation.* New York: Ballantine Books.

Tannen, D. 1994. *Talking from 9 to 5: How women's and men's conversational styles affect who gets heard, who gets credit, and what gets done at work.* New York: Morrow.

Tannenbaum, A. S., Kavcic, B., Rosner, M., Vianello, M., & Wieser, G. 1974. *Hierarchy in organizations.* San Francisco: Jossey-Bass.

Tayeb, M. H. 1995. *Supervisory styles and cultural contexts: A comparative study.* Oxford: Elsevier Science.

Taylor, M. S. 1990. American managers in japanese subsidiaries. *Human Resource Planning, 14,* 43–49.

Taylor, S., Beechler, S., & Napier, N. 1996. Toward an integrative model of strategic international human resource management. *Academy of Management Review, 21,* 959–985.

Taylor, S., & Napier, N. K. 1995. *Western women working in Japan: Breaking corporate barriers.* Westport, CT: Greenwood Press.

Teagarden, M. 1995. Toward a theory of comparative management research: An idiographic case study of the best international human resources management project. *Academy of Management Journal, 38,* 1261–1287.

Thatcher, M. 1995. *Path to power.* New York: HarperCollins.

Thomas, A. 1993. Psychologie interkulturellen Lernen und Handelns. In A. Thomas (Ed.), *Kulturvergleichende Psychologie—Eine Einführung* (pp. 377–424). Göttingen: Hogrefe.

Thomas, A. 1995. Die Vorbereitung von Mitarbeitern für den Auslandseinsatz: Wissenschaftliche Grundlagen. In T. M. Kühlmann (Ed.), *Mitarbeiterentsendung ins Ausland* (pp. 85–118). Göttingen: Verlag für Angewandte Psychologie.

Thomas, A. 1996a. Analyse der Handlungswirksamkeit von Kultur-standards. In A. Thomas (Ed.), *Kulturstandards in der internationalen Begegnung* (pp. 55–69). Saarbrücken: Breitenbach.

Thomas, A. (Ed.). 1996b. *Psychologie interkulturellen Handelns.* Göttingen: Hogrefe.

Tichy, N. M. 1989. GE's crotonville: A staging ground for corporate revolution. *Academy of Management Executive, 3* (2), 99–106.

Tichy, N. M. 1992. Global development. In V. Pucik, N. M. Tichy, & C. K. Barnett (Eds.), *Globalizing management: Creating and leading the competitive organization* (pp. 206–224). New York: John Wiley & Sons.

Tichy, N. M., Brimm, M., Charan, R., & Takeuchi, H. 1992. Leadership development as a lever for global transformation. In V. Pucik, N. M. Tichy, & C. K. Barnett (Eds.), *Globalizing management: Creating and leading the competitive organization* (pp. 47–60). New York: John Wiley & Sons.

Tindale, R. S., & Larson, J. R. 1992a. Assembly bonus effect or typical group performance? A comment on Michaelsen, Watson and Black 1989. *Journal of Applied Psychology, 77,* 102–105.

Tindale, R. S., & Larson, J. R. 1992b. It's not how you frame the question, it's how you interpret the results. *Journal of Applied Psychology, 77,* 109–110.

Ting-Toomey, S. 1988. Intercultural conflict styles: A face-negotiation theory. In Y. Y. Kim & W. B. Gudykunst (Eds.), *Theories in intercultural communication* (pp. 213–235). Newbury Park, CA: Sage.

Torbiörn, I. 1982. *Living abroad: Personal adjustment and personnel policy in the overseas setting.* New York: Wiley.

Triandis, H. C. 1972. *The analysis of subjective culture.* New York: Wiley.

Triandis, H. C. 1988. Collectivism v. individualism: A reconceptualization of a basic concept in cross-cultural social psychology. In G. K. Verma & C. Bagley (Eds.), *Cross-cultural studies of personality, attitudes, and cognition.* New York: St. Martin's Press.

Triandis, H. C. 1995. *Individualism–Collectivism.* Boulder, CO: Westview.

Triandis, H. C., Kurowski L. L., & Gelfand, M. 1994. Workplace diversity. In H. C. Triandis, M. D. Dunnette, & L. M. Hough (Eds.), *Handbook of industrial and organizational psychology* (2d ed., Vol. 4, pp. 769–827). Palo Alto: Consulting Psychologists Press.

Trompenaars, F. 1993. *Riding the waves of culture: Understanding cultural diversity in business.* Avon: Bath Press.

Trompenaars, F. 1994. Developing the international manager. In M. Johnson & L. A. Allard (Eds.), *Global management 1995* (Vol. 1, pp. 63–74). London: Sterling.

Tung, R. L. 1981. Selection and training of personnel for overseas assignments. *Columbia Journal of World Business, 16,* 68–78.

Tung, R. L. 1982. Selection and training procedures of U.S., European, and Japanese multinationals. *California Management Review, 25,* 57–71.

Tung, R. L. 1987. Expatriate assignments: Enhancing success and minimizing failure. *Academy of Management Executive, 1,* 117–125.

Tung, R. L. 1988a. Career issues in international assignments. *Academy of Mangement Executive, 2,* 241–244.

Tung, R. L. 1988b. *The new expatriates: Managing human resources abroad.* Cambridge, MA: Ballinger.

Tung, R. L. 1988c. Selection and training procedures of U.S., European and Japanese multinationals. *California Management Review, 25* (1), 57–71.

Tung, R. L. 1998. American expatriates abroad: From neophytes to cosmopolitans. *Journal of World Business, 33,* 125–144.

Tung, R. L., & Miller, E. 1990. Managing in the twenty-first century: The need for global orientation. *Management International Review, 30,* 5–18.

Turner, J. 1978. Social categorisation and social discrimination in the minimal group paradigm. In H. Tajfel (Ed.), *Differentiation between social groups: Studies in intergroup behaviour.* London: Academic Press.

Ulrich, E. 1994. *Arbeitspsychologie* (3d ed.). Stuttgart: Pöschel.

Unctad. 1998. *World Investment Report.* New York: U.N. Press.

Underhill, E. 1911. *Mysticism: A study in the nature and development of man's spiritual consciousness.* New York: Dutton.

Van Houten, G. 1990. The implications of globalism: New mangement realities at Philips. In P. Evans, J. Doz, & A. Laurent (Eds.), *Human resource mangement in international firms* (pp. 101–111). London: Macmillan.

Vardi, Y., Shrom, A., & Jacobson, D. 1980. A study of leadership beliefs of Israeli managers. *Academy of Management Journal, 23,* 367–374.

Vesperini, H. 1990, June. Thomson Consumer Electronics: Switched on to thinking internationally. *Business International Council,* pp. 7–9.

Von Glinow, M. A. 1993. Diagnosing best practice in human resource management practices. In B. Shaw et al. (Eds.), *Research in personnel and human resources* (supplement 3, pp. 612–637). Greenwich, CT: JAI Press.

Von Glinow, M. A. in press. Toward achieving best practices in IHRM: Lessons learned from a 10 country/regional analysis. *Human Resource Management Journal.*

Ward, C. 1996. Acculturation. In D. Landis & R. S. Bhagat (Eds.), *Handbook of intercultural training* (2d ed., pp. 124–147). Thousand Oaks, CA: Sage.

Watson, W. E., Kumar, K., & Michaelsen, L. K. 1993. Cultural diversity's impact on interaction process and performance: Comparing homogeneous and diverse task groups. *Academy of Management Journal, 36,* 590–602.

Watson, W. E., Michaelsen, L. K., & Sharp, W. 1991. Member competence, group interaction, and group decision making. A longitudinal study. *Journal of Applied Psychology, 76,* 803–809.

Webber, R. H. 1969. Convergence or divergence. *Columbia Journal of World Business, 4* (3), 185–195.

Weber, W., & Festing, M. 1996. Wiedereingliederung entsandter Führungskräfte—Idealtypische Modellvorstellungen und realtypische Handhabungsformen. In K. Macharzina & J. Wolf (Eds.), *Handbuch internationales Führungskräfte-Management* (pp. 455–479). Stuttgart: Raabe.

Weber, W., Festing, M., Dowling, P. J., & Schuler, R. S. 1998. *Internationales Personalmanagement*. Wiesbaden: Gabler Verlag.

Weick, K. E. 1995. *Sensemaking in organizations*. Thousand Oaks, CA: Sage.

Weick, K. E. 1996. *Sensemaking in organizations*. Beverly Hills, CA: Sage.

Weick, K. E., & Van Orden, P. W. 1990. Organising on a global scale: A research and teaching agenda. *Human Resource Management, 29*, 49–61.

Weidenbaum, M. 1999. All the world's a stage. *Management Review, 88*, 42–48.

Weisman, S. R. 1986, April 11. A daughter returns to Pakistan to cry for victory. *The New York Times*, p. 12.

Welch, D. E., & Welch, L. S. 1991, August. *Using personnel to develop networks: An approach to subsidiary management* (Working Paper 1991/34). Sandvika: Norwegian School of Management.

Wellington, S. W. 1996. *Women in corporate leadership: Progress and prospects*. New York: Catalyst.

Wernerfelt, B. 1984. A resource-based view of the firm. *Strategic Management Journal, 5*, 171–180.

Wernerfelt, B. 1995. The resource-based view of the firm: Ten years after. *Strategic Management Journal, 16*, 171–174.

West, M. A. 1996. Reflexivity and work group effectiveness: A conceptual integration. In M. A. West (Ed.), *Handbook of work group psychology* (pp. 555–579). Baffins Lane, Chichester: John Wiley & Sons.

White, M. 1988. *The Japanese overseas*. New York: Free Press.

Wierzbicka, A. 1991. *Cross-cultural pragmatics*. Berlin: Mouton de Gruyter.

Williams, K. D., & Karau, S. J. 1991. Social loafing and social compensation: The effects of expectations of co-worker performance. *Journal of Personality and Social Psychology, 61*, 570–581.

Williamson, O. E. 1975. *Markets and hierarchies: Analysis and antitrust implications*. New York: Free Press.

Williamson, O. E. 1984. Efficient labor organization. In F. H. Stephen (Ed.), *Firms, organisation and labour* (pp. 87–118). London: Macmillan.

Williamson, O. E. 1985. *The economic institutions of capitalism*. New York: Free Press.

Williamson, O. E. 1990. *Die ökonomischen Institutionen des Kapitalismus*. Tübingen: J.C.B. Mohr.

Williamson, O. E., Wachter, M. L., & Harris, J. E. 1975. Understanding the employment relation: The analysis of idiosyncratic exchange. *Bell Journal of Economics, 6*, 250–278.

Windham International & National Foreign Trade Council. 1994. *Global relocation trends 1994 survey report*. New York: Windham International.

Winogard, T., & Flores, F. 1986. *Understanding computers and cognition*. Reading, MA: Addison-Wesley.

Winter, G. 1994. Was eigentlich ist eine kulturelle Überschneidungssituation? In A. Thomas (Ed.), *Psychologie und multikulturelle Gesellschaft* (pp. 221–227). Göttingen: Verlag für Angewandte Psychologie.

Wirth, E. 1992. *Mitarbeiter im Auslandseinsatz.* Wiesbaden: Gabler.

Witte, E. H. 1989. Köhler rediscovered: The anti-Ringelmann effect. *European Journal of Social Psychology, 19,* 147–154.

Wolf, J. 1994. *Internationales Personalmanagement: Kontext, Koordination, Erfolg.* Wiesbaden: Gabler.

Woolf, V. 1938. *Three guineas.* New York: Harcourt Brace.

Wright, J. C., & Mischel, W. 1987. A conditional approach to dispositional constructs: The local predictability of social behavior. *Journal of Personality and Social Psychology, 53,* 1159–1177.

Wright, P. M., & McMahan, G. C. 1992. Theoretical perspectives for strategic human resource management. *Journal of Management, 18,* 295–320.

Wunderer, R. 1992. Internationalisierung als strategische Herausforderung für das Personalmanagement. *Zeitschrift für Betriebswirtschaft, 62,* 161–181.

Yeung, A., Ulrich, D. O., Nason, S., & Von Glinow, M. A. 1999. *Learning organizations, culture change and competitiveness: How managers can build learning capability.* Working Paper, University of Michigan.

Yeung, A. K., & Ready, D. A. 1995. Developing capabilities of global corporations: A comparative study in eight nations. *Human Resource Management, 34,* 529–547.

Yukl, G. 1998. *Leadership in organizations* (4th ed.). Saddle River, NJ: Prentice Hall.

Zahra, S. A. 1998. Competitiveness and global leadership in the 21st century. *Academy of Management Executive, 12* (4), 10–12.

Zander, L. 1997. *The license to lead: An 18 country study of the relationship between employees' preferences regarding interpersonal leadership and national culture.* Stockholm: Institute of International Business, Stockholm School of Economics.

Zeira, Y., & Banai, M. 1985. Selection of expatriate managers in MNCs: The host-environment point of view. *International Studies of Management and Organization, 15,* 33–51.

Zimbardo, P. G. 1996. *Psychologie.* Berlin: Springer-Verlag.

Index

Uncertainty: corporate strategy
influences, 44; derivation, 44;
asset specificity, 46; variation of
management tasks relative to, 46
Unity, women leaders as symbols
of, 92

Volkswagen, 102

Volkswagen Foundation, 181
Vision: component of global
leadership, 40, 77–78; global
nature of, 38; women global
leaders and, 92–93

Williamson, Oliver, 43, 45

About the Editors and Contributors

Nancy J. Adler is Professor of Management at McGill University in Montreal, Canada. Dr. Adler consults with global companies and government organizations on projects in Asia, Europe, North and South America, and the Middle East. She conducts research on strategic international human resource management, global leadership, and global women leaders. She has authored more than 100 articles and produced the film, *A Portable Life*. Her books include *International Dimensions of Organizational Behavior, Women in Management Worldwide,* and *Competitive Frontiers: Women Managers in a Global Economy*. Professor Adler is a Fellow of both the Academy of Management and the Academy of International Business.

Zeynep Aycan is Assistant Professor of Cross-Cultural Industrial and Organizational Psychology at Koc University. Her research interests include cross-cultural approaches to HRM practices, leadership and motivation, women in management, and work–family conflict. On these topics, she published twenty research articles as academic journal articles and book chapters. She also edited two books, *Expatriate Management: Theory and Research* (1997); and *Leadership, Management and Human Resource Practices in Tur-*

key (in press). Dr. Aycan is the cofounder and coeditor, with Terence Jackson, of the *International Journal of Cross-Cultural Management*. She provides consulting services to local and multinational corporations (e.g., Alcatel, Bechtel) on expatriate management and influence of culture on HRM practices.

Allan Bird holds the Eiichi Shibusawa–Seigo Arai Chair of Japanese Studies at the University of Missouri in St. Louis. He has worked and lived overseas for eight years. His research and consulting focus on international HRM, particularly managerial effectiveness in international contexts and the performance of Japanese MNCs. He has authored numerous articles and books and recently coedited, with Schon Beechler, *Japanese Multinationals Abroad: Individual and Organizational Learning*.

J. Stewart Black is Managing Director of the Center for Global Assignments, which produces research and publications and provides consulting services related to international assignments. His research and consulting focus on the areas of global leadership, strategic human resource management, international assignments, and cross-cultural management. He has consulted and presented seminars in these areas to a variety of firms including American Express, Black & Decker, Boeing, Exxon, General Motors, IBM, Kodak, Motorola, NASA, and Honda Motors. He has authored numerous articles, some of which have been published in *Harvard Business Review, Academy Management Journal, Academy of Management Review, Journal of International Business Studies, Human Relations, Human Resource Management,* and *Sloan Management Review*.

Paula M. Caligiuri is currently Assistant Professor in the Department of Human Resource Management, School of Management and Labor Relations, Rutgers University. She received her Ph.D. from Pennsylvania State University in industrial and organizational psychology. Her primary area of research is in the strategic human resource practices in multinational organizations. Specifically, her current research includes selection, retention, and performance management of global assignees. Her research has appeared in the *International Journal of Human Resource Management, Journal of World Business, Journal of Applied Psychology,* and *International Journal of Intercultural Relations*.

C. Brooklyn Derr is Professor of Human Resource Management and the Knowles Faculty Scholar at the University of Utah. His areas of expertise are management development, work–family issues, conflict management, cross-functional and cross-cultural teams, and internationalizing top management. He has taught at Harvard, UCLA, IMD, Ecole Superieur de Commerce (Lyon), and INSEAD. Professor Derr has written four books and published numerous articles, and has been a consultant to international corporations and government organizations in Europe and North America. His consulting specialties are in the areas of management development, high-potential management, internationalizing managers, and conflict management.

Marion Festing is Assistant Professor of Management and Human Resources at the University of Paderborn. She has worked and studied in various countries and her research and teaching interests include strategic international human resource management and the application of transaction cost theory to human resource management. She is a coauthor of the book *Internationales Personalmanagement* with Wolfgang Weber, Peter J. Dowling, and Randall S. Schulter (1998). Recently she edited a special issue of *Management International Review* on "Strategic Issues in International Human Resources Management." She is a member of the editorial board of *Career Planning International*; serves as a reviewer for *Management International Review* and *Zeitschrift für Personalwirtschaft*; and is a member of the European International Business Academy and the Academy of International Business.

Hal B. Gregersen is Associate Professor of International Management at the Marriott School of Management, Brigham Young University. His primary research focuses on managing international assignments strategically, developing global leaders, and implementing international strategy. He has authored numerous articles, book chapters, and cases on these subjects, some of which have been published in *Harvard Business Review, Academy of Management Journal, Journal of Applied Psychology, Journal of International Business Studies, Personnel Psychology,* and *Sloan Management Review.* As a senior partner at the Center for Global Assignments, he consults with a variety of North American, European, and Asian firms.

Torsten M. Kühlmann is Chair of Human Resource Management at the University of Bayreuth. He holds a doctorate in business administration from the University of Erlangen–Nürnberg. His research and teaching deal with industrial and organizational psychology, entrepreneurship, and (international) human resource management. He serves as a reviewer of *Ergonomics, Journal of*

Occupational and Organizational Psychology, Zeitschrift für Arbeits- und Organisationspsychologie, Management International Review, and *Journal of Applied Psychology.* He is actively involved in international executive education and has consulted with a variety of organizations. A member of several advisory committees, he also belongs to the Deutsche Gesellschaft für Psychologie.

Mila Lazarova is a Ph.D. student in the School of Management and Labor Relations at Rutgers University. She has a master's degree in International Economic Relations from the University of National and World Economics in Sofia, Bulgaria. Her primary research interests include international human resource management, and more specifically, issues related to management of global assignees. She has also done research on the topics of integration of the labor market of the European Union, as well as on impact of technology on the workplace.

Martha L. Maznevski is Assistant Professor at the McIntire School of Commerce, University of Virginia, and a visiting scholar at the Institute of International Business, Stockholm School of Economics. She received her Ph.D. in organizational behavior from the University of Western Ontario, specializing in cross-cultural management. Her two major streams of research involve developing an instrument to measure elements of culture in individuals (the Cultural Perspectives Questionnaire), and understanding and increasing effectiveness in cross-cultural management situations. She teaches courses in organizational behavior and international management, and works with managers in many multinational corporations to help them improve their effectiveness. Maznevski is coauthor of the textbook *International Management Behavior,* as well as author of several articles and book chapters on international management.

Mark E. Mendenhall holds the J. Burton Frierson Chair of Excellence in Business Leadership at the University of Tennessee in Chattanooga. In 1998, he held the Ludwig Erhard Stiftungsprofessur endowed chair at the University of Bayreuth in Germany, and in 1999 he was a visiting professor at the Europa Institute at the University of Saarland in Germany. He has published numerous books and journal articles on expatriate management and other international human resource management issues. He is active in the Academy of Management, and is past president of the International Division of that organization. His other research and consulting interests are in the areas of leadership and organizational change, the nonlinear dynamics of organizational systems, and Japanese organizational behavior.

Edwin L. Miller is a Fellow of the Academy of Management and a recently retired professor and associate dean from the University of Michigan Business School. He has made important contributions to two areas of research and publication. The first contribution has been to international human resource management, and his research and publications have blanketed the entire range of the staffing cycle, including the expatriate selection decision process, management succession planning, and executive development programs. He has also directed his attention toward the future challenges of the international human resource management function and the contribution of the function to the overall corporate strategic planning process. Second, Professor Miller has occupied a pivotal position in the process to internationalize the faculty, curricula, and doctoral education within U.S. schools and colleges of business administration.

Alois Moosmüller is Professor of Intercultural Communication in the Department of Cultural Anthropology at Munich University. From 1992 to 1997, he lectured at Keio University in Tokyo, and did research on intercultural issues of German–Japanese and U.S.–Japanese collaboration in multinational companies in Japan. In 1984 and 1987, he conducted ethnographical fieldwork in Indonesia. Currently he does research on cross-cultural issues in international collaboration in multinational companies and on emerging cultural patterns in overseas expatriate communities. In addition, he is an experienced intercultural trainer and consultant, and has worked with numerous companies in improving their international HRM expertise.

Bernd Müller-Jacquier is Professor of Intercultural Communication at the University of Chemnitz. He received his academic training at the universities of Bonn, Toulouse, Tübingen, and Indiana. Since 1976, he has served as lecturer and assistant professor at the universities of Tübingen, Coimbra, Paris, Montpellier, and Bayreuth. His research interests include discourse analysis of intercultural situations and intercultural training. He has edited a number of books, is series editor of *Reihe Interkulturelle Kommunikation* (München), and has contributed to numerous academic journals. His publications are written in German, English, and French, and most of them have appeared under his former name, Bernd-Dietrich Müller. Since 1998 he has been president of the German branch of the Society for Intercultural Education, Training, and Research (SIETR).

Gary Oddou is Department Head of the Management and Human Resources Department at Utah State University. He has coauthored or coedited the books *Cases in International Organizational Behavior, Readings and Cases in International Human Resource Management,* and *Managing Internationally: A Personal Journey.* His research and consulting experience is primarily in the area of international human resource management. He has authored numerous journal articles which have appeared in such journals as the *Academy of Management Review, Human Resource Management, Journal of Management Education, European Management Journal,* and *Columbia Journal of World Business.* He has been affiliated with IMD, Ecole de Management–Lyon, Monterey Institute of International Studies, and the University of Sarajevo.

Joyce S. Osland is Associate Professor at the University of Portland. She lived and worked overseas in seven countries, primarily in West Africa and Latin America for fourteen years, working as a manager, researcher, consultant, and professor. Dr. Osland's current research and consulting focus includes expatriates, cultural sense making, Latin American management, and global leadership. She is the author of *The Adventure of Working Abroad* (1995) and coauthor of *Organizational Behavior: An Experiential Approach,* and *The Organizational Behavior Reader* (2000).

Astrid Podsiadlowski is a Ph.D. student at the Institute of Psychology, Department for Industrial and Organizational Psychology, and lectures at the Department for Cross-Cultural Communication at the University of Munich. Her research and teaching activities as well as publications focus on the field of multicultural work groups and international human resource management (expatriation, intercultural team building and training) mainly in North America and Southeast Asia.

Erika Spieß is Associate Professor of Organizational Psychology at the Institute of Psychology at the University of Munich in Germany. She received her doctoral degree in psychology from the Maximilians–University of Munich. She has published many articles and books in the fields of industrial and organizational psychology. Her research interests focus on the role of women at work, cooperation in organizations, and international organizational behavior.

Günter K. Stahl is Assistant Professor of Human Resource Management and Leadership at the University of Bayreuth, Germany. He has published books and articles in the fields of leadership development, cross-cultural management, and international human resource management, in particular the management of expatriates. He has conducted research projects in Japan and the United States and his current research interests include careers in multinational corporations, trust within and between organizations, and integration processes in mergers and acquisitions. He has also done consulting work for various organizations, including Daimler-Chrysler, Siemens, and Lufthansa.

Siegfried Stumpf is Assistant Professor of the Department of Social and Organizational Psychology at the University of Regensburg. He studied psychology and philosophy at the University of Regensburg, and after receiving his doctorate from the University of Goettingen, he worked for several years in the human resource department of the Bayerische Landesbank in Munich. His main interests in research and teaching are group processes and effectiveness, simulation of organizational processes, methods and instruments for human resource development, and cross-cultural psychology.

Mary Ann Von Glinow is Professor of Management and International Business and the Director of the Center for International Business Education and Research (CIBER) at Florida International University. Dr. Von Glinow was the 1994–1995 president of the Academy of Management, the world's largest association of academicians in management, and is a member of eleven editorial review boards. She has authored more than 100 journal articles and eight books. She is presently writing up a decade's worth of work based on the international consortium she heads of researchers delving into "Best International HRM Practices." Dr. Von Glinow consults with a number of domestic and multinational enterprises, and holds a mayor appointment to the Shanghai Institute of Human Resources in China. Since 1989, she has been a consultant in General Electric's Work-Out and Change Acceleration programs, and has led change initiative activities throughout the world. She serves on the board of the Fielding Institute, Friends of Bay Oaks, Animal Alliance in Los Angeles, and is a senior advisor to Miami's One Community–One Goal, having worked extensively in their jobs-creation process. She is actively involved in animal welfare organizations from Miami to Los Angeles, and won the 1996 Humanitarian Award of the Year from Adopt-A-Pet.

Ellen M. Whitener is Professor of Commerce at the McIntire School of Commerce at the University of Virginia where she teaches organizational behavior and human resource management. Her articles have been published in journals such as the *Academy of Management Review, Journal of Applied Psychology, Journal of Vocational Behavior, Human Resource Management Review, Computers in Human Behavior, Communications of the ACM,* and *Journal of Management.* Her recent research has focused on building employee morale, trust, and performance, understanding cross-cultural differences in trust, and using human resource practices to build a high commitment workforce.

Lena Zander is Assistant Professor at the Institute of International Business, Stockholm School of Economics, specializing in cross-cultural management. Her multiple award-winning dissertation, "The License to Lead," examined preferences for interpersonal leadership in eighteen countries. She teaches courses in cross-cultural management to both MBA and executive education audiences. She has lived and worked in Botswana, France, and the United States, and she continues to work with managers and executives from throughout the world. She has coedited two books on culture and management together with Annick Sjögren, and is author of book chapters on leadership and culture. Her current research focuses on extending her leadership studies, and examining cross-cultural interaction and leadership in multinational teams.

Ulrich Zeutschel is a consultant and trainer with Kronshage, Bauer & Partner, Organizational and Personnel Development in Hamburg, as well as a freelance consultant. He conducts training seminars, team facilitation, conference moderation and documentation, and program evaluation for corporations, NGOs, and public service organizations. Other areas of professional experience include international youth exchanges and research in intercultural communication and educational exchanges. From 1995 to 1998 he coordinated a research project on intercultural cooperation in work groups at the University of Regensburg.